FABRICATING ISRAELI HISTORY

By the same author

Empires of the Sand: The Struggle for Mastery in the Middle East, 1789–1922 (with Inari Karsh)

The Gulf Conflict 1990–1991: Diplomacy and War in The New World Order (with Lawrence Freedman)

Saddam Hussein: A Political Biography (with Inari Rautsi)

Soviet Policy towards Syria Since 1970

Neutrality and Small States

The Soviet Union and Syria

The Iran–Iraq War: A Military Analysis

The Cautious Bear: Soviet Military Engagement in Middle East Wars in the Post-1967 Era

Between War and Peace: Dilemmas of Israeli Security (editor)

Peace in the Middle East: The Challenge for Israel (editor)

Israel at the Crossroads (co-editor)

Non-Conventional Weapons Proliferation in the Middle East:Tackling the Spread of Nuclear, Chemical, and Biological Capabilities (co-editor)

The Iran–Iraq War: Impact and Implications (editor)

In Search of Identity: Jewish Aspects in Israeli Culture (co-editor)

Israel: the First Hundred Years (editor)

FABRICATING ISRAELI HISTORY

The 'New Historians'

Second Revised Edition

Efraim Karsh

Professor of Mediterranean Studies at the
University of London

FRANK CASS
LONDON • PORTLAND, OR

First Published in 1997 in Great Britain by
FRANK CASS & CO. LTD.
Newbury House, 900 Eastern Avenue
London, IG2 7HH

and in the United States of America by
FRANK CASS
c/o ISBS, 5804 N.E. Hassalo Street
Portland, Oregon, 97213-3644

Second Revised Edition 2000

Copyright © 1997, 2000 Frank Cass & Co. Ltd.

British Library Cataloguing in Publication Data:

Karsh, Efraim
  Fabricating Israeli history: the 'new historians'. – 2nd
  rev. ed. – (Cass studies in Israeli history, politics and
  society)
  1. Arab–Israeli conflict – Historiography 2. Jewish–Arab
  relations – Historiography 3. Zionism – Historiography
  4. Israel – History – 20th century – Historiography
  5. Palestine – History – 20th century – Historiography
  I. Title
  956.9'405

ISBN 0-7146-5011-0 (cloth)
ISBN 0-7146-8063-X (paper)

Library of Congress Cataloging-in-Publication Data:

A catalog record for this book is available
from the Library of Congress

Typeset by Vitaset, Paddock Wood, Kent
Printed in Great Britain by
Bookcraft (Bath) Ltd, Midsomer Norton, Somerset

What the reviewers said about the first edition

'*The first serious, comprehensive analysis of the revisionist school of national historians in Israel in the State's fifth decade of sovereignty. A frontal, no-holds barred assault that cannot fail to sharpen the debate between the established school and its opponents. It is required reading for the inquisitive no less than the engaged professional historians.*'

Professor J. C. Hurewitz, Columbia University

'*The first full-length and detailed rebuttal to those Israeli scholars who call themselves the "new historians" ... Karsh's key strength is the application of unprejudiced common sense to clarify issues clouded by the pseudo-scholarship of propagandists.*'

Daniel Pipes, *Middle East Quarterly*

'*... a skilful surgical probing and occasionally a savage attack on the New Historians.*'

Jerusalem Post

'*... Karsh seems to have scored a palpable hit on the contentious issue of the strategic thinking of Ben-Gurion.*'

The Economist

'*Efraim Karsh, whose scholarship in all the relevant documentation in English, Hebrew, and Arabic far outweighs that of the New Historians, has delivered a crushing blow to them, revealing how hollow and superficial their theses are.*'

Hyam Maccoby, *Midstream*

'Fabricating Israeli History *is an incisive analysis of the origins of the Arab–Israeli conflict ... Efraim Karsh is a witty and an eloquent writer as well as a reputable historian with all the necessary methodological and linguistic tools (Hebrew, Arabic, and English) to demolish the "new historians" who have created the myths which dominate the airwaves and headlines of much of the media ... The book is only 205 pages long and there is not a word that can be called "extraneous".'*

Norman Berdichevsky, *Contemporary Review*

'In this easy-to-read and thoroughly convincing volume of historical detective work, Efraim Karsh strips away the academic cloak with which the New Historians have wrapped themselves. Not only has Karsh shattered the myths created by the New Historians by ripping apart their historiography, but he has also produced a very important contribution to the literature on the Arab–Israeli conflict. For in the process of debunking the debunkers, he has powerfully supported the traditional interpretation of the conflict's origins.'

David Rodman, *The Partisan Review*

'Karsh has done a good service in questioning and probing certain assumptions of the revisionists ...'

Martin Kolinsky, *Times Higher Education Supplement*

'Efraim Karsh is a fine scholar, an absorbing writer and a well-respected director of Mediterranean Studies at King's College, London. In Fabricating Israeli History, *he takes to task the new school of Israeli historians who are challenging what they see as the myths that have cast a rosy glow over their country's past. In doing so, he demonstrates how the pen can be, not just mightier, but much nastier that the sword.'*

Bernard Josephs, *The Jewish Chronicle*

CASS SERIES: ISRAELI HISTORY, POLITICS AND SOCIETY
Series Editor: Efraim Karsh
ISSN: 1368-4795

This series provides a multidisciplinary examination of all aspects of Israeli history, politics and society, and serves as a means of communication between the various communities interested in Israel: academics, policy-makers, practitioners, journalists and the informed public.

1. *Peace in the Middle East: The Challenge for Israel*, Edited by Efraim Karsh.

2. *The Shaping of Israeli Identity: Myth, Memory and Trauma*, Edited by Robert Wistrich.

3. *Between War and Peace: Dilemmas of Israeli Security*, Edited by Efraim Karsh.

4. *US-Israeli Relations at the Crossroads*, Edited by Gabriel Sheffer.

5. *Revisiting the Yom Kippur War*, Edited by P R Kumaraswamy.

6. *Israel: The Dynamics of Change and Continuity*, Edited by David Levi-Faur.

7. *In Search of Identity: Jewish Aspects in Israeli Culture*, Edited by Dan Urian.

8. *Israel at the Polls, 1996*, Edited by Daniel J Elazar and Shmuel Sandler.

9. *From Rabin to Netanyahu: Israel's Troubled Agenda*, Edited by Efraim Karsh.

10. *Fabricating Israeli History: The 'New Historians'*, Second Revised Edition, by Efraim Karsh.

11. *Divided Against Zion: Anti-Zionist Opposition in Britain to a Jewish State in Palestine, 1945–1948*, by Rory Miller.

12. *Peacemaking in Israel after Rabin*, Edited by Sasson Sofer.

For my children
Rachel, Ro'i, and Matan

Contents

'Thou shalt take in vain the name of the archives.'
THE 'NEW HISTORIAN'S' FIRST COMMANDMENT

Preface to the Second Revised Edition

The original edition of this book was published in the spring of 1997. Its arrival sparked a heated debate. Arguments were traded in journals, newspapers, radio programmes, and lecture halls in Europe, the United States, and Israel; letters of support and vilification poured in.

Such a response is not difficult to understand. Israel has always aroused deep passions, both positive and negative, unprecedented in scope and intensity for a state of its minuscule size. As the first frontal assault on Israel's fashionable 'revisionist' school of thought, *Fabricating Israeli History: The 'New Historians'* touched a raw nerve among its many partisans, enticing them into a concerted effort to fend off this new threat. At the same time, it was welcomed by those who had long been troubled by the 'revisionist' rewriting of history in a manner casting the birth of the Jewish State as the source of all evil.

Yet I was taken aback by the malevolence of some of the responses. I certainly did not expect my publisher to be harassed, at a prestigious academic gathering in the United States, by an erstwhile critic of Israel urging his colleagues to boycott him for publishing my book. And while this might have been a somewhat unorthodox form of scholarly discourse, it was by no means more violent than that person's review of *Fabricating Israeli History*.

This is not to say that I am averse to criticism of my book. Quite the reverse. Provoking a debate is the scholar's ultimate reward; and in this respect, *Fabricating Israeli History* has been more than rewarding. Yet, in order to qualify as a debate, *criticism must grapple with the issue it takes to task*, not with a distorted caricature of it. For otherwise debate will have lost its *raison d'être* altogether. Hence, when my publisher informed me of his intention to issue a second edition of the book, I welcomed this as an opportunity both to return to the heart of the matter and flesh out further evidence of historical fabrication, and to tell the story behind the book – the circumstances of its conception and the attempt of the 'new historians' and their partisans to give it an unceremonious early burial. For while the debate is far from over, its tone and demeanour are no less revealing of the oppressive atmosphere which has gained hold of contemporary Middle Eastern studies than the pattern of historical fabrication exposed by the book.

It all began in the most unexpected way. Several years ago, as my working day was drawing to a close, my office door was flung open and in dashed a complete stranger. He took a seat, introduced himself as a visiting professor from the University of Haifa, and with a nonchalant familiarity, as if we had been lifelong friends, began to heap abuse on a fellow member of my department. Baffled by this unexpected outburst, I later asked my colleague about the nature of his relationship with the Israeli professor. It transpired that he too had been paid a surprise visit by the same person, whom he had never heard of before, and been subjected to a virulent sermon on the 'original sins' of the Zionist movement and the State of Israel. When my colleague made it clear that, as a Jewish person, he had no interest in this tirade, the uninvited guest, who was totally unaware of my colleague's Jewishness, was evidently embarrassed and swiftly took his leave.

This was by no means my first encounter with Israeli self-debasement during my years in London. Yet its intensity left me puzzled. What drives a person, who clearly belongs to his country's intellectual and social elite, to attack his native country in front of complete strangers, in terms well beyond the reasonable bounds of constructive criticism? This meeting might well have remained a passing episode had it not been for a chance encounter in its immediate wake with a published manifestation of this self-flagellation. After all, there is a fundamental difference between voicing an opinion at a private meeting, or even a public gathering, and the investment of years of archival research geared solely to laying the basis for such an anti-Israel indictment.

The text in question was a book on the birth of the Palestinian refugee problem by Israeli academic Benny Morris (of Ben-Gurion University in Beersheba). While leafing through the book's English-language version, I came across a quote from a letter, written by David Ben-Gurion to his son Amos in 1937, stating that 'we must expel Arabs and take their places'.[1] This rang a distant bell. Having read the book's Hebrew edition several years earlier, I recalled the letter as saying something quite different. Indeed, an examination of the Hebrew text confirmed my recollection. It read as follows: 'We *do not wish, we do not need* to expel Arabs and take their place ... All our aspiration is built on the assumption ... that there is enough room in the country for ourselves and the Arabs.'[2]

Though I was surprised by this fundamental contradiction, I gave Morris the benefit of the doubt. Perhaps this was merely a mistranslation, or even a typographical mistake? To set my mind at rest I looked up the entire documentation used by Morris with regard to the Zionist position regarding the expulsion of the Palestinians to the neighbouring Arab states, or 'transfer' as it is commonly known, to which Ben-Gurion's letter allegedly referred. To my bewilderment I

---

1   Benny Morris, *The Birth of the Palestinian Refugee Problem, 1947–1949* (Cambridge: Cambridge University Press, 1987), p. 25.
2   Benny Morris, *Leidata shel Be'ayat Ha-plitim Ha-falestinim 1947–1949* (Tel-Aviv: Am Oved, 1991), p. 45 (emphasis added).

discovered that there was scarcely a single document quoted by Morris which had not been rewritten in a way that distorted its original meaning altogether.

By now my curiosity was growing by the hour. Morris, after all, is not just another historian interacting with his facts. He is a prominent and vociferous member of a rapidly expanding group of Israeli and Jewish 'revisionists', or 'new historians' as they call themselves, claiming to have uncovered the 'historical truth' about the creation of the State of Israel and the advent of the Arab–Israeli conflict. Could it be that his research methods are representative of this group's common practice?

Until then, I had kept away from the heated historiographical debate about the creation of Israel and its implications. My own research on the history and politics of the Middle East had led me to question some of the central claims of the 'new historians', as well as the extent of their familiarity with the wider historical context of their research; but I ascribed these differences to contending approaches and interpretations – a common and constructive attribute of a scholarly discourse. The possibility of *falsification of documentation* by these revisionist historians had never occurred to me: not merely because of the presumed existence of elementary academic integrity, but also because such distortion would have undermined the foundations of scholarly and/or scientific research, which must necessarily draw on earlier studies by way of accumulating an aggregate body of knowledge.

Yet, having discovered the pervasiveness of Morris's distortions, I could no longer avoid thinking the unthinkable. And indeed, an examination of the documentation used by several key 'new historians', as well as of sources withheld from their readers, led to the disturbing conclusion that Morris's distortions were neither a fluke nor an exception. Rather, they typified the *modus operandi* of a sizeable group of academics, journalists, and commentators, who had predicated their professional careers on rewriting Israel's history in an image of their own choosing so as to cast it in the role of the regional villain. This is *not* a matter of contending interpretations or different readings of documents – both of which are perfectly legitimate aspects of scholarly research. It is a deliberate attempt at historical distortion. Nothing more, nothing less.

Had such professional misconduct occurred in the natural or physical sciences there would doubtless have been serious consequences: e.g. the collapse of a bridge following phoney engineering calculations aimed at cutting construction costs; dangerous side-effects hidden during the development of a new medicine, etc. Yet it would seem that when it comes to the social sciences and the humanities, especially to historical research which has no direct bearing on daily life, and which deals with subjective and largely unquantifiable social phenomena, the researcher can escape punishment for the worst kinds of malpractice. More seriously, partisan rewriting of history has apparently become the accepted norm in those fields of research dealing with highly contentious political, social, and historical phenomena, such as the Arab–Israeli conflict. In this Orwellian world, where war is peace and ignorance is strength, not only are falsifiers not censured by their professional milieu – they are applauded.

This has indeed been the foremost driving force behind the 'new historians': the precise opposite of the assiduously cultivated heroic image of a small and courageous minority, persecuted by Israel's academic and intellectual establishment for its uncompromising quest for truth and justice. Benny Morris, for one, has presented himself for years as the hapless victim of a 'system' which has allegedly prevented him from embarking on a tenure-track position in an Israeli university – a claim which has received much publicity in the Israeli and foreign media.[3] (The fact that other candidates might have been better qualified than Morris for the few

3   See, for example, Ruti Sinai, 'Not in Our School', *Ha-aretz*, 27 May 1997.

positions offered by the competitive Israeli higher education system apparently did not occur to these reporters.)

Similarly, in a foreword to the French edition of his book *Binyan Uma o Tikun Hevra?* (Nation Building or Reforming a Society?), Israeli political scientist Ze'ev Sternhell (of the Hebrew University of Jerusalem) presented himself as being on the receiving end of the intolerant and vindictive Israeli society. 'The historian who reveals undesirable truths, who challenges or explodes myths – in other words, the historian with a non-conformist interpretation', he argued, 'is perceived as a troublemaker, an enemy of the people.'[4] To which one can only say that if an established Chair at Israel's veteran university, ubiquitous presence in the media, and generous institutional financial assistance for a book blackening the state's founding fathers are part of the treatment meted out to 'an enemy of the people', then one wonders how Israeli society rewards its favourite members.

The same applies to Morris. Whatever the reasons for his (relatively) slow integration within Israeli academia, these have had nothing to do with a state-sponsored 'persecution'. Not only are Israeli universities teaming with academics holding far more extreme views than Morris regarding the essence of Zionism and the State of Israel, but they constitute the heart of the academic establishment in the social sciences and the humanities: Ilan Pappé, Benjamin Beit Hallahmi, and Uri Ben-Eliezer at the University of Haifa; Joseph Grodzinski, Yoav Peled, and Tania Reinhardt at Tel-Aviv University; Israel Shahak, Baruch Kimmerling, Ze'ev Sternhell, and Moshe Zimermann of the Hebrew University in Jerusalem; Gabriel Piterberg and Uri Ram from Ben-Gurion University – even this far from complete list would easily refute Morris's claim of ideological persecution.

Moreover, Morris himself has repeatedly rebutted his own

4   Quoted in *Rive – Review of Mediterranean Politics and Culture*, December 1996, p. 48. To Sternhell's 'credit' it should be noted that he acknowledges that this alleged phenomenon 'is not only intrinsic to Israeli society; it is also very well known in France'.

charge. In his response to the attack by Israeli author Aharon Meged on the 'new historians' in the summer of 1994, Morris argued that 'the new historiography is the present and future direction of the research in the country [i.e., Israel]'.[5] In his assault on the first edition of *Fabricating Israeli History*, published in the *Journal of Palestine Studies*, Morris went further to boast that 'the books and articles produced by the New Historians [are] taught in all of Israel's universities and in a variety of courses and disciplines (history, sociology, political science, etc.)'.[6] A similar view was voiced by Joel Beinin (of Stanford University) who questioned my findings on the grounds that 'many of the arguments of the "new historians" are widely accepted today in liberal Israeli intellectual circles'.[7] And 'new historian' Tom Segev (of *Ha-aretz* newspaper) put a lighter touch on this group's growing popularity. 'We perform at weddings and bar mitzvas', he jokingly told an admiring American journalist.[8]

Of course, fashion and popularity cannot authenticate incorrect historical facts and arguments. Yet this claim underscores the fact that far from being a persecuted minority in Israeli, let alone in Western universities, the 'new historians' and like-minded 'revisionists' constitute the hard core of the academic establishment, if not a persecuting majority. Hence the steadily enfeebling criticism of the 'new historians' by their erstwhile opponents, anxious to avoid stigmatization as 'old' or reactionary.

This state of affairs is scarcely surprising. Half a century after the creation of the State of Israel and the attendant 1947–49 War (for Israelis, the War of Independence; for Palestinians, *al-Nakba*: the Catastrophe), these momentous events have lost much of their meaning for contemporary

---

5   Benny Morris, 'Objective History', *Ha-aretz Weekly Magazine*, 1 July 1994, p. 40.
6   Benny Morris, 'Refabricating 1948', *Journal of Palestine Studies*, XXVII, 2 (Winter 1998), p. 82.
7   Joel Beinin, review of *Fabricating Israeli History* in the *Middle East Journal*, 52, 3 (Summer 1998), p. 449.
8   Michael Kennedy, 'Rewriting History', *Inquirer Magazine*, 1 February 1998, p. 12.

Israelis. Many participants, not to mention decision-makers, are no longer alive, and later generations lack the first-hand experience which could have easily foiled the revisionist attempt to turn Israeli history on its head through documentary manipulation. For young Israelis, the events of the late 1940s are very remote – just another episode in history books that has to be read for exams, the odd television documentary; as such, the revisionist version of history seems as good as any.

The situation is all the more acute in the Western world, the United States in particular. Not only is there widespread ignorance regarding the origins of the Arab–Israeli conflict, but Middle Eastern studies have increasingly fallen under the sway of Arabists and their disciples (i.e., veterans of institutions dealing with the region, such as the Department of State, oil companies, economic/financial organizations, etc.), and/or scholars of Arab descent, as even a glance at the membership list of the American Middle East Studies Association (MESA) and its European counterparts will easily reveal. Moreover, for quite some time the Arab oil-producing countries have been penetrating the foremost Western universities and academic publishing houses by subsidizing publications and extending generous grants for the establishment of Chairs and research centres, on which they exercise a lasting control, however indirect.

There is yet another side to the ledger. Since democracy is an extremely rare commodity in the Middle East, and since students of the region's contemporary politics, history, and society are anxious to maintain free access to its countries, they exercise a strict self-censorship, avoiding like the plague anything that smacks of criticism of local societies and regimes. Take, for example, a former doctoral student who wanted to research contemporary Syrian state-sponsored terrorism. It did not take him long to realize that the topic would make him *persona non grata* in Syria (and Lebanon), and would isolate him among fellow Arabists. Because of this he changed both his research focus and its time-frame so as to avoid any potential current implications. There is of course nothing wrong in historical research, which, unlike contemporary studies, can be backed by solid archival evidence; but the underlying cause of this particular change of tack, which had nothing to do with scholarly considerations, is fundamentally wrong.

Consider also an international conference on Iraq, held at the Royal Institute of International Affairs (or Chatham House as it is commonly known after the building in which it resides), shortly before the Iraqi invasion of Kuwait in August 1990. All participants, British, Europeans, and Americans, went out of their way to heap praise on Saddam Hussein's regime and to rub shoulders with the senior Iraqi officials in attendance (notably Nizar Hamdoon, then Iraq's Deputy Foreign Minister). A respected American academic even applauded the desert concentration camps, in which the Iraqi authorities had herded many thousands of Kurds exiled from their homes during and after the Iran–Iraq War, as decent hamlets. When the handful of Iraqi expatriates, who had somehow managed to obtain invitations to the conference, tried to voice criticism of the repressive nature of the Iraqi regime, they were peremptorily silenced by the moderators, with some of them being unceremoniously ushered out of the discussion hall.

In this disturbing atmosphere, where intellectual and professional integrity is subordinated to expedience and fashion, it is scarcely surprising that demand for Israel-bashing is ever on the rise. Notwithstanding the inherent anti-Israel prejudice of the Arabists, by virtue of their education and careers, Israel of the 1980s and the 1990s, of the Lebanon War and the *intifada* is a soft target. The image of a young and brave David fighting for his life against an uncompromising enemy has ceased to exist; instead it has been transformed into a Goliath, subjugating another people and denying them the right of national self-determination. And the distance from here to the anachronistic projection of a contemporary reality 50 years back is very short indeed.

This trend has not been confined to academic life. In today's 'global village', where events in one part of the world are transmitted instantaneously around the globe, reaching the public and policy-makers at the same moment, Arabists have gradually become key shapers of public opinion in their field of specialty. It is they who interpret the Middle East to the general public whenever there is a fresh conflagration in this highly volatile area; it is they who often give the benefit of their opinion to Congress and government. The Arabist presence has been particularly conspicuous on television, where a mutually beneficial partnership between broadcaster and pundit has been forged: the former is in constant need of commentary, given the explosion in news channels broadcasting around the clock; the latter is eager to sell his merchandise come what may. Consequently, Israel has been implicated in every Middle Eastern crisis over the past two decades, regardless of any actual involvement in those events. During the 1990–91 Gulf crisis, from Iraq's invasion of Kuwait and its expulsion from the emirate six months later, numerous commentaries suggested that the crisis could be resolved if only Israel made some concessions to the Palestinians, as if Saddam Hussein had the slightest concern for Palestinian well-being. (After all, had he wished to 'liberate occupied Palestine' he would have marched his forces westwards rather than southwards to Kuwait.)

The peace process during the Rabin–Peres government (1992–96) somewhat curbed this phenomenon; but the anti-Israel prejudice quickly resurfaced as the initial euphoria attending the Oslo Accords subsided and the process ran into recurrent difficulties. Paradoxically, the closer Palestinians and Israelis have come to resolving their historic feud, the more ferocious the historiographical assault on Israel has become: both as a tactical ploy to extract substantial Israeli concessions on such sensitive issues as the return of the refugees, and as part of the broader design to transform the prospective peace accords into official public acknowledgement of the justness of the Palestinian cause, thereby recasting collective memory by deleting past blunders and their devastating consequences and presenting the Palestinians as hapless victims of Zionist/Israeli aggression.

In this reinvigorated historiographical assault, the 'new historians' have come to occupy pride of place. For what could conceivably provide better 'proof' of the correctness of the 'Palestinian narrative' than the ostensible debunking of Israel's 'founding myths' by Israeli historians? And the more vociferous this self-flagellation the better. Thus, for example, Gabriel Piterberg concludes an article in the *British Journal of Middle Eastern Studies*, in which he thoroughly misrepresented the contents of Israeli textbooks, so as to prove the (allegedly) patronizing attitude of Israel's (allegedly) Ashkenazi education system over Sephardi Israelis, with the political statement that 'I am a product of a nationalist-colonial state and society, in opposition to which I seek to stand.'[9] How bold, how touching, how irrelevant.

Would it be conceivable for Americans, Canadians, Argentineans, Australians, etc., whose colonial past is infinitely clearer than Israel's, to conclude academic articles in a similar politicized fashion? Hardly. The proper place of such a statement (even if it were not totally misconceived) would be in a propaganda pamphlet or a political treatise – not in a scholarly journal.

In these circumstances, where propaganda is often substituted for scholarship, it is scarcely surprising that the partisan *Journal of Palestine Studies* (*JPS*) has not only opened its doors to the 'new historians' but has wholeheartedly embraced them as its favourite contributors. Since the late 1980s the *JPS* featured at least seven articles by Avi Shlaim (of Oxford

---

9   Gabriel Piterberg, 'Domestic Orientalism: The Representation of "Oriental" Jews in Zionist/Israeli historiography', *British Journal of Middle Eastern Studies*, 23, 2 (November 1996), p. 145.

University); and Benny Morris, a late-comer to this forum, has been breathing down Shlaim's neck with six articles: far more than any Palestinian or Arab scholar, with the sole exception of Edward William Said (who published ten articles during the journal's 26 years of existence).

The *JPS* has also used the 'new historians' as its foremost demolition team, particularly against works by Israeli historians deemed most damaging to the 'Palestinian narrative'. In 1994, for example, Morris wrote a lengthy and venomous review of *The Road Not Taken* by Itamar Rabinovich (of Tel-Aviv University); and this review pales in comparison to his 15-page assault on the first edition of *Fabricating Israeli History*.[10] Apparently the longest review-essay ever published by the *Journal of Palestine Studies* – four times longer than the review of Edward William Said's *Orientalism* – this assault underscores the *JPS*'s anxiety to discredit my work. To this end, the *JPS* had also denied me access to its readers – by rejecting an article of mine on the idea of transfer in Zionist thinking under the odd pretext that it 'does not fit in with our needs at the time' – while presenting these readers with a distorted picture of my research by the least impartial person possible.

The *JPS*, to be sure, has not been the only journal seeking to shield the 'new historiography' from legitimate criticism. The *International Journal of Middle East Studies* (*IJMES*), MESA's scholarly journal, declined an article of mine on similar grounds. Rather than address my factual assertions, the journal's readers chose to denigrate the article as, *inter alia*, 'situated on the extreme right of Israeli academic politics in its attack on the new Israeli historians'. Since when are scholarly works judged not by their intrinsic merit but by the perceived national and/or ideological identity of their authors? And why should there be any discrimination on the basis of one's background in the first place? Are scholarly

---

10 Benny Morris, 'A Second Look at the "Missed Peace", or Smoothing Out History: A Review Essay', *Journal of Palestine Studies*, XXIV, 1 (Autumn 1994), pp. 78–88; idem, 'Refabricating 1948'.

journals not supposed to provide a forum for a true intellectual discourse, which by definition involves challenging
the received wisdom? Besides, having spent the lion's share
of my academic career at a British university, I have never
been part of the 'Israeli academic establishment', let alone a
participant in 'Israeli academic politics'. Moreover, as a longtime advocate of Palestinian statehood, my political views
would be on the 'extreme left' of the spectrum rather than the
other way round. But then, the possibility that one could be
sympathetic towards Palestinian rights without refashioning
the past does not seem to have occurred to *IJMES*'s referees.

Not surprisingly, the *JPS* seems to subscribe to the same
approach. Apart from using the 'new historians' to provide
(ostensible) credibility for its version of Palestinian history, it
has recently made them, Shlaim and Morris in particular,
regular commentators on contemporary Israeli–Palestinian
affairs; [11] and their adherence to the facts in this newly assumed
role is no stricter than that demonstrated in their 'historical'
studies. Thus, for example, having traced the origins of Yitzhak
Rabin's assassination to a mixture of 'national–religious tradition of ideological and actual lawlessness', and 'the older
tradition of "Revisionist" terrorism', Morris went on to argue
that 'during the late 1960s and the 1970s, Gush Emunim
continuously broke the law in its campaign to set up Jewish
settlements in the West Bank. The Labour-led governments
of the day, under Prime Ministers Levi Eshkol, Golda Meir,
and Yitzhak Rabin, continually bent to their will'.[12] But Gush
Emunim was established in March 1974, in the twilight of the
Yom Kippur War,[13] and hence could not have 'continuously
broke[n] the law' during the late 1960s. Nor could Prime
Ministers Meir and Eshkol have 'continually bent to their

11 See, for example, Avi Shlaim, 'Prelude to the Accord: Likud, Labor and the Palestinians',
    Journal of Palestine Studies, 2 (Winter 1994), pp. 5–19; idem, 'The Oslo Accord', XXIII, 3
    (Spring 1994), pp. 24–40.
12 Benny Morris, 'After Rabin', *Journal of Palestine Studies*, XXV, 2 (Winter 1996), pp. 84, 86.
13 Ehud Sprinzak, *The Ascendance of Israel's Radical Right* (New York: Oxford University
    Press, 1991), p. 65.

will', if only because the former had resigned her post before the start of the Gush's activities and the latter had died five years before its establishment. But then why be bothered by facts?

Similarly, in a commentary on the armed Israeli–Palestinian confrontation in September 1996, following Israel's opening of a tunnel in Old Jerusalem, Ilan Pappé argued that 'the bloodshed in September … was caused by [Prime Minister Benjamin] Netanyahu's decision to send the IDF (Israeli Defense Forces) back into areas already evacuated by Israel'.[14] It is not clear from where Pappé derived this fantastic claim, which was not even made by Yasser Arafat's Palestinian Authority. But why lose a golden opportunity for Israel-bashing?

In a proper academic field such propagandistic comments would have raised a serious question mark as to the professional credibility of the persons making them. Not so in contemporary Middle Eastern studies. For such is the politicization of this field that the New Historiography's partisanship has been its entry ticket to the Arabist club and its attendant access to academic journals, respected publishing houses, and the mass media. Shlaim, for one, was the foremost academic adviser to a six-part BBC television series about the Arab–Israeli conflict, produced on the occasion of Israel's 50th anniversary and casting the Jewish State in the role of the regional villain.[15] Morris, for his part, was the moving spirit behind a televized documentary on the Palestinians by an Israeli expatriate. Favourable reports on the 'new historians' feature regularly in the Western press. Indeed, there is no business like the bash-Israel business. Whoever dares endanger this prosperous industry is subjected to a massive retaliation, or rather a defamation campaign, aimed at eliminating the messenger before he/she has been given the opportunity to speak out.

14 Ilan Pappé, 'Netanyahu: The Worst Case Scenario', *Rive*, Spring 1997, p. 59.
15 See Efraim Karsh, 'Who Started It?', *Daily Telegraph*, 7 April 1998, p. 22.

Such was the reaction of the 'new historians' and their erstwhile supporters to *Fabricating Israeli History*: a litany of personal smear and innuendo regarding the purity of my motives, *accompanied by no attempt to rebut my factual assertions.* But it was the timid response of scholars who do not belong to this group, indeed reject its fundamental tenets, which is particularly revealing of how fashionable the 'new historiography' has become, and how politically incorrect it is to challenge this fad.

First, there were those who disowned the book without taking the trouble to read it. Thus, for example, I was told by a London-based colleague that she was doubtful whether she would agree with me once she had read my book. She never did read it, yet remained entrenched in her disagreement. Dan Perry, *Associated Press* correspondent in Israel, went a significant step further. He telephoned me for my views, for an article he was preparing on the 'new historiography', and we held a lengthy conversation. I clarified for Perry in no uncertain terms that my quarrel with the 'new historians' was *not* about the interpretation of this or that document but rather about professional and intellectual integrity, without which there could be no scholarly discourse; I also told him that my book contained numerous examples of systematic falsification of evidence aimed at portraying a distorted picture of the birth of Israel. He promised to look these examples up. Yet, when his dispatch was published a few days later, it contained not a shred of this evidence, nor indeed indicated the slightest familiarity with my book. Instead, Perry wrongly claimed that 'the essence of the historians' debate appears to be mostly about emphasis and interpretation' – the precise opposite of what it actually is.[16]

Yet another kind of reaction to *Fabricating Israeli History* involved speaking from both sides of the mouth, saying one thing in private and its opposite in public. Thus, for example,

---

16 Dan Perry, 'Historians Question Israel's Early Treatment of Palestinians', *Washington Times*, 31 December 1997.

an Israeli historian wrote to me approvingly that 'there is no doubt that the tendency to twist documents is a malady'; then went on to approach a leading 'new historian' for a foreword to his own book. Bernard Wasserstein (at the time at the Oxford Centre for Hebrew and Jewish Studies) went one step further. Having read my first criticism of the 'new historians' in an American scholarly journal,[17] he wrote to me that, notwithstanding his basic affinity with this group, 'you do make some telling points, I admit'. Yet when my book triggered a heated debate in the *Times Literary Supplement*, Wasserstein chose to damn it in a manner which stood in stark contrast to what he had said in his letter.

Similarly, a leading Israeli political scientist wrote to me that while he fully accepted my rebuttal of Morris's claim that the 'transfer idea' constituted an integral part of mainstream Zionist thinking in the late 1930s and 1940s, he thought I was too judgemental of Morris: 'He works with integrity and one should argue with him, in my opinion, without resorting to personal slander.' To which one can only say that professional integrity is not the first thing to come to mind given that there is scarcely a single document quoted by Morris on the transfer issue free from twisting and distortion. Besides, since when does the exposure of wrongdoing constitute 'personal slander'?

A far more revealing demonstration of timidity has been provided by the review of *Fabricating Israeli History* by Emmanuel Sivan (of the Hebrew University of Jerusalem).[18] Several years earlier, when the Hebrew-language edition of Morris's *The Birth of the Palestinian Refugee Problem* first appeared, Sivan damned it as seriously flawed and one-sided, mainly on account of its virtual overlooking of Arab and/or Arabic-language sources. Since then, however, the

---

17 Efraim Karsh, 'Rewriting Israel's History', *Middle East Quarterly*, III, 2 (June 1996), pp. 19–31.
18 Emmanuel Sivan, 'The New Historians and the Unfulfilled Promise', *Sfarim*, 26 June 1997, p. 1.

'new historians' have become media favourites and a force to be reckoned with in the Israeli academic establishment. Sivan, the quintessential veteran Orientalist, whose like are regularly vilified by the 'new historians', attempts to have his cake and eat it at the same time. He compliments me for debunking Avi Shlaim's conspiracy theory about a Zionist–Transjordanian collusion to abort the UN Partition Resolution of November 1947 and to divide Mandatory Palestine between themselves; at the same time he seeks to belittle both the significance of this rebuttal by claiming that 'Shlaim has already retracted some of his interpretations', and the originality of my research by stating that I had relied 'to a large extent on Avraham Sela's pioneering work'. Neither of these claims is true. This would have been evident to anyone who read my book. Shlaim has not backed an inch from his conspiracy theory and my book in no way relies on Sela's work. On the contrary, Sela accepts in principle the existence of a Zionist–Transjordanian collusion to divide Palestine, but claims that it had been overtaken by events in the months following its clinching in November 1947. In contrast, my book proves that there was no such collusion in the first place; and Sivan himself concedes that on this issue I demolished Shlaim's conspiracy theory.

Even more peculiar is Sivan's attempt to trivialize the exposure of Morris's falsifications regarding the transfer issue. In his opinion, the question of whether the Zionist movement was genuinely interested in peaceful coexistence with the Palestinians within the framework of a two-state solution (i.e., partition), or wished to dispossess them of their land is 'a marginal aspect of Morris's book'. To my mind, this question not only constitutes the hinge on which Morris's book rests: it stands at the core of the historiographical debate raging to this very day about the origins of the Palestinian refugee problem. This no doubt is also the view of the shapers of the 'Palestinian narrative', as evidenced *inter alia* by the sustained effort of the *Journal of Palestine Studies* to (mis)attribute such intention to the Zionist movement.[19] Even Morris himself claimed at a recent conference at Ben-Gurion University that 'it is impossible to understand the spirit of transfer and partial ethnic-cleansing in 1948 without taking into account Ben-Gurion's thinking and wishes'.[20] Yet, for Sivan this is but a marginal aspect of Jewish-Israeli–Palestinian relations.

Needless to say, the response of the 'new historians' and their partisans to *Fabricating Israeli History* has been anything but timid. Not once have they grappled with the book's central thesis, let alone attempted to refute its factual assertions. Instead they have misrepresented its essence altogether through a string of distortions, misquotations, and bogus claims, then laughed it off as an odious caricature.

William Quandt (of the University of Virginia), is perhaps the only sympathizer of this group to have acknowledged both the nature of my anti-revisionist charge and its severity. 'Karsh is not talking about differences of interpretation, of nuanced readings of texts', he wrote in a review of my book, 'he is making a different and more damaging accusation – namely, that these academics are deliberately misleading readers. That is, they know what the record says and choose to distort it'. 'Along with plagiarism', he continued, 'fabrication is the worst accusation one academic can make against another.'

Do I succeed in making my case? Here, Quandt closes ranks: 'I do not come away convinced, although in some cases he does raise points that seem to warrant examination of the originals.'[21] But then, why not press this point to its logical conclusion and conduct this warranted 'examination of the

19 See, for example, Walid Khalidi, 'Plan Dalet Revisited', *Journal of Palestine Studies*, XVIII, 1 (Autumn 1988), pp. 3–71; Israel Shahak, 'A History of the Concept of "Transfer" in Zionism', *Journal of Palestine Studies*, XVIII, 3 (Spring 1989), pp. 22–38; Nur Masalha, 'A Critique of Benny Morris', *Journal of Palestine Studies*, XXI, 1 (Autumn 1991), pp. 90–97; idem, '1948 and After Revisited', *Journal of Palestine Studies*, XXIV, 4 (Summer 1995), pp. 90–95; Norman Finkelstein, 'Myths, Old and New', *Journal of Palestine Studies*, XXI, 1 (Autumn 1991), pp. 66–89; Benny Morris, 'Response to Finkelstein and Masalha', *Journal of Palestine Studies*, XXI, 1 (Autumn 1991), pp. 98–114.
20 *Ha-aretz*, 20 November 1997.
21 William Quandt, review of *Fabricating Israeli History*, in *MESA Bulletin*, 32 (1998), p. 118.

originals' before writing the review? Don't the readers deserve a thorough analysis which gets to the bottom of things, rather than leaving the key question hanging in the air? Quandt has applauded works by 'revisionist' Israeli historians, notably Nur Masalha's book on the role of 'transfer' in Zionist thinking. Isn't he interested in discovering whether or not this praise has been fully warranted?

Still, Quandt has at least given a general indication of what my book is all about, something which regrettably cannot be said of like-minded academics. Joel Beinin, for one, totally misrepresents the nature of my criticism of Morris by claiming that 'by returning the debate to the arena of intellectual history, Karsh … avoids engaging [Benny] Morris's archival discoveries'.[22] This could not be further from the truth. My book has nothing to do with 'the arena of intellectual history'. It has everything to do with engaging the 'archival discoveries' of Morris and his fellow 'new historians'.

Similarly, Avi Shlaim charges me of predicating my rebuttal of his thesis that Britain was an active party to a Transjordan–Zionist collusion to partition Mandatory Palestine between themselves on a single 'unimportant and insignificant document', written by 'a middle-level career civil servant' and deemed 'not suitable for circulation outside the Foreign Office'.[23] This is a very odd claim indeed. For even a glance at my book would easily reveal that two full chapters, containing hundreds of documents from official British archives, including that of St Antony's College, Oxford – Shlaim's own institution – are dedicated to the rebuttal of the above claim.

But the story does not end here. Shlaim chose to misrepresent the nature of the above document and its significance. First, this was not an obscure document by a middle-level career civil servant but rather a summary of a

---

22 Beinin, review of *Fabricating Israeli History*, p. 448.
23 Avi Shlaim, 'A Totalitarian Concept of History', *Middle East Quarterly*, III, 3 (September 1996), p. 55; Shlaim's response to an interview with me in *Ha-aretz Weekly Magazine*, 2 May 1997, p. 18.

highly important consultation, held by the British Foreign
Secretary, Ernest Bevin, with his key advisers immediately
after his meeting with the Transjordanian Prime Minister,
Tawfiq Abu al-Huda; the consultation discussed the critical
issue of Transjordan's possible incursion into Palestine after
the termination of the Mandate, raised by Abu al-Huda
during his meeting with Bevin, and its implications. Secondly,
contrary to Shlaim's claim, the memorandum was considered
suitable for circulation outside the Foreign Office, as clearly
evidenced by the comment on its bottom: 'This was briefly
discussed with the S. of S. [i.e. Bevin] who did not object to
the substance of the above minute being confidentially discussed with the State Depat. I attach a draft tel.'[24]

In short, Shlaim has inverted the above memorandum,
turning black into white. This is not a matter of having a
different interpretation from mine; it is a blatant misrepresentation of the substance of a historical document. I challenged
Shlaim to publish the sources of his (mis)representation of the
document.[25] He never did.

But if Shlaim attempts, however disingenuously, to rebut
some of my claims, Ilan Pappé does not even bother. Instead
he derided me as a 'court historian' failing to grasp the tenets
of the 'post-Zionist' thesis, such as the claim 'that there was
parity on the battlefield in the 1948 war'. 'Perhaps in the
patriotic Israeli colony in London there are still the fighting
spirit and the readiness to fight for Zionism to the last drop
of ink', he wrote.[26]

What can one say in reply to such arguments? That the
debate is not about perceived political views but about
elementary professional and intellectual integrity? That if
'parity on the battlefield in the 1948 war' constitutes a central
tenet of the 'de-Zionized view' of history, then most Israeli

24 Memorandum by B.A.B. Burrows, 9 February 1948, FO 371/68368/E2696.
25 Efraim Karsh, 'Historical Fictions', *Middle East Quarterly*, III, 3 (September 1996), p. 60.
26 See, Ilan Pappé, 'My Non-Zionist Narrative', *Middle East Quarterly*, III, 3 (September 1996), pp. 51–2; idem, letter to *Ha-retz Weekly Magazine*, May 1997.

writings on the war, including David Ben-Gurion's war diaries and autobiographical account, are 'de-Zionized'? That when one retreats to the 'patriotic' line of defence, one has lost the argument? For years Pappé has proudly presented himself as a staunch opponent of Israel's existence. 'Jews are nothing more than a religion', he uncritically reiterated the misconceived adage, used by generations of anti-Zionists from Arnold Toynbee to Hafiz al-Asad. 'To have a "Jewish state" is like having "a Catholic state" in France.'[27] Now all of a sudden he exhorts the virtues of patriotism. Could it be that it has all been a façade and that in his heart of hearts Pappé has always been a true Zionist/Israeli patriot? But then, why does he deem it incongruous for a London-based Israeli academic to criticize the pervasive anti-Israel partisanship, but not for Israeli expatriates to indulge in this partisanship in the first place? It would seem that as far as Pappé's patriotism is concerned, expatriate Israelis (not to speak of those living in Israel) should 'fight Zionism to the last drop of ink'.

This is also the view of Omer Bartov, an expatriate Israeli teaching history at Rutgers University in New Jersey. In a review of my book in the *Times Literary Supplement*,[28] Bartov made no attempt to refute any of my factual assertions, which in itself is hardly surprising since he has done no independent research on the subject himself; instead he hurled a string of personal smears. He claimed, for example, that I began my 'specialization in Middle Eastern affairs as an officer in Israeli army intelligence',[29] when in fact I had already acquired my first academic degree in modern Middle Eastern history prior to joining the army; nor did I deal with Arab affairs during my service but rather with superpower involvement in the Middle East. Similarly, Bartov finds a fundamental incongruity between my criticism of the 'revisionist' partisanship and

---

27   Quoted in Dan Perry, 'After Half-century, Historians Debate Israel's Birth', *Associated Press*, 21 December 1997.
28   Omer Bartov, 'Of Past Wrongs – and Their Redressing', *Times Literary Supplement*, 31 October 1997, pp. 13–14.
29   Ibid., p. 14.

my longstanding support for the Palestinian right to self-determination, as if one's political views should necessarily mould one's historical research!

But the most revealing response to my book has been that of Benny Morris. For years Morris had had it easy. By inundating his readers with primary sources, he created the impression, one that even his critics accepted unquestioningly, that his work is solidly grounded in facts, thus earning himself a reputation as the most thorough and meticulous of 'new historians'. It was scarcely surprising therefore that when I proved this picture to be false, Morris was besides himself with rage. 'Efraim Karsh's "Rewriting Israel's History" is a mélange of distortions, half-truths, and plain lies that vividly demonstrates his profound ignorance of both the source material ... and the history of the Zionist–Arab conflict', he retorted to my first criticism of the 'new historians', published in the June 1996 issue of the *Middle East Quarterly*. 'It does not deserve serious attention or reply.'[30] He reiterated the very same position in response to a lengthy interview I gave *Ha-aretz Weekly Magazine*, following the publication of *Fabricating Israeli History*. While emphasizing that he had not taken the trouble to read my book, he dismissed my findings as 'idiotic slander indicative of the man himself, who is perhaps seeking this way to promote personal interests'.[31] Needless to say, he never stated which personal interests could be promoted by going against the grain.

Before long, however, Morris was forced to shed his façade of indifference. When *The Economist* and the *Times Literary Supplement* (London) published several examples of his falsification of archival documentation,[32] Morris begrudgingly

---

30 Benny Morris, 'Undeserving of Reply', *Middle East Quarterly*, III, 3 (September 1996), p. 51.
31 For my interview and Morris's response see, 'The Charge: Historical Fabrication', *Ha-aretz Weekly Magazine*, pp. 16–18.
32 'The Unchosen People', *The Economist*, 19 July 1997, p. 92; *Times Literary Supplement*, 14 November 1997, p. 19.

conceded the correctness of my interpretation of every single document published by the two magazines, while simultaneously seeking to disguise the real nature of his misconduct. 'Karsh has a point', he wrote to the *Times Literary Supplement*. 'My treatment of transfer thinking before 1948 was, indeed, superficial.' He also acknowledged my refutation of his misinterpretation of an important speech made by David Ben-Gurion of 3 December 1947: 'he is probably right in rejecting the "transfer interpretation" I suggested in *The Birth* to a sentence in that speech'.[33] In his attack on my book in the *Journal of Palestine Studies* Morris went a step further by admitting that, with regard to the same quote, 'Karsh appears to be correct in charging that I "stretched" the evidence to make my point.'[34]

The truth is fundamentally different. What is at hand here is neither the misinterpretation of a certain sentence in Ben-Gurion's speech nor even the 'stretching of evidence': it is a deliberate and complex attempt to misrepresent the contents of this speech so as to portray a false picture of the moral and political world-view of Israel's founding father.[35]

An insightful glimpse into the depth of Morris's anxiety following the publication of my book is afforded by his *JPS* review. How is it possible that until the publication of *Fabricating Israeli History* nobody else has charged the 'new historians' of such professional misconduct? He feigned innocence – as if the failure to uncover a felony can be equated with its non-occurrence (besides, as noted in the Introduction below, Shabtai Teveth did expose some of Morris's distortions already in 1990). Morris also clings to some of Israel's veteran Orientalists, such as Moshe Maoz and Emmanuel Sivan, the likes of whom he has repeatedly dismissed as 'old historians'; yet he 'forgets' to tell his readers of either Sivan's acknowledgement of my rebuttal of Shlaim's collusion myth, or his past scathing criticism of Morris's own book.

---

33   Benny Morris, *Times Literary Supplement*, 28 November 1997, p. 17.
34   Morris, 'Refabricating 1948', p. 83.
35   For a detailed exposure of Morris's distortion of this speech see below, pp. 61–67.

Morris also reverts to his common practice of identifying (alleged) marginal errors, typographical and otherwise, as a means to discredit his opponents and divert attention from the real issues. Thus, for example, he charges me of mis-naming Teveth's book in one footnote as *Ben-Gurion and the Palestine Arabs*, when it should have actually read *Ben-Gurion and the Palestinian Arabs*. But Morris, in his own book, repeat-edly quotes Teveth's book as *Ben-Gurion and the Palestine Arabs*.[36] So, what is the point?

Yet in his determination 'to shore up the crumbling walls' of the New Historiography to use his own words,[37] Morris shuns no means – he even compares my work to that of Holocaust deniers. This below-the-belt accusation seems incredible indeed given the following two facts.

- My book offers a scathing criticism of the appalling treatment of Holocaust survivors by the British Govern-ment, Foreign Secretary Ernest Bevin in particular, while the 'new historians' whitewash this behaviour and applaud Bevin as the 'guardian angel' of the Jewish State;
- The 'new historians' have been at the forefront of the campaign to dilute the uniqueness of the Holocaust and downplay its significance, whether by charging Israel of exploiting this tragic event for political capital, or by depicting the Palestinians as the Holocaust's 'real victims', or by putting Israeli and Nazi actions and behaviourial patterns on a par.

Indeed, in an article in the *Journal of Palestine Studies*, Morris himself sought to conceal the significance of the Holocaust in Jewish contemporary thinking by withholding Ben-Gurion's exasperation, at a Cabinet meeting on 16 June 1948, with the

36 For Morris's charge see, *Refabricating 1948*, p. 84. For Morris's own quotes of Teveth's book see, *The Birth*, pp. 304 (n. 27), 369. I am grateful to Alan Miller for bringing this point to my attention.
37 Morris, 'A Second Look', p. 87.

international indifference to the pan-Arab attack on Israel in May 1948:

> The world must understand that 700,000 people are confronted with 27 million. One against forty. And it is not that easy to stand up. I cannot understand what has happened to human decency: how could they stand idly by when 27 million [Arabs] attacked 700,000 Jews, after six million Jews had just been slaughtered? ...[38]

Moreover, Morris made the same omission *twice* in the course of the same article – once when citing Ben-Gurion's book; the second time when citing the official protocol.[39] And then Morris proceeds to accuse Ben-Gurion of falsifying the record ...

One can only hope that academic and intellectual integrity in the study of the Arab–Israeli conflict, sacrificed on the altar of popularity and fashion, will be restored before too long. Both Israelis and Arabs have suffered too much and for too long for their collective memories to be shaped by this kind of false history.

E.K., Winter 1999

---

38   Israel State Archives, Protocol of the Provisional Government Meeting of 16 June 1948, pp. 35–6.

39   Benny Morris, 'Falsifying the Record: A Fresh Look at Zionist Documentation of 1948', *Journal of Palestine Studies*, XXIV, 3 (Spring 1995), pp. 57–8.

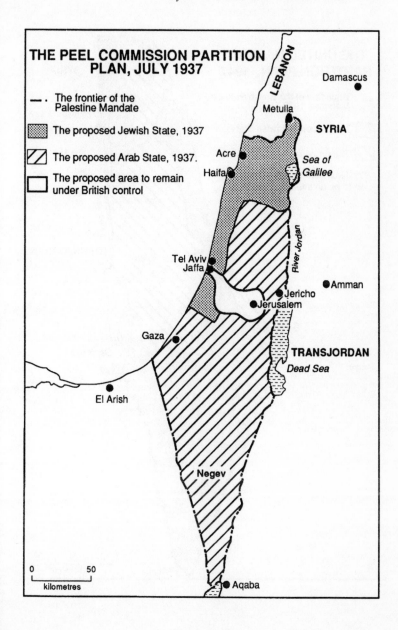

THE PEEL COMMISSION PARTITION PLAN, JULY 1937

— . The frontier of the Palestine Mandate

The proposed Jewish State, 1937

The proposed Arab State, 1937.

The proposed area to remain under British control

Damascus

LEBANON

Metulla

SYRIA

Acre

Sea of Galilee

Haifa

River Jordan

Tel Aviv
Jaffa

Amman

Jericho

Jerusalem

Gaza

TRANSJORDAN

Dead Sea

El Arish

Negev

0   50
kilometres

Aqaba

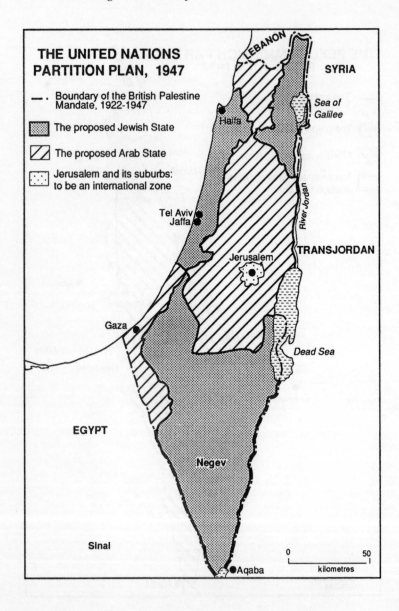

THE UNITED NATIONS PARTITION PLAN, 1947

—· Boundary of the British Palestine Mandate, 1922-1947

The proposed Jewish State

The proposed Arab State

Jerusalem and its suburbs: to be an international zone

LEBANON

SYRIA

Sea of Galilee

Haifa

River Jordan

TRANSJORDAN

Tel Aviv
Jaffa

Jerusalem

Gaza

Dead Sea

EGYPT

Negev

Sinai

Aqaba

0   50
kilometres

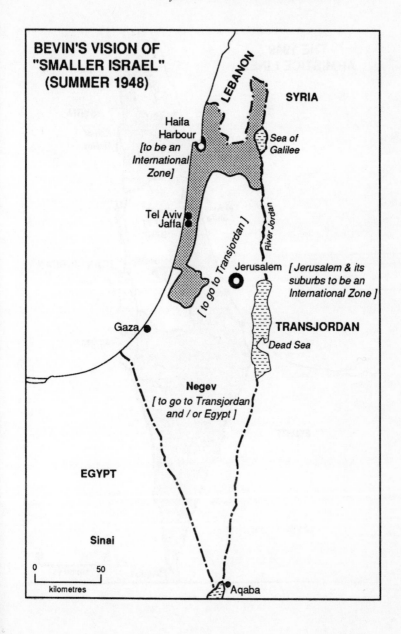

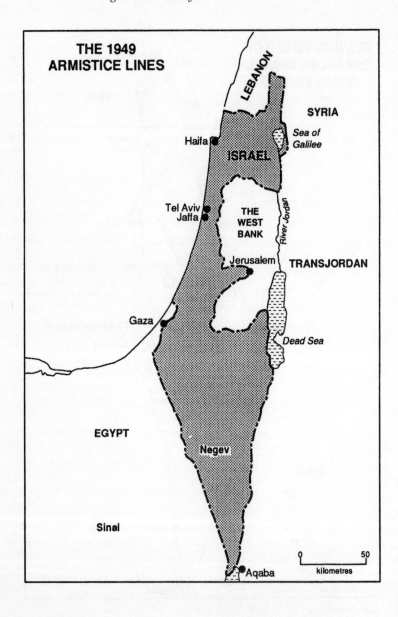

Introduction

> The purpose of Newspeak was not only to provide
> a medium of expression for the worldview and
> mental habits proper to the devotees of Ingsoc [or
> English Socialism], but to make all other modes of
> thought impossible.
>
> GEORGE ORWELL, *Nineteen Eighty-Four*

For quite some time Israeli historiography has been subjected to a sustained assault by a cohort of self-styled 'new
historians' vying to debunk what they claim to be the distorted 'Zionist narrative' of Israeli history in general, and of
the Arab–Israeli conflict in particular. Deriding alternative
interpretations as 'old' or 'mobilized', they have portrayed
Zionism as the 'original sin' underlying the region's violent
history. To some, Zionism is an archaic remnant of Western
colonialism destined to wither away sooner or later as Israel
will enter its 'post-Zionist' phase. To others it is 'merely' an
exploitative and aggressive movement which brought
about the Palestinian tragedy and bears the responsibility
for perpetuating the conflict with its Arab neighbours,
failing time and again to seize their extended hand for
peace.

Before long these views sparked a heated debate, spil-
ling over from the ivory tower of academe to the public
domain. This was brought to a head in the summer of 1994
following a frontal attack on the 'new historians' by the
respected author Aharon Megged. In an article titled 'The
Israeli Suicide Drive', published in the weekly magazine of

the prestigious newspaper *Ha-aretz*, Megged accused this self-styled group of having a political-ideological axe to grind. 'It would be erroneous to call this [genre of historio-graphical writing] "myth debunking"', he claimed. 'The work done before our eyes is merely the rewriting of the one-hundred-year Zionist history in the spirit of its enemies and opponents'.[1]

The response of the 'new historians' was quick in coming, ranging from the vitriolic, to the patronizing, to the pious. Benny Morris (of the Ben Gurion University of Beer Sheba) defined this criticism as 'slander which Megged himself does not even know whether or not it has a basis, since he has never bothered to read a single book by those new historians'.[2] Gabi Piterberg (of Ben-Gurion University of Beersheba) castigated Megged as a Stalinist whose article proves 'that emotional problems are not necessarily the exclusive domain of the new historians'.[3] Baruch Kimmerling (of the Hebrew University) accused Megged of being the front man for a group of senior Israeli academics who feel that 'the earth is shaking under-neath their status since their theories no longer withstand the test of changes undergone by the social sciences and historiography'. 'One could have dismissed Megged's article with a bemused nod of the head and ask what does an author understand in academic history and social sciences', he wrote, 'except that this article ... serves as a mouth-piece for a highly distinguished group of veteran academics, and is part of an incremental effort to delegitimize the works of other scholars, normally those who have not yet managed to secure their place within the Israeli academic establishment'.[4]

1   Aharon Megged, 'The Israeli Suicide Drive', *Ha-aretz Weekly Magazine*, 10 June 1994, pp. 27, 92.
2   Benny Morris, 'Objective History', ibid., 1 July 1994, p. 40.
3   Gabi Piterberg, 'The Stalinist', ibid., 17 June 1994, p. 44.
4   Baruch Kimmerling, 'The Historian's Ethics', ibid., 24 June 1994, p. 52. Strictly speaking Kimmerling does not fall within the category of 'new historians' but rather within that of the similarly self-styled 'critical sociologists'.

Leaving aside this thick veil of personal smear and innuendo, the anti-Megged case can be summarized as follows: not being a professional historian, he cannot and, indeed, did not challenge the theses of the 'new historians'; rather, he demanded their loyalty to the 'mobilized Zionist narrative' regardless of its correspondence to the 'historical truth', something that is totally unacceptable to 'true historians'. In the words of Ilan Pappé (of the University of Haifa): 'Since nobody questions the academic competence of the new historians, what is left is to unleash on them'.[5]

The truth of the matter is that both the theses of the 'new historians' and their research methods have precisely been questioned by fellow historians. The claim that Israel's recalcitrance was mainly to blame for the failure to make peace at the end of the 1947–49 War and in its aftermath was debunked by Itamar Rabinovich (of Tel-Aviv University).[6] Benny Morris's account of the birth of the Palestinian refugee problem[7] has been seriously challenged by Shabtai Teveth, David Ben-Gurion's foremost biographer.[8] Similarly, the 'new historiographical' allegation that Israel and Transjordan agreed in advance of that war to limit their war operations so as to avoid an all-out confrontation between their forces was demolished by Avraham Sela (of the Hebrew University).[9] In fact, one need not look further than the pattern of the Israeli–Transjordanian hostilities to realize the absurdity of this claim: the exorbitant human toll and the onerous dislocation occasioned by this conflict, the near-loss of Israel's capital, Jerusalem, and the destruction of all Jewish settlements in the part of Mandatory Palestine awarded by the UN Partition Resolution of

5   Ilan Pappé, 'A Lesson in New History', ibid., 24 June 1994, p. 54.
6   Itamar Rabinovich, *The Road Not Taken: Early Arab–Israeli Negotiations* (New York: Oxford University Press, 1991).
7   Benny Morris, *The Birth of the Palestinian Refugee Problem* (Cambridge: Cambridge University Press, 1987).
8   Shabtai Teveth, 'The Palestine Arab Refugee Problem and its Origins', *Middle Eastern Studies*, 26, 2 (April 1990), pp. 214–49.
9   Avraham Sela, 'Transjordan, Israel and the 1948 War: Myth, Historiography, and Reality', *Middle Eastern Studies*, 28, 4 (October 1992), pp. 623–89.

29 November 1947 to the Arab State, something that was by
no means necessary.[10]

At the methodological level, the 'new historians' have been
criticized for one-sidedness, clinging to every shred of
'incriminating evidence' against Israel while turning a blind
eye to at least equally 'incriminating evidence' on the Arab
side, or even overlooking it altogether; a corollary criticism
has been the almost exclusive reliance by most 'new historians'
on Israeli and Western sources to the glaring neglect of Arab
source material. This last criticism in particular has touched a
sensitive nerve, enticing the 'new historians' into a riposte.
Protesting foul play, Morris claimed 'that the archives of the
Arab Governments are closed to researchers, and that historians interested in writing about the Israeli–Arab conflict
perforce must rely mainly on Israeli and Western archives'.[11]
In a follow-up argument he claimed that 'at least as regards
the *Birth*, none of them [i.e., Morris's critics] argues that had
I used the available Arab (or Arabic) "sources", I would have
emerged with a significantly different picture of the Arab
exodus and its causes'. 'In short', he concluded,

> so long as these critics are unable to show exactly how
> a given Arab (Arabic) source could and would sub-
> stantially and accurately alter, enhance, or correct the
> picture painted in the *Birth* and in *1948 and After*, the
> criticism regarding the (relative) non-use of Arab

10   For example, following a visit to the Arab Legion's headquarters in Jerusalem on 24 May
    1948, a British official reported: 'So far as can be gathered the intention is to occupy the
    whole city, a policy that is at variance with the advice of Glubb Pasha [the Legion's
    British commander]. Morale is at a high level. These views are largely based on the belief
    that the Jerusalem population cannot bear siege conditions for much longer than
    another ten days and that a military decision will be forced during that period'.
    'Conversation with Major Abdullah al-Tal[l], Military Governor of Jerusalem and Dr.
    Mousa Husseini, 24th May 1948', FO 371/68641/E7589, Public Record Office (PRO), Kew
    Gardens, London (hereinafter, unless otherwise indicated, all British archival source-
    material cited in this book is taken from the PRO).
        For Arab Legion officers' impatience with Glubb's strategy see also Suleiman Musa,
    Ayyam La Tunsa: al-Urdun fi Harb 1948 (Days not to be Forgotten: Jordan in the 1948 War)
    (Amman, 1982), pp. 129–30.
11   Benny Morris, 'A Second Look at the "Missed Peace", or Smoothing Out History: A
    Review Essay', *Journal of Palestine Studies*, XXIV, 1 (Autumn 1994), p. 86.

sources is irrelevant, a red herring designed, perhaps, to impress, mislead, and ultimately befuddle
unsuspecting readers.[12]

This argument reflects a fundamental lack of understanding
of the historian's task, all the more so when it comes from a
self-styled 'new historian' whose claim to 'newness' is
predicated on the (alleged) uncovering of hitherto untapped
source material. It is not for Morris's critics (whose professional credentials he dismisses in the first place) to show him
how certain sources which he has consciously overlooked –
presumably due to his insufficient mastery of the Arabic
language – would have refined his thesis; it is up to him to
prove to his readers that he has used all available categories
of source material on the research phenomenon. Whether or
not the use of Arab source material would have changed the
general picture painted by Morris, or parts of it, is immaterial;
the elementary principle of historical investigation is that no
category of source material should be excluded *a priori*, let
alone primary sources on the objectives, perceptions and
activities of one party to a bilateral conflict. Failure to use such
vital information would *ipso facto* condemn any historical
study to one-sidedness, like a dancer tangoing alone. Morris
does not escape this flaw.

Moreover, Morris's excuse that Arab official archives have
been totally inaccessible to researchers has been recently
demolished by Robert Satloff (of the Washington Institute for
Near East Policy). Reviewing Morris's latest book,[13] Satloff
wryly notes that 'in a book that proposes to examine "Arab
infiltration and Israeli retaliation", Arabs are virtually non-
existent. While we are told the name of almost every Israeli
who uttered a word on retaliation in the Knesset, Cabinet,
Mapai plenum and Jewish Agency Executive session, Arab

---

12 Benny Morris, *1948 and After: Israel and the Palestinians* (Oxford: Clarendon Press, 1994),
    p. 44.
13 Benny Morris, *Israel's Border Wars, 1949–1956* (Oxford: Clarendon Press, 1993).

politicians are noticeable only by their absence ... and when Arabs are cited, the reference is often wrong'. He then proves how Morris's lack of Arab sources results in a shallow, stereotypical and often incorrect description of Arab politics and society before lending the *coup de grâce* to Morris's pretext for not using Arab sources:

> In his preface Morris states that 'No Arab state has opened its state papers to researchers, Arab or non-Arab' – this is not true. In a small, antiquated building across the street from what is now the Philadelphia Hotel off the third circle in Amman, the Jordanian national archives contain hundreds of government files from the period in question, piled floor to ceiling. At least two years prior to Morris's completion of this book, I read through papers on such relevant topics as 'Military File, 1952–57' (all originally labelled secret); 'Directives of the Ministry of Interior, 1954–55'; and 'Qibya, 1953', complete with the handwritten testimony of participants and witnesses. Though there were no xerox facilities, the staff was courteous throughout.

Having exposed the hollowness of Morris's pretext, Satloff continues his demolition job:

> Even if Morris's Israeli passport precluded him (though surely not a research assistant) to check this source, it did not stop him from examining the dozens of published Arab sources that could shed light on this period. These range from government publications (e.g., minutes of parliamentary sessions; collections of royal or presidential speeches) to local newspapers and radio broadcasts (virtually all of which are located in the extensive Newspaper Documentation Centre in the Dayan Center, Tel-Aviv

University) to memoirs and secondary sources. Again, Morris's preface states that he 'tapped some relevant Arab memoirs', but the bibliography makes mention of only Heikal, Salah Khalaf, Nasser and Sadat, all either in their English or Hebrew translations. Published but untranslated memoirs, such as those by Jordanian Prime Minister Hazza al-Majali or Jordanian military attache in Cairo Abdullah al-Tal (who is mentioned in the book), apparently were not checked.[14]

While fully subscribing to Satloff's penetrating criticism, this book takes an altogether different approach. Rather than concentrate on those vital categories of source material ignored or neglected by the 'new historians', it will prove that *the very documentation* used by these self-styled champions of 'truth and morality' reveals a completely different picture from that which they have painted.

Violating every tenet of *bona fide* research, the misrepresentation of the historical record by the 'new historiography' has ranged from the more 'innocent' act of reading into documents what is not there, to tendentious truncation of documents in a way that distorts their original meaning, to 'creative rewriting' of original texts by putting words in people's mouths and/or giving false descriptions of the contents of these documents. The 'New Israeli Distortiography' would not be an inaccurate description of this foul play.

---

14 Robert Satloff's review of Morris's *Israel's Border Wars*, in *Middle Eastern Studies*, 31, 4 (October 1995), p. 954.

1 New Bottles – Sour Wine

One of the reasons I gave up political history was
that it is very difficult not to direct it towards
the future, towards your idea of what ought to
happen. And that somehow distorts your view of
what has happened.

ALBERT HOURANI

Ever since Edward Said (of Columbia University in New
York) launched his vehement attack against the so-called
'Orientalists' some two decades ago, Middle Eastern studies
have been politicized to an extent that is unprecedented even
by the standards of this highly partisan field. Works are
judged not on their intrinsic merit but in terms of the perceived national and/or ideological identity of the respective
scholars, and their conformity to the fashionable fad; boldness
of critical thinking has been on the wane as writers have
anxiously sought to avoid stigmatization as 'Orientalists', that
vague and elusive term used by Said and his followers to
deride intellectual opponents as 'imperialistically-minded'.
Such outstanding historians as Bernard Lewis and Elie
Kedourie have been grouped in this 'politically incorrect'
category, together with a younger generation of prominent
scholars like Fouad Ajami, who dares to criticize pan-Arabism,
and, most recently, the expatriate Iraqi intellectual Kanan
Makiya, alias Samir al-Khalil, whose only 'sin' was to
denounce Iraq's genocidal policies in Kurdistan in the late
1980s, to support the international effort to end its violation

of Kuwait, and to call for the overthrow of Saddam Hussein.[1]

In this repressive intellectual atmosphere it is scarcely surprising that Israel has been cast in the role of the regional villain bearing the sole responsibility for the cycle of violence in the Middle East during the past 50 years. As Edward Said himself candidly admitted, he was convinced that 'Israel were the bad guys' long before doing any research on the Arab–Israeli conflict;[2] and he is not alone in thinking so. From its earliest days Zionism has been castigated by its detractors – Jewish and Arab, Western and Soviet – as an offshoot of Western imperialism, a predatory colonial movement bent on occupying a land that is not its own and dispossessing the indigenous population. What distinguishes Said from the earlier detractors, though, is that he has cloaked his anti-Zionist prejudice in a glossy 'scholarly' wrapping by incorporating it into a wider crusade against the 'Orientalist' bogey.

Since the late 1980s a group of Israeli academics have been pining for admission to this fashionable club. Their dowry: the 'historical evidence' to substantiate Said's *idée fixe* that 'Israel were the bad guys'. Their *modus operandi*: the crude methods of the Manhattan guru such as derogation of opponents through personal innuendo and blanket stigmatization, creation of straw theories (painted as 'Zionist myths') pre-destined for demolition, and misuse of historical evidence to serve preconceived dogmas.

---

1   A vivid illustration of this disturbing trend is afforded by Nancy Elizabeth Gallagher's *Approaches to the History of the Middle East: Interviews with Leading Middle East Historians* (Reading: Garnet, 1994), from which Lewis and Kedourie, among some other prominent historians, are glaringly missing. Citing approvingly Gallagher's pretension that 'taken together, their [i.e., her interviewees'] works represent the central historiographical transitions of the post-world war II era', Malcolm Yapp of the University of London comments: 'Indeed, they represent the generation which succeeded the Orientalists properly so-called, that is the scholars trained in classical philology'. He expresses surprise at the lack of any reference in the book to the *Encyclopedia of Islam*, but not at the absence of the field's foremost historians. Nor does he bother to explain why the Manchester-born Albert Hourani and the Paris-born Maxime Rodinson (both born in 1915) 'represent the generation which succeeded the Orientalists' while the Baghdad-born Elie Kedourie, 11 years their junior, does not. For Yapp's review see *British Journal of Middle Eastern Studies*, 22, 1 and 2 (1995), pp. 136–37.

2   *Sunday Times*, 20 June 1993.

This is already borne out by their self-proclamation as 'new historians'. In donning this pretentious and self-laudatory mantle, the 'new historians' have shrewdly positioned themselves as *avant-garde* and their critics as reactionaries, and have fended off any potential opposition to their views; for which young Israeli scholar would like to be tainted as an 'old historian', the parochial equivalent of the much-maligned 'Orientalist'? Moreover, by creating a bogus 'official Zionist line' of the Arab–Israeli conflict and attaching it to their academic opponents,[3] the 'new historians' have cast doubt on the latter's intellectual integrity and reduced them to propagandists in the service of a devious state ideology.

This derision, to be sure, is not only absurd but also sinister. The very choice of the term 'Zionist' rather than 'Israeli' to describe the imaginary 'official line' allegedly pursued by the fictitious 'old historians' is highly insidious, echoing not only the long-standing Arab castigation of Israel as 'the Zionist entity' but also the standard anti-semitic propaganda connecting Zion and its 'Elders' to bogus doctrines. It is true of course that no society in a prolonged state of war with implacably hostile neighbours, however progressive and open-minded it may be, can eradicate all traces of self-righteousness; yet the blanket stigmatization of an entire academic and intellectual community (a few 'privileged' individuals excepted) in a democratic and pluralistic society of subscribing to an 'official' or 'semi-official' historiographical narrative by virtue of a national affiliation is mind-boggling. Just as there has never been an 'official' monolithic American or British scholarly doctrine of French foreign policy, or for that matter of any non-Anglo-Saxon society, so earlier generations of Israeli academics have been guided by their own research interests, ideas and findings – not by some Orwellian Ministry of Truth. Some scholars have naturally possessed

---

3   Avi Shlaim, 'The Debate About 1948', *International Journal of Middle East Studies*, 27, 3 (August 1995), p. 289.

better professional skills or greater intellectual integrity than others; still others have undoubtedly been more conservative and less imaginative than their counterparts; but in no way, shape or form has this bulk of earlier studies ever amounted to an 'official Zionist line'.

In short, by creating a bogus 'old' or 'official' history the 'new historians' have cleverly diverted the debate from where it should actually be conducted, namely good versus bad scholarship; and for very good reason, for a thorough examination of their works will reveal not just a clear agenda but also basic poor scholarship.

Interestingly enough, the thought that Arab and/or Palestinian contemporaries of these 'Zionist propagandists' might have been infected with the same 'nationalist virus' to the extent of creating an 'official Arab line' has not seriously crossed the minds of the 'new historians'.[4] To them they are fair-minded and impartial observers of the Arab–Israeli conflict if not 'eminent historians', as a leading 'new historian'[5] described Palestinian partisan Walid Khalidi, whose own use of historical source material leaves much to be desired.[6]

---

4 The only ostensible exception to this rule is Ilan Pappé, who talks about the existence of parallel 'Zionist' and 'Palestinian/Arab' narratives. But this is a mere lip service, since Pappé not only fails to offer any criticism of the 'Palestinian/Arab narrative' or its practitioners that is remotely reminiscent of his assault on the 'Zionist narrative', but openly accepts its fundamental articles of faith, namely the perception of Zionism as a colonial usurper which has deliberately disinherited the indigenous population of a land that is not its own. See, for example, Pappé, 'A Lesson in New History', p. 54.

5 Avi Shlaim, *Collusion Across the Jordan: King Abdullah, the Zionist Movement, and the Partition of Palestine* (Oxford: Clarendon Press, 1988), pp. 2, 120.

6 For example, the veteran Israeli geographer Moshe Brawer has proved Khalidi's *All That Remains: The Palestinian Villages Occupied and Depopulated by Israel in 1948* (Washington: Institute for Palestine Studies, 1992) to be highly partisan and fundamentally flawed. Brawer points to several categories of invaluable source material totally overlooked by Khalidi, ranging from 'Village Notebooks' in which headmen recorded for the administration, until 1947, social and economic information of their respective villages, to air-photos taken by the RAF in the early 1940s, to the 'village files' compiled by the Hagana Jewish underground military organization. Failing to use these vital sources, Khalidi drew his entire information from a single source – the *Village Statistics 1945* – which in itself is of doubtful reliability. Worse than that, Khalidi did not even consult this source in the original, but relied on a tampered-with version published in Beirut in 1970, and edited by Sami Hadawi. See Moshe Brawer, 'All that Remains?', *Israel Affairs*, I, 2 (Winter 1994) pp. 334–46.

Similarly, much of Khalidi's edited tome *From Haven to Conquest: Readings in Zionism and the Palestine Problem Until 1948* (Beirut: Institute for Palestine Studies, 1971),

But let us assume for argument's sake that this non-existent 'official Zionist line', or the 'Zionist narrative', as it is stigmatized by some, did actually exist. What then would make certain Israelis better qualified than others to transcend their 'Zionist' upbringing, let alone assume the dual role of 'judge and hangman' *vis-à-vis* their colleagues?[7] Is it because they have miraculously been spared the 'Zionist indoctrination' afflicting the rest of their compatriots? Or because they belong to a different socio-economic-cultural milieu from their opponents? Or are their superior faculties of judgement and self-criticism due to the fact that 'most of them, born around 1948, have matured in a more open, doubting, and self-critical Israel than the pre-1967, pre-1973, and pre-Lebanon-War Israel of the old historians'?[8] Of course, biological age indicates little about outlook. The opponents of the 'new historians' also matured 'in a more open, doubting, and self-critical Israel',

particularly his own essays in the volume, are little more than sheer propaganda. His 'Note on Arab Strength in Palestine' (Appendix VIII, pp. 858–60), for example, is a transparent exercise in deflating Palestinian military strength so as to portray them as hapless victims of an aggressive and well-armed predator. He mentions only the rifle strength of the Palestinian Arabs, totally ignoring categories of more lethal weaponry such as mortars, machine guns and sub-machine guns which, according to contemporary Arab and British sources, were at Palestinian disposal. Needless to say, when it comes to Jewish military strength Khalidi does not 'forget' these categories.

Moreover, even the Palestinian rifle strength cited by Khalidi is woefully under-reported. Had he taken the trouble to read the far more scholarly and comprehensive study of the 1947–49 War by fellow Palestinian Arif al-Arif, he would have easily realized the absurdity of his own figures. According to Khalidi, for example, the Arabs of Jaffa possessed a mere 264 rifles; al-Arif, giving a detailed breakdown of the distribution of weapons in Jaffa, sets this number on 574, not including 18 machine guns and 56 sub-machine guns – a total of 648 weapons.

Likewise, Khalidi puts the total strength of the Arab forces invading the State of Israel at a mere 13,876 (p. 867), 'forgetting' to mention their substantial increase within a few weeks. Al-Arif puts the initial Arab strength at 20,000, then cites Jon Kimche's figures on the subsequent doubling of these forces to some 45,000 troops. He points to the lack of official Arab confirmation of Kimche's figures but does not dispute them altogether. Indeed the veracity of Kimche's estimates is borne out, *inter alia*, by a contemporary report by Sir John Bagot Glubb (Glubb Pasha), Commander of the Arab Legion, assessing the strength of the Iraqi army in the Nablus area between 15,000 and 20,000 troops. Kimche's figure for the Iraqi strength is 15,000; Khalidi's figure, 3,000–4,000.

See Glubb Pasha, 'Transjordan and Palestine, 5 October 1948', FO 371/68642/E13240; Arif al-Arif, *al-Nakbah* (The Catastrophe) (Beirut: Manshurat al-Maktaba al-Asriyah li-l-Tiba'ah wa-l-Nashr, 1956), vol. I, pp. 245, 342, vol. III, pp. 566–7; Jon Kimche, *Seven Fallen Pillars: The Middle East, 1915–1950* (London: Secker & Warburg, 1950), pp. 250–51.

7 Morris, *1948 and After*, p. 45.
8 Ibid., p. 7.

many of them belonging to the same age group and having lived in the same milieu as the 'new historians'. Moreover, some 'new historians' are older than the 'old historians', or at least the 'new old historians', a pejorative invented to surmount this embarrassing fact of life. This is particularly applicable to the founding father of the 'new historiography', the left-wing political activist Simha Flapan who was born in 1911 and thus was precisely a member of that generation which 'had lived through 1948 as highly committed adult participants in the epic, glorious rebirth of the Jewish commonwealth' and that was consequently derided by the 'new historians' as being 'unable to separate their lives from the events they later recounted, unable to distance themselves from and regard impartially the facts and processes through which they had lived'.[9]

Or do the 'new historians' enjoy the high moral and intellectual ground since their hands have not been 'stained' by serving in the Israeli establishment in one form or another? Benny Morris, probably the most self-righteous of this self-styled group, certainly thinks so. 'A new wave of scholars has emerged in Israel, whom one might justly dub "New Old Historians"', he patronizes a whole generation of younger critics; and the ultimate 'proof' of this 'oldness': 'Some of them have served, often as career officers, in the IDF Intelligence Branch, and have since then done service in and for the Government in various ways. Most are connected to the Middle East Studies departments of the various universities'.[10] One of them, Heaven forbid, even served as his country's Ambassador to the United States.

Much as it is irrelevant, this McCarthyist linkage between the Israeli intelligence services and the Middle East Studies departments raises 'a blatant problem of stones and glass houses', to use Morris's own words.[11] For one thing, it is of

9   Ibid.
10   Ibid., p. 40.
11   Ibid., p. 43.

course a common practice for Western academics to advise their governments in their fields of expertise (I have heard many strands of criticism of Francis Fukuyama's 'End of History' thesis, but not one based on his service in the Department of State's Policy Planning Staff), for another, it is not at all clear how real-time exposure to classified information on the Arab World of the sort that Morris and his fellow 'new historians' will be busy screening in archives in 30 or 40 years' time detracts from one's understanding of this research pheno- menon, or how Ambassador Itamar Rabinovich's doubling as one-time chief peace negotiator with Syria impinges on his comprehension of contemporary Syrian affairs. Besides, Morris himself is a research fellow at the 'orientalist' Truman Institute of the Hebrew University in Jerusalem, whose present Head, Moshe Ma'oz, not unlike some of his pre- decessors, is the quintessential 'orientalist' – professor of modern Middle Eastern History, reserve colonel in the Israeli army and former adviser to the Israeli government and defence establishment on Arab affairs. Yet surprisingly enough Morris has spared Ma'oz his rod, together with several other senior officers who 'have done service in and for the Government in various ways', notably the late Generals Yehoshafat Harkaby (former Head of the Israel Defence Forces' Intelligence Directorate) and Matityahu Peled, both of whom embarked on a second career as 'orientalists' at Israeli universities. Nor does Morris seem to be perturbed by the fact that fellow 'new historians', such as Avi Shlaim and Ilan Pappé, have been members of similar 'orientalist' institutions: the former at the Middle East Centre at St Antony's College, Oxford University, the latter of the Politics and Middle East Departments of the University of Haifa. Pappé has even been a visiting fellow at the Dayan Center for Asian and African Studies of Tel-Aviv University, often portrayed as perhaps the foremost bastion of the 'old historiography'.

All this leads to the inevitable conclusion that Morris's pious standards, so selectively and arbitrarily applied, are aimed at the *a priori* discreditation of critics rather than at expressing real concern over the (imaginary) detrimental effects of one's institutional affiliation or past career on one's historiographical worldview. In other words, those who accept the gospel of Morris & Co., or at least do not contest it in public, to them all sins are forgiven; those who do not are castigated as Trojan horses of the defence establishment within academe.

OLD MERCHANDISE REPACKAGED

But just how new is this gospel of the 'new historiography'?

Not very, if one is to believe Avi Shlaim, one of its leading apostles. As he put it: 'Many of the arguments that are central to the new historiography were advanced long ago by Israeli writers, not to mention Palestinian, Arab, and Western writers'.[12] He could not be more right. The moralistic message of the 'new historiography' has been foreshadowed by legions of academic Israel-bashers, from Arnold Toynbee and Alfred Lillienthal, to Noam Chomsky and Edward Said, not to mention Arab and Soviet propaganda; its more neutral 'findings' have been public knowledge for quite a long time.

Take Shlaim's own book on the secret contacts between the Zionist movement and Transjordan's King Abdullah, provocatively entitled *Collusion Across the Jordan*. Shlaim himself admits that the fact 'that there was traffic between these two parties has been widely known for some time and the two meetings between Golda Meir and King Abdullah in November 1947, and May 1948 have even been featured in popular films'.[13] Yet he claims that 'it is striking to observe how great is the contrast between accounts of this period written without access to the official documents and an account such as this one, based on documentary evidence'.[14]

---

12   Shlaim, 'The Debate', p. 289.   13   Ibid., p. 296.   14   Shlaim, *Collusion*, p. viii.

Nothing could be further from the truth. If anything it is striking to observe how little our understanding of these specific meetings has been enriched following the release of the relevant state documents. Not only was the general gist of the Abdullah–Meir conversations common knowledge by the early 1960s,[15] but there is little doubt that the authors of most of the early works had access to the then-classified official documents. Dan Kurzman's 1970 account of the November 1947 meeting,[16] in which according to Shlaim the 'collusion' to divide Palestine between Transjordan and the prospective Jewish State was clinched, is a near verbatim narration of the report prepared after the meeting by Ezra Danin, the Jewish Agency's Political Department's adviser on Arab affairs. Shlaim, using the same report as his primary source of information on the meeting, adds nothing new to Kurzman's revelations of 18 years earlier. Similarly, the description of the same conversation in the personal memoirs of the Israeli leader Zeev Sharef, published nearly three decades before its 'discovery' by Shlaim, is undoubtedly based on Meir's then-classified verbal account of the meeting, given to the Provisional State Council six months after the event.[17] As we shall see later, Shlaim has chosen to ignore this crucial report despite his keen awareness of its existence. Is this for the simple reason that it destroys his ill-conceived conspiracy theory?

Another key element of Shlaim's thesis – that in a February 1948 meeting with Transjordan's Prime Minister Tawfiq Abul Huda, British Foreign Secretary Ernest Bevin gave his blessing to the alleged Hashemite–Jewish agreement to divide Palestine between themselves – was already 'revealed' in 1957 by the former commander of the Arab Legion, Sir John Bagot Glubb, or Glubb Pasha as he was widely known, and quoted

15   Jon Kimche and David Kimche, *Both Sides of the Hill* (London: Secker & Warburg, 1960), p. 60; Marie Syrkin, *Golda Meir: Woman with a Cause* (London: Victor Gollancz, 1964), pp. 195–202.
16   Dan Kurzman, *Genesis 1948: The First Arab–Israeli War* (New York: New American Library, paperback edition, 1972), pp. 42–4.
17   Zeev Sharef, *Three Days* (London: W.H. Allen, 1962), pp. 72–3.

by most early works on the Arab–Israeli conflict.[18] If the newly-released official British documents shed fresh light on the Bevin–Abul Huda meeting – as indeed they do – it is in the completely opposite direction from that suggested by Shlaim.

Nor has Shlaim pioneered the examination of declassified Israeli and British documents unavailable to the earlier generations of writers; in this he was preceded by such mainstream Israeli historians as Avraham Sela (of the Hebrew University), Aharon Klieman (of Tel-Aviv University), Yosef Nevo, Dan Schueftan and Yoav Gelber (of the University of Haifa), as well as Canadian academic Neil Caplan,[19] none of whom belong to the self-styled 'new historiographical' club.

As far as interpretation is concerned, Shlaim concedes that his charge of collusion is not new: 'It was made in a book published by Colonel Abdullah al-Tall who had served as a messenger between King Abdullah and the Jews, following Tall's abortive coup and defection to Egypt. A similar charge was levelled against Ben-Gurion by Lieutenant Colonel Israel Baer in the book he wrote in his prison cell following his conviction of spying for the Soviet Union. Tall condemned King Abdullah for betraying his fellow Arabs and selling the Palestinians down the river. Baer condemned Ben-Gurion for forming an unholy alliance with Arab reaction and British imperialism'.[20] In fact, as aptly noted by Avraham Sela, this conspiracy theory has been far more pervasive than merely

18   Sir John Bagot Glubb, *A Soldier with the Arabs* (London: Hodder & Stoughton, 1957), pp. 63–6. For its use in early works see, for example, Kurzman, *Genesis*, pp. 116–17; Sharef, *Three Days*, p. 77; Kimche and Kimche, *Both Sides*, pp. 39, 105–6.
19   See, for example, Aharon Klieman, *Du Kium Le-lo Shalom* (Unpeaceful Coexistence: Israel, Jordan, and the Palestinians) (Tel-Aviv: Ma'ariv, 1986), pp. 15–16; Yosef Nevo, *Abdullah Ve-arviyei Eretz Israel* (Abdullah and the Arabs of Palestine) (Tel-Aviv: Dayan Center, 1975); Avraham Sela, *Me-maga'im Le-masa U-matan: Yahasei Ha-sochnut Ha-yehudit U-medinat Israel im Ha-melech Abdullah, 1946–1950* (From Contacts to Negotiations: the Relations between the Jewish Agency and the State of Israel with King Abdullah, 1946–1950) (Tel-Aviv: Shiloah Center, 1985); Yoav Gelber, 'The Negotiations between the Jewish Agency and Transjordan, 1946–1948', *Studies in Zionism*, 6, 1 (1985), pp. 53–83; Dan Schueftan, *Optsia Yardenit: Israel, Yarden, Veha-palestinaim* (A Jordanian option: the Yishuv and the State of Israel *vis-à-vis* the Hashemite Regime and the Palestinian National Movement) (Tel-Aviv: Yad Tabenkin, 1986); Neil Caplan, *Futile Diplomacy, Vol. II: Arab–Zionist Negotiations and the End of the Mandate* (London: Frank Cass, 1986).
20   Shlaim, 'The Debate', p. 296.

Baer's and Tall's accounts. On the Israeli side it has been an integral part of the criticism of the government's conduct of the 1947–49 War by both left- and right-wingers, while in anti-Hashemite Arab historiography 'the collusion myth became the crux of an historical indictment against the king for betraying the Arab national cause in Palestine'.[21] Why Shlaim has chosen to give these partisan accounts a scholarly seal of approval is not for me to say. It is clear, however, that in choosing to stroll along this beaten track he has precluded himself from breaking any new ground.

What then qualifies Shlaim's conspiracy theory for inclusion in the self-proclaimed 'new historiographical' club? In his own account, it is its challenging of 'the conventional view of the Arab–Israeli conflict as a simple bipolar affair in which a monolithic and implacably hostile Arab world is pitted against the Jews'.[22] But this claim to newness is patently false, for the simple reason that the 'conventional view of the Arab–Israeli conflict' it pretends to challenge has never existed: it is merely one of those bogus concepts created by the 'new historians' to allow them to sell old merchandise in glossy new wrapping. Even such passionately pro-Israeli feature films on the 1947–49 War as *Exodus* and *Cast a Giant Shadow*, to which presumably Shlaim alluded earlier, do not portray a picture of 'a monolithic and implacably hostile Arab world pitted against the Jews', but rather of divided Arab communities in which some leaders would rather not fight the Jews while others would even cooperate with the Jews against their Arab 'brothers'. And what applies to this most popularized medium is all the more applicable to writings on the 1947–49 War. None of the early works mentioned above, not to mention later works by 'old historians', subscribes to the stereotypic approach attached to them by Shlaim. In fact,

---

21 Sela, 'Transjordan, Israel and the 1948 War', pp. 623–4. See also his article: 'Arab Historiography of the 1948 War: The Quest for Legitimacy', in Laurence J. Silberstein, ed., *New Perspectives on Israeli History* (New York: New York University Press, 1991), pp. 124–54.
22 Shlaim, 'The Debate', p. 297.

Shlaim's alleged challenge of the 'conventional view of the Arab–Israeli conflict' is a replica of the (equally misconceived) claim to novelty made by the quintessential 'Zionist' historian Aharon Klieman in his study of Hashemite–Zionist relations, published two years prior to the appearance of Shlaim's own book. As Klieman put it: 'It has been a commonplace to present the Palestine or the Arab–Israeli conflict in all its historical stages as a simple bilateral conflict ... It is a mistake to present the Arab side to the equation as a monolithic bloc. The "Arab camp" has always been divided and at war with itself'.[23]

The truth is that even at the height of their most critical confrontation with the Arab World in 1947–49, Jewish leaders did not adopt the simplistic 'conventional view' of the conflict *à la* Shlaim, as demonstrated by David Ben-Gurion's public address on 25 November 1947, four days before the UN vote on partition:

> We have no reason to despair of friends and supporters even in the Arab World, something is already emerging over the horizon. We have recently heard not only hostile words and threats. And it should be borne in mind that the masses of the Arab people – forcibly silenced and deprived of political expression – are not keen to rush to battle. This does not mean that agitation cannot entice them into action – it would be a dangerous illusion [to think so] – but the task of the agitators is not easy. And the way in which these masses will act depends in no small measure upon us. The more they know they have to respect our strength and trust our integrity – the more difficult the task of the agitators will be.[24]

What applies to Shlaim is equally applicable to Benny Morris's study of *The Birth of the Palestinian Refugee Problem*. His general

23   Klieman, *Du Kium*, pp. 15–16.
24   David Ben-Gurion, *Ba-ma'araha* (In Battle) (Tel-Aviv: Hotsa'at Mifleget Poalei Eretz Israel, 1959), vol. IV, 2, p. 254.

conclusion that 'the Palestinian refugee problem was born of war, not by design, Jewish or Arab'[25] will be amenable to any 'old' Israeli historian, though not necessarily his entire depiction of the dynamics and development of that war. His claim that 'what happened in Palestine/Israel over 1947–9 was so complex and varied ... that a single-cause explanation of the exodus from most sites is untenable'[26] echoes not only Aharon Cohen's and Rony Gabbay's conclusions of decades earlier,[27] but also the standard explanation of the Palestinian exodus by such 'official Zionist' writers as Joseph Schechtman: 'This mass flight of the Palestinian Arabs is a phenomenon for which no single explanation suffices. Behind it lies a complex of apparently contradictory factors'.[28]

Nor is there any novelty in Morris's periodization of the Arab flight into four distinct stages. Though hotly contested by Shabtai Teveth, this periodization was pre-dated by four decades by Asher Goren of the Israeli Foreign Office, whose memorandum on the subject was incorporated into later works such as Michael Asaf's *Toldot Hit'orerut Ha-arvim Be-eretz Israel U-brihatam* (The History of the Awakening of the Arabs in the Land of Israel and their Flight); Rony Gabbay divided the Palestinian flight to three phases, not that dissimilar from Morris's four stages.[29] Even Morris's foremost self-laudatory 'revelation', namely that expulsion of Arabs from certain places by Israeli forces did take place, at times through the use of violence, was preceded by decades by such works as Jon and David Kimche's *Both Sides of the Hill*;

25　Morris, *The Birth*, p. 286.
26　Ibid., p. 294.
27　Aharon Cohen, *Israel and the Arab World* (London: W.H. Allen, 1970), pp. 458–66; Rony Gabbay, *A Political Study of the Arab–Israeli Conflict: the Arab Refugee Problem (A Case Study)* (Geneva: Libraire E. Droz, 1959), pp. 54, 85–98.
28　Joseph B. Schechtman, *The Arab Refugee Problem* (New York: Philosophical Library, 1952), p. 4.
29　Michael Asaf, *Toldot Hit'orerut Ha-arvim Be-eretz Israel U-brihatam* (The History of the Awakening of the Arabs in the Land of Israel and their Flight) (Tel-Aviv: Tarbut Vehinuch, 1967), pp. 180–82; Gabbay, *A Political Study*, Chapter 1. For Shabtai Teveth's criticism of Morris's periodization see: 'The Palestine Arab Refugee Problem', pp. 219–20; and 'Charging Israel With The Original Sin', *Commentary*, 88, 3 (Sept. 1989), pp. 28–9.

Gabbay's *A Political Study of the Arab–Israeli Conflict*, and Nadav Safran's *From War to War*.[30]

Finally, in their eagerness to debunk the perception of the 1947–49 War as a heroic struggle of the few against the many, the 'new historians' have pointed to the existence of an approximate numerical parity on the battlefield during that conflict.[31] Ilan Pappé has carried this claim so far as to argue that the war's outcome had been predetermined in the political and diplomatic corridors of power 'long before even one shot had been fired', as if the decision of the Palestinians and the Arab States to resort to violence to subvert the UN Partition Resolution was a heavenly dictate and the war they brought about an insignificant sideshow of the 'real' political and diplomatic struggle, an optical illusion for mass consumption.[32]

Had this actually been the case, then the newly-established State of Israel certainly paid an exorbitant price for such a predetermined outcome: the war's 6,000 fatalities represented one per cent of Israel's total Jewish population, a higher human toll than that suffered by Great Britain in the Second World War and approximately four times the American toll during the same conflict, not to mention the Korea and Vietnam Wars where American fatalities accounted for one fiftieth and one thirtieth of one per cent of the total population respectively. Translated into British and US Second World War terms, the Jewish death toll during the 1947–49 War would have equalled some 467,468 British and 1,342,818 American fatalities (the actual figures being 355,276 and 362,561 fatalities respectively).[33]

---

30 Gabbay, *A Political Study*, pp. 109–11; Nadav Safran, *From War to War: The Arab–Israeli Confrontation 1948–1967* (Indianapolis: Pegasus, 1969), pp. 34–5; Kimche and Kimche, *Both Sides*, pp. 227–8.

31 See, for example, Morris, *1948 and After*, pp. 13–16; Shlaim, 'The Debate', pp. 294–5.

32 Ilan Pappé, *The Making of the Arab–Israeli Conflict, 1947–1951* (London: I.B. Tauris, 1992), p. 271.

33 Britain suffered 264,433 army, navy and air force deaths during the Second World War, as well as 60,595 civilian deaths from bombing, and 30,248 merchant navy deaths, a total of 355,276, or 0.76 of one per cent of the total population. The 362,561 American fatalities

Moreover, the Israeli battlefield losses during the war were even heavier in relative (if not absolute) terms than that suffered by the Palestinians. According to official British figures, by 3 April 1948, some four months after the Palestinians resorted to violence to subvert the UN Partition Resolution, their casualties had amounted to 967 dead and 1,911 wounded, as compared with 875 and 1,858 Jewish casualties respectively.[34] During the next few weeks Palestinian casualties rose sharply due to a string of Jewish successes resulting in the fall of the major Arab towns of Jaffa, Haifa, Tiberias, Safad and Acre, among other territories. While it is difficult to assess the precise number of Palestinian casualties, if one accepts the somewhat inflated figures given by Arif al-Arif, who has written the most comprehensive Palestinian study of the 1947–49 War, then by the time of the Arab States' attack on Israel on 15 May 1948 Palestinian/Arab fatalities (including apparently those of the pan-Arab Liberation Army which had gradually penetrated Palestine since the beginning of the year) had amounted to some 4,000.[35]

represented 0.27 of 1 per cent of the total population. See, for example, Martin Gilbert, *The Second World War* (London: Fontana, 1990), p. 746; National Register of the United Kingdom and the Isle of Man, *Statistics of Population on 29 September 1939* (London: HMSO, 1939); Maldwyn A. Jones, *The Limits of Liberty: American History 1607–1992* (Oxford: Oxford University Press, 1995).

34 'Casualties in Palestine since the United Nations Decision, Period 30th November, 1947 to 3rd April, 1948', CO 733/483/5, p. 19.

35 Al-Arif, *al-Nakba*, vol. I, pp. 222, 281, 296, 309. A vivid illustration of the precariousness of casualty estimates is afforded by the rumours that some 23,000 Arabs were killed in the battle over Haifa. The actual Arab casualty toll, according to British military commanders on the spot, was 100 dead and 100 wounded (compared with 14 Jews killed and 40 wounded).

'Jewish attack at Haifa was direct consequence of continuous attacks by Arabs on Jews in Haifa over previous four days', the British High Commissioner in Palestine, General Sir Alan Cunningham, cabled the Colonial Secretary, Arthur Creech-Jones, on 25 April 1948. 'Attack was carried out by Hagana and there was no "massacre". Arabs in Haifa were thus themselves responsible for this outbreak in spite of our repeated warnings'. Al-Arif's casualty figure is 150 Arab fatalities and 350 wounded (he notes an additional estimate of 300 dead), as compared with 363 Jewish fatalities: approximately 25 times the actual Jewish death toll (p. 222). Indeed, as far as Jewish casualty figures are concerned, al-Arif's book is on extremely shaky ground.

For the 'massacre' rumours see *The Memoirs of Field-Marshal Montgomery* (London: Fontana, 1960), pp. 480–2. For the real figures see Cunningham's cable to Creech-Jones on 25 April (no. 1127), Cunningham Papers, III/4/52, St. Antony's College, Oxford University, p. 168.

In the following months Jewish battlefield casualties grew rapidly while Palestinian casualties (both military and civilian) remained relatively low. This was due to the shift in the nature of the war from a Jewish–Palestinian confrontation to a struggle between Israel and the invading Arab armies on the one hand, and to the total collapse of the Palestinian war effort and their mass exodus on the other. Hence, apart from certain instances such as the battle of Lydda in July 1948,[36] there was no real fighting between Israel and the Palestinians during this period. Even if we assume that despite their lack of direct involvement in the fighting, Palestinian fatalities grew by yet another 50 per cent to 6,000, this overall death toll would still be identical to that of the Jewish community, or the *Yishuv* as it is called in Hebrew. Given that the Yishuv's population was roughly half the size of the Palestinian Arab community, Israel lost proportionately twice the percentage of the Palestinians. Still the Yishuv stayed its course while the Palestinian community unravelled rapidly.

Mass Palestinian flight from major urban centres, notably Haifa, already began before the passing of the UN Partition Resolution (and not in December 1947 as wrongly claimed by Morris).[37] On 21 November 1947, for example, a British intelligence report narrated that 'in this state of uncertainty, many Arabs of Haifa are evacuating their families to neighbouring Arab countries in anticipation of the period of disorder they foresee'.[38] As hostilities intensified, this mass flight quickly snowballed into a haemorrhage. Even if we accept Morris's figures, by February–March 1948 'some 75,000 Arabs, mostly from the urban upper and middle classes of Jaffa, Haifa and Jerusalem, and from villages around Jerusalem and in the Coastal Plain, had fled to Arab centres to the east, such as Nazareth

---

36 Al-Arif puts the number of Palestinian fatalities in this battle at 426 (*al-Nakba*, vol. III, p. 605); Morris gives the lower figure of 'more than 250' (*1948 and After*, p. 1).
37 *The Birth*, p. 41; *1948 and After*, p. 18.
38 Sixth Airborne Division, Historical Section: GHQ MELF, 'Weekly Intelligence Review', issued on 21 November 1947, WO 275/120, No. 138.

and Nablus, or out of the country'.[39] Morris attributes this flight to 'Jewish – Hagana, IZL or LHI – attacks or fear of impending attack, and from a sense of vulnerability to such attack', though conceding that 'until the end of March, the Hagana's operations conformed to the general principle of limiting the conflagration', and that during these months the Yishuv had no policy of 'removing or moving the Arabs out of Palestine or the Jewish-dominated parts of Palestine'.[40]

What Morris fails to mention, however, is that the Jewish community was subjected to the same dislocations and pressures as its Arab rival and still did not take to the road. In fact the mass Palestinian flight began at a time when they were still on the winning side and the Yishuv dangerously cornered, as a report on the military situation by the British authorities in Palestine put it in early April 1948:

> Arab terrorism in Jerusalem and Haifa makes an ordered Jewish existence in either town difficult. As long as mortar bombs are fired from Jaffa at Tel-Aviv, life in that city is also precarious. Haifa and Tel-Aviv can at least be victualled from the sea. Jerusalem is a much more serious problem … The 100,000 Jews of Jerusalem have been held to ransom and it is doubtful whether the Arab economic blockade of the city can be broken by Jewish forces alone. If the Jewish leaders are not prepared to sacrifice the 100,000 Jews of Jerusalem, then they must concede, however unwillingly, that the Arabs have won the second round in the struggle which began with a Jewish victory in the first round on the 29th November.[41]

This in turn belies the 'new historiographical' contention that 'the final outcome of the war was thus not a miracle but a

---

39   Morris, *The Birth*, p. 30.
40   Ibid., pp. 36, 59–60.
41   'An Analysis of the Palestine Situation, April 1948', Cunningham Papers, IV/5/33.

faithful reflection of the underlying Arab–Israeli military balance',[42] let alone Pappé's absurd claim that the outcome of the war had been predetermined 'long before even one shot had been fired'. The Jewish–Palestinian conflict was not won by the militarily stronger party but rather by the more resilient society. Two communities were thrown into the whirlpool of war, enduring similar hardships and dislocations: both suffered a painful human toll, including mutual atrocities; and both experienced sustained widespread disruption to daily life in the form of urban and rural guerrilla warfare and bouts of terrorism. Yet one of them managed to weather the storm by extreme effort, while the other fragmented to small pieces.

It is true that the Palestinian upper and middle classes felt vulnerable; but so did their Jewish counterparts, as even a cursory examination both of British documents and of the discussions at the Jewish Agency Executive, the effective 'government' of the Yishuv, would easily reveal.[43] Yet what makes a certain social group into a nation is precisely the readiness to stay put, to endure the hardships and to make the necessary sacrifices for defending its collective existence on its own land. The Yishuv, being the cohesive national movement that it was, mustered these vital resources; the atomized Palestinian community, lacking an equivalent sense of corporate identity, did not – hence the mass desertion of its most

42   Shlaim, 'The Debate', p. 295. See also Morris, *1948 and After*, p. 14.
43   See, for example, the protocols of the Jewish Agency Executive (JAE) meetings of 17 March, 10, 11, 16, 21 April 1948, Central Zionist Archives (all transcripts of the JAE meetings cited in this book are taken from the CZA). At the 16 April meeting JAE Chairman David Ben-Gurion told his colleagues: 'We are still far away from the required force to meet 15th May. We lack almost half of the necessary manpower, about 80 per cent of the vehicles, and substantial additional equipment'. Similarly, according to a British report from the same period: 'It is becoming increasingly apparent that the Yishuv and its leaders are deeply worried about the future. The intensification of Arab attacks on communications and particularly the failure of the Kfar Etzion convoy – probably the Yishuv's strongest armoured transport unit – to force a return passage has brought home the precarious position of Jewish communities both great and small which are dependent on supply lines running through Arab controlled country. In particular it is now realized that the position of Jewish Jerusalem, where a food-scarcity already exists, is likely to be desperate after 16th May'. Cunningham to Creech-Jones, 3 April 1948, telegram 835, Cunningham Papers, III/3.

vital social classes; and the moment this élite chose to save its skin before the going got tough, leaving the confounded Palestinian 'masses' leaderless, the struggle was lost. Would Britain have survived the Second World War if Winston Churchill had fled the country together with 3,000,000 members of the classes and groups that mattered most (just over 6 per cent of the total population, as was the case with the Arabs of Palestine) – the political, military, social, administrative, economic, and cultural élites? Of course not! Neither did the Palestinian masses. As the British High Commissioner for Palestine, General Sir Alan Cunningham, put it in a typical British understatement in a letter to the Colonial Secretary, Arthur Creech-Jones:

> You should know that the collapsing Arab morale in Palestine is in some measure due to the increasing tendency of those who should be leading them to leave the country. For instance in Jaffa the Mayor went on 4 days leave 12 days ago and has not returned, and half the National Committee has left. In Haifa the Arab members of the municipality left some time ago; the two leaders of the Arab Liberation Army left actually during the recent battle. Now the Chief Arab Magistrate has left. In all parts of the country the effendi class has been evacuating in large numbers over a considerable period and the tempo is increasing.[44]

A week later Cunningham seemed to be losing all hope of shoring up the Palestinian campaign. 'Wherever the Arabs are in contact with the Jews their morale has practically collapsed and we are finding increasing difficulty in bolstering them up', he reported to Creech-Jones:

---

44 Cunningham to Secretary of State, 26 April 1948, telegram 1148, Cunningham Papers, III/4/71, p. 189.

Jaffa is rapidly emptying of all its inhabitants and I
am told that the Iraqis with the ALA [Arab Liberation
Army] there are also threatening to leave ... It may
interest you to know that the Arab in command in
the Katamon battle [in Jerusalem] also left in the
middle. The Arabs had been shooting at the Jews
from this quarter for weeks and really brought the
attack on themselves.[45]

He was not the only one to think this way. Hussein Khalidi,
Secretary of the Arab Higher Committee was no less scathing
in his criticism of his fellow Palestinians. 'I tell you', he
complained in a phone conversation intercepted by the
Jewish intelligence service, 'in 1936 there were 60,000 troops
and [the Arabs] did not fear, now we deal with 30,000 Jews
and they are trembling in fear. Now everyone wants to work
for a fee'.[46]

And the Lebanese Minister of the Interior, Camille Chamoun,
was no more complimentary of Palestinian conduct. 'The
people of Palestine, in their previous resistance to imperialists
and Zionists, proved they were worthy of independence', he
said in a press conference on 7 May 1948. 'But at this decisive
stage of the fighting they have not remained so dignified in
their stand; they lack organization and omitted to arm themselves as well as their enemy did. Many of them did not assist
their brothers from nearby Arab countries who hastened to
help them. I think the explanation is that they were absorbed
in local disputes'.[47]

Going back to the size of the opposing armies during the
1947–49 War, it is true that the battlefield balance of forces was
more or less even in terms of engaged manpower, but this
fact, just as most other aspects of the 'new historiographical'

45 Cunningham to Creech-Jones, 1 May 1948, telegram 1217, Cunningham Papers, III/5/25.
46 David Ben-Gurion, *Yoman Ha-milhama* (War Diary) (Tel-Aviv: Misrad Ha-bitahon, Ha-
    hotsa'a La-or, 1982), 4 January 1948, vol. I, p. 113.
47 Beirut Radio, 7 May 1948, 'BBC Monitoring Service – Summary of World Broadcasts',
    Caversham Park, Reading, III, 50, 13 May 1948, p. 57.

gospel has been an open secret in Israel long before its miraculous 'discovery': school-children could find it in historical atlases, students in academic books. Even Ben-Gurion's autobiographical account of Israel's history, published some two decades before the 'new historians' made their debut on the public stage, contains illuminating data on the Arab–Israeli military balance; his edited war diaries, published by the Ministry of Defence Press in 1982, give a detailed breakdown of the Israeli order of battle – not the slightest attempt at a cover-up.[48]

Whether these figures confirm the simplistic conclusions drawn by the 'new historians' is an altogether different matter given the complex nature of war in the modern epoch. The size of armed forces tells only part of the story. The quantity and quality of weapons at the disposal of the warring parties are equally crucial, and at the initial and most critical stage after the Arab invasion of its territory, Israel was overwhelmingly inferior to its adversaries in every category of major weaponry, be it armoured vehicles, artillery or aircraft. Even Shlaim concedes that 'during three critical weeks, from the invasion of Palestine by the regular armies of the Arab States on 15 May until the start of the first truce on 11 June, this community [i.e., the Yishuv] had to struggle for its very survival'.[49]

That the Yishuv managed to survive this concerted onslaught was primarily due to the same factor that allowed it to outlive the pressures that brought about Palestinian disintegration, namely strong national cohesion and an unwavering sense of purpose. This again proves that the

---

48 See, for example, Moshe Lissak, Yehuda Wallach, and Eviatar Nur, eds, *Atlas Karta Le-toldot Medinat Israel: Shanim Rishonot* (Karta Atlas of Israel: the First Years, 1948–61) (Jerusalem: Karta, 1978); Ted Berkman, *Cast a Giant Shadow: The Story of Mickey Marcus Who Died to Save Jerusalem* (Garden City: Doubleday & Co., 1962), pp. 212–13; Safran, *From War to War*, p. 30; Jon and David Kimche, *Both Sides*, pp. 160–2; David Ben-Gurion, *Medinat Israel Ha-mehudeshet* (The Restored State of Israel) (Tel-Aviv: Am Oved, 1969), Vol. I, pp. 70–1, 98, 102, 106, 115–16; idem, *Israel: A Personal History* (London: New English Library, 1972), pp. 61, 90; idem, *Yoman Ha-milhama*, particularly vol. III, pp. 1013–19.

49 Shlaim, 'The Debate', p. 294.

overall might of nations extends far beyond the number of soldiers they can field, indeed beyond their military strength; and there is little doubt that in such critical components of national power as demography, territory, geo-strategic location and wealth, the Arabs were (and are still) overwhelmingly superior to Israel. This superiority has been somewhat blunted by Israel's national cohesion and qualitative edge – a self-evident fact since otherwise the Jewish State would not have had the slightest chance of survival. But it has never been fully eradicated. The Arabs possess a stronger staying power than Israel in a protracted conflict; they need not close the qualitative gap with Israel, only narrow it to a point that would allow their overwhelming quantitative superiority to be brought to bear; and they can absorb successive setbacks while Israel cannot afford a single military defeat.

Indeed it has been the Arabs' keen awareness of this fundamental asymmetry which drove them to attempt to abort Israel at birth and has sustained their hopes for the eventual destruction of Jewish State for so long. Suffice it to note the confident assessment of the then Secretary-General of the Arab League, Abd al-Rahman Azzam, to realize that the 1947–49 War involved a far wider national struggle than the simplistic head-count offered by the 'new historians'. 'Alternative to this [i.e., a last-minute nullification of partition] was civil war in which Arabs were fully confident of ultimate success though it might take some years', Azzam told the British Ambassador to Cairo, Sir Ronald Campbell, on 17 April 1948, days before the Jews turned the tables on the Palestinians. 'It would be a war of attrition since manpower reserves upon which the Arab side could draw were inexhaustible'.[50]

Greater military authorities than Azzam have articulated this strategic prognosis, notably President Hafiz al-Asad of Syria, the self-styled champion of the pan-Arab cause. In the

50   Sir R. Campbell to Foreign Office, 18 April 1948, telegram no. 478, PREM 8/859, III.

view to which he subscribed until the late 1980s, if not to this very day, the Arab–Israeli conflict is a mortal struggle over 'existence' and 'destiny' that must eventually be settled in favour of one of the two protagonists; and since the Arabs enjoyed a marked superiority over Israel in the most fundamental elements of national power they were bound to triumph at the end of the day, provided they adopted a long-term historical perspective, kept their nerve, and rejected easy solutions and short-cuts:

> We view the matter from the perspective of the future of the nation and not that of the next few hours, months or years in which we shall live ... If we, as a generation, fail to do and to achieve what must be done, there will be future generations which will deal with this issue in the proper manner ... What I am saying here is not new. I am just reviewing some facts in our history. Let us go back to the Crusaders' invasion. Although they fought us for 200 years, we did not surrender or capitulate. They, too, were a big power and had scored victories, while we had been defeated. After 200 years, however, we triumphed. Why are we now expected either to score a decisive victory in approximately thirty years or completely surrender?[51]

51 Asad's interview with *al-Rai al-Amm* (Kuwait), as brought by Damascus Domestic Service, 13 December 1981. See also his interview with *Libération* (Paris), 14 February 1986, and his speeches on the anniversary of the Ba'th revolution as brought by the Damascus Domestic Service on 8 March 1988 and 1989; Vice-President Zuhair Mashariqa's interviews with *al-Ba'th*, 24 January 1987, 8 March 1987; Foreign Minister Farouq al-Shara's interview with the *Damascus Domestic Service*, 31 May 1989.

That Asad has not abandoned this historical vision altogether, despite his grudging participation since 1991 in the American-led peace process, has been evidenced by his negotiating style which has been geared more to placating 'the only remaining superpower', as the United States came to be called after the disintegration of the Soviet Union, than to convincing Israel of the sincerity of his intentions. Notwithstanding the clear signals from the late Prime Minister, Yitzhak Rabin, and his successor, Shimon Peres, that they are resolved to withdraw from the Golan Heights provided that such issues as the precise location of the border, the use of water resources and the necessary security arrangements can find a satisfactory formula, Asad has acted as if he is in no hurry to regain his lost territories. He has refused to accelerate the peace talks by

ARCHAIC FETISHISM OF FACTS

If the claim for 'newness' is not based on the discovery of
hitherto unknown facts, or the provision of fresh interpretations, or the development of novel historical methodo-
logies (since most 'new historians' adhere to the old-fashioned
'positivist' approach),[52] where does it lie? In the realm of archival
documentation, argues Shlaim, in what represents the standard
position of the 'new historians':

> Although many of the arguments of the new historio-
> graphy are not new, there is a qualitative difference
> between this historiography and the bulk of the
> earlier studies, whether they accepted or contra-
> dicted the official Zionist line. The difference, in a nut-
> shell, is that the new historiography is written with
> access to the official Israeli and Western documents,
> whereas the earlier writers had no access, or only
> partial access, to the official documents. This is not a
> hard and fast rule; there are many exceptions and
> there are also degrees of access. Nevertheless, it is
> generally true to say that the new historians, with

elevating them from ambassadorial to ministerial level, let alone to meet his Israeli
counterparts in person. He also continues to make a Syrian–Israeli peace conditional
on the complete resolution of the Palestinian problem yet keeps on raising the threshold
of such a deal: as long as the Palestine Liberation Organization (PLO) openly called for
the destruction of Israel, Asad pledged allegiance to any solution amenable to the
organization; once the PLO recognized Israel in 1988, Syria immediately castigated this
move; and when the PLO carried this recognition a step further by signing the
September 1993 Declaration of Principles (DOP) with Israel, chilly winds blew from
Damascus and the Syrian-based Palestinian terrorist, Ahmad Jibril, threatened PLO
Chairman Yasser Arafat with death. An equally hostile reception was given to the
Israel–PLO follow-up agreement of September 1995 on the withdrawal of Israeli forces
from most of the West Bank. Last but not least, while maintaining the low-keyed
diplomatic channel in Washington, Asad has been conducting a nasty war by-proxy
against Israel in South Lebanon through the Hizbullah guerrilla organization and has
sheltered the worst enemies of peace from among the Palestinian organizations, some
of which have been engaged in a brutal terrorist campaign aimed at derailing the very
same process of which Syria ostensibly is a part.

52 Ilan Pappé offers a partial exception to this rule by allegedly subscribing to an inter-
disciplinary, rather than to the 'empirical positivist' historical approach. But thus far he
has had little to show for this pretension. See the Conclusions of this book.

the exception of the late Simha Flapan, have carried
out extensive archival research in Israel, Britain, and
America and that their arguments are backed by hard
documentary evidence and by a Western-style scholarly
apparatus. Indeed, the upsurge of new histories would
not have been possible without the declassification
of the official government documents.[53]

Much as it is pretentious, this archaic 'fetishism of facts', to
paraphrase the eminent British historian E.H. Carr,[54] is totally
misconceived. Since the discovery of new facts and their
organization in a way that will shed fresh light on the past
lies at the core of the historical investigation, any claim to a
new school of thought has to rest on a far more substantial
scholarly contribution than the mere acts of collection and
organization, let alone access to newly released materials.
Were every historian to stake such a claim on the basis of access
to documents hitherto unaccessed by earlier scholars, the
advent of a 'new historiography' would become an annual event
throughout the democratic world in concomitance with the
latest release of state documents to the public. Conversely, if
one were to press Shlaim's flawed argument to its logical conclusion, there can be no room for any 'new historiography' of
pre-mid-twentieth-century history since archival source
material from this period has been accessible to researchers
for quite some time. This perhaps explains why works on early
Zionist history by such historians as David Vital and Isaiah
Friedman have never qualified for inclusion in the 'new
historiography', though their 'arguments are backed by hard
documentary evidence and by a Western-style scholarly
apparatus'.

The absurdity of the claim to 'newness' on the basis of access
to recently released documents is further underscored by the

53   Shlaim, 'The Debate', p. 289. See also Morris, 1948 and After, p. 7.
54   E.H. Carr, What is History (Harmondsworth: Penguin, 1984), p. 16.

following two facts. First, the declassification of documents does not, in and of itself, guarantee fresh information that will alter one's perception of past events in any major, or even minor way; it may well be that the documentary crop of some years will be rather insignificant as far as certain research phenomena are concerned. Second, and more importantly, these newly declassified documents have also been available to recent 'old historians', some of whom, as noted above, have indeed preceded their 'new' counterparts in the use of these very sources, and they came up with very different conclusions. But while the use of newly released documents by Klieman, Rabinovich, Sela and like-minded historians buys them the epithet of 'new old historians', the utilization of the same documents by Shlaim, Morris and Co. amounts to a 'new historiography'.

Which again leads to the self-evident realization that it is not the *availability* of new documents that distinguishes the 'new historians' from their opponents but the *interpretation* they give to this source material. It is not the 'pure' facts that inexorably thrust a certain reality upon the historian; it is the historian who constructs reality out of the facts. Some facts may be found in official State documents, others may not – as certain aspects of social and political activity defy straightforward official recording. But the identification of sociopolitical occurrences, whether to be found in documents or not, and their transformation into 'historical facts' is wholly of the historian's own making. As noted by E.H. Carr more than 30 years ago:

> The facts are really not at all like fish on the fishmonger's slab. They are like fish swimming about in a vast and sometimes inaccessible ocean; and what the historian catches will depend, partly on chance, but mainly on what part of the ocean he chooses to fish in and what tackle he chooses to use – these two factors being, of course, determined by the kind of

fish he wants to catch. By and large, the historian will
get the kind of facts he wants. History means
interpretation.[55]

In other words, more than anything else the 'new historiography' is a state of mind or, rather, a fashion. What unites its
practitioners, by and large, is subscription to the all-too-
common perception of Zionism as an offshoot of European
imperialism, or at the very least as an aggressive and expansionist national movement.[56] That is the part of the ocean in
which the 'new historians' have chosen to fish and the tackle
they have chosen to use; the rest flows from there.

Some members of this group, notably Ilan Pappé, would
not only concede this research bias but would argue that it is
incumbent upon historians to bring their political values and
beliefs to bear on their work. Others, like Avi Shlaim, would
wrap this prejudice with Carr's general truism that 'the
historian's fundamental task is not to record but to evaluate'.[57]
Benny Morris takes a far more pious tack. He accepts 'that the
political views of the New Historians and current political
concerns were among the factors that led these historians to
research particular subjects', but rejects Pappé's view of the

55 Ibid., p. 23.
56 Avi Shlaim writes: 'At the time of the Basle Congress, Palestine was under the control of
     the Ottoman Turks. It was inhabited by nearly half a million Arabs and some 50,000 Jews
     ... But, in keeping with the spirit of the age of European imperialism, the Jews did not
     allow these local realities to stand in the way of their own national aspirations'. He then
     cites approvingly Walid Khalidi's characterization of the origins of the Arab–Israeli
     conflict in this vein (*Collusion*, pp. 2–3).
         In fact, Shlaim is out-Khaliding Khalidi as the latter was somewhat less explicit on
     this particular instance in making the standard linkage between Zionism and
     colonialism. As Khalidi put it: 'At the time of the Basle Congress 95% of the population
     of Palestine was Arab and 99% of its land was Arab-owned. In excluding these realities
     from their ken, the Jewish leaders assembled at Basle were behaving in a spirit
     characteristic of their age and continent' (Khalidi, *From Haven to Conquest*, p. xxii).
         Ilan Pappé has been far more outspoken in articulating Zionism as a brand of Western
     colonialism which 'gained control over a land that is not theirs at the end of the
     nineteenth century'. See, for example, 'Damning the Historical Forgery', *Kol Ha-ir*,
     6 October 1995, p. 61.
57 Avi Shlaim, *The Politics of Partition: King Abdullah, the Zionists and Palestine, 1921–1951*
     (Oxford: Oxford University Press, 1990), p. ix (this is an abridged and somewhat revised
     edition of *Collusion Across the Jordan*); Carr, *What is History?*, p. 21.

nature of the historical investigation. The historian should not be judgmental, argues Morris who has coined the full panoply of patronizing labels 'new', 'old', and 'new old' historiographies, but 'must remain honour-bound to gather and present his facts accurately and must "warn" his readers that he has such-and-such beliefs and that they have influenced his work in such-and-such manner ... historiography can and should attempt to be objective and impartial'.[58]

Alas, as we shall see in the next chapter, Morris is the last person to abide by these lofty principles. Pappé, the self-professed 'relativist', has at least the decency to admit that the line between fact and fiction is very thin indeed and that history can be 'imagined', to borrow the term coined by one of his intellectual gurus, Benedict Anderson.[59] Morris, and – somewhat less piously so – Shlaim, pretend to use documents as their 'Ark of covenant in the temple of facts',[60] but the history they construct is no less imagined than Pappé's. To return to Carr's metaphor, the 'new historians' have been trying to pass the sardine they have caught for a salmon, if not a whale.

58 Morris, *1948 and After*, p. 47.
59 Benedict Anderson, *Imagined Communities* (London: Verso, 1991). For Pappé's clinging to this tree see, for example, 'Zionism as an Interpretation of Reality', *Ha-aretz*, 26 May 1995.
60 Carr, *What is History*, p. 16. Shlaim writes: 'I did not set out with the intention of writing a revisionist history. It was the official documents I came across in the various archives that led me ... to re-examine some of my own assumptions as well as the claims of previous historians'. Shlaim, *Collusion*, p. viii.

2 'Falsifying the Record': Benny Morris, David Ben-Gurion, and the 'Transfer' Idea

> I think that for good history there must be a basic
> integrity in the use of the evidence.
>
> ALBERT HOURANI

The idea of 'transfer', or the expulsion of the Palestinians to the neighbouring Arab States, has been one of the most charged issues in the historiography of the Arab–Israeli conflict. The Palestinian view, based on an historical assessment that ascribes sole responsibility for the events of 1947–49 to 'Zionist aggression', sees the Palestinians as the hapless victims of a Jewish grand design to disinherit them from their land. In contrast, Israelis deny the existence of any such intention and view the Palestinian tragedy as primarily a self-inflicted disaster by an extremist and short-sighted leadership which consistently rejected all compromise solutions that would have averted its people's tragic fate.

In his study on the origins of the Palestinian refugee problem, Benny Morris reached the commonsensical conclusion that this tragedy 'was born of war, not by design, Jewish or Arab'.[1] He found no evidence in support of the standard Arab claim that the Yishuv entered the 1947–49 War with a

---

1 Morris, *The Birth*, p. 286.

master plan to expel the Arabs, or that its political and military leaders had ever adopted such a plan.[2] Yet he maintained that 'from the mid-1930s most of the Yishuv's leaders, including Ben-Gurion, wanted to establish a Jewish State without an Arab minority, or with as small an Arab minority as possible, and supported a "transfer solution" to this minority problem'.[3]

Not surprisingly, partisans of the Arab cause have been quick to point to this ostensible contradiction: if the 'transfer solution' did indeed have 'a basis in mainstream Jewish thinking, if not actual planning, from the late 1930s and 1940s',[4] as claimed by Morris, then how can he account for its glaring absence from Israeli political and operational planning during the 1947–49 War? The possibility that Morris has erred in claiming that 'transfer' was etched on 'mainstream Jewish thinking', as indeed he has, does not seem to have occurred to them. As far as they are concerned, for all his self-proclaimed 'revisionism', Morris is yet another 'Israeli-Zionist propagandist', and one of the more devious of them. After all, is he not a research fellow at 'one of the most prestigious and mainstream academic institutions in Israel'? Has his book not been published by 'a Labour party publishing house founded by the Mapai leadership of the early 1940s'?[5]

While one cannot avoid the irony of Morris being given a healthy dose of his own medicine, this below-the-belt tactic totally misses the point unless, of course, it is proven that Morris's academic affiliation or choice of publisher have led him to distort his findings. Until then, and so long as no other historian produces any incriminating evidence of an Israeli master plan to expel the Palestinian Arabs, Morris cannot be

2   Ibid., pp. 288–9, 292; Morris, *1948 and After*, p. 17.
3   Morris, *1948 and After*, p. 17.
4   Morris, *The Birth*, p. 24.
5   Nur Masalha, '1948 and After Revisited', *Journal of Palestine Studies*, XXIV, 4 (Summer 1995), pp. 90–1. See also idem, 'A Critique of Benny Morris', *Journal of Palestine Studies*, XXI, 1 (Autumn 1991), pp. 90-97; Norman Finkelstein, 'Myths, Old and New', *Journal of Palestine Studies*, XXI, 1 (Autumn 1991), pp. 66–89; criticism by Sharif Kanaana of Bir Zeit University, cited in Morris, *1948 and After*, p. 35.

faulted for an act of omission in this respect. In contrast, on the issue of 'transfer' Morris has made serious acts of commission which totally invalidate his claim that this idea 'had a basis in mainstream Jewish thinking, if not actual planning, from the late 1930s and 1940s'.

In the first place, Morris fails to place the Zionist discussion of the transfer idea within its true context, namely in response to the British Peel Royal Commission recommendations of July 1937. In its report the commission suggested the partition of Mandatory Palestine (west of the Jordan River) into two states – an Arab state in some 85 per cent of this territory and a Jewish State in the rest; and by way of reducing future friction between the two communities the commission suggested a land and population exchange between the Jewish and the Arab States, similar to that effected between Turkey and Greece in the wake of the First World War.[6] Since there were far more Arabs in the Jewish State-to-be than the other way round (225,000 as compared with a mere 1,250), some Zionist proponents of partition (such as David Ben-Gurion) viewed this exchange, or transfer as it came to be known, as offering partial compensation for the confinement of the prospective Jewish State to a tiny fraction of the Land of Israel, provided it was carried out by Great Britain and received the blessing of the League of Nations. A 'Population Exchange Committee' was thus established by the Jewish Agency Executive (JAE) in November 1937 to study the matter, only to disband quietly and unofficially the following summer after concluding that the idea was stillborn, not least because the British backed down from their initiative. Hence not one of the 30 odd submissions made by the JAE to the Palestine Partition Commission (the Woodhead Commission, 1938) suggested population exchange and transfer.[7] Indeed the

---

6 Palestine Royal Commission, *Report*, Presented by the Secretary of State for the Colonies to Parliament by Command of His Majesty, July 1937, Cmd. 5479 (London: HMSO, 1937), pp. 291–5.
7 Teveth, 'The Palestine Arab Refugee Problem', p. 232.

commission reported that 'on behalf of the Jews it was made clear to us that *Jewish opinion was opposed to the exercise of any degree of compulsion*'.[8] In short,

> Transfer as a concrete political possibility never exceeded the bounds of the 1937 royal commission report – it was born and buried there. It was not even mentioned in the United Nations partition plan of 1947. Had transfer not been included in the Peel commission report, it would not have been placed on the political agenda of the Zionist movement, even though the idea itself had been mentioned occasionally in the past.[9]

While Morris mentions the Peel Commission's recommendation of transfer, he does so only in passing, as one of several (unidentified) schemes addressing this issue in the mid-1930s and not necessarily the most important of them. Worse than that, not only does Morris fail to give the commission its due credit as the originator of transfer as a political option, but he also creates the false impression that it was the Zionists who thrust the idea on the indifferent, if not reluctant British Mandatory Power rather than vice versa, and that Zionist interest in transfer as a political option outlived the Peel Commission by far. 'In the run-up to the UN General Assembly Partition Resolution of November 1947, the Yishuv leaders usually ignored the subject. The British had made it clear that they opposed a transfer and certainly would not implement it on behalf of the Jews', Morris writes, whereas in reality it was the British Labour Party which made transfer part of its election platform in 1945, only to be rejected by the Zionists.[10]

8   Palestine Partition Commission, *Report*, Cmd. 5854 (London: HMSO, 1938), p. 52 fn. (emphasis added).

9   Itzhak Galnoor, *The Partition of Palestine: Decision Crossroads in the Zionist Movement* (Albany: State University of New York Press, 1995), pp. 179–80.

10   Morris, *The Birth*, pp. 25, 28. In fact Morris contradicts himself by conceding that Ben-Gurion dismissed the British Labour's 'transfer' solution out of hand (p. 28). Yet the false impression of Zionist interest in the idea has already been etched on the reader.

That Morris fails to prove this fallacy is vividly illustrated by the fact that the lion's share of his 'evidence' comes from the 1937–38 period, or more precisely, from three JAE meetings (on 7, 9, and 12 June), though he misleads his readers into the belief that there were actually four such meetings.[11] Moreover, Morris has painted a totally false picture of the actual proceedings of these meetings. Contrary to his claim that these meetings 'debated at length various aspects of the transfer idea', the issue was discussed only in the last meeting, and even then as one element in the overall balance of risks and opportunities attending Britain's suggested partition, rather than as a concrete policy option.[12] Not only did the other

11   Morris does so by discussing the 7 June meeting on two different occasions, separated by several paragraphs, without noting its precise date. See, *The Birth*, pp. 24, 25–26. Morris brings two other items from the same period: Ben-Gurion's diary entry for 12 July 1937, and a letter to his son, Amos, on 5 October 1937, both of which are incidentally cited from a secondary source, namely, Shabtai Teveth's study of Ben-Gurion's attitude to the Palestinian Arabs.

12   Contrary to Morris's claim, the transfer issue did *not* take up 'almost the whole of the day-long executive meeting of 12 June, which was also attended by members of the Political Committee of the Zionist Actions Committee' (*The Birth*, p. 26), but approximately 20 per cent of the overall deliberations. Transfer was not discussed at all during the morning session which was dedicated to a review of the meeting held the previous week between the JAE and the Woodhead Commission. The agenda of the afternoon session included four major items expected to be raised by the Woodhead Commission: a) the rights of the non-Jewish minorities in the Jewish State; b) the stages in the transition to statehood; c) the transfer issue; d) frontier settlements in the prospective Jewish and Arab states.
   As for the actual proceedings, Morris resorts to selective quotations by omitting certain passages that could place their substance in context. For example, he cites Avraham Menahem Ussishkin, Head of the Jewish National Fund (JNF) as seeing nothing immoral in transfer: 'It is the most moral [thing to do] ... We will not be able to begin our political life in a state in which Arabs will constitute 45% [of the population]' (ibid.}. The full text reads as follows: 'If you ask me whether it is moral to take 60,000 families from the places in which they presently reside and transfer them to a different location, while giving them of course all the means for [re]settlement – then I will tell you that it is moral, for if it is possible to rob the Jewish People of nine-tenths of its historic homeland (including Transjordan), to deny them any foothold there and to forbid them to go and settle and purchase [land] there –and this after all the hopes instilled in us and all the commitments undertaken by the Balfour Declaration and the League of Nations' Mandate etc. etc. If all this is moral, then to give us one small stretch [of land] and to take a part of the Arabs and transfer and settle them in a better-off manner [than that in which they are today] is as moral as can be. I am prepared to stand before the Lord and the League of Nations and defend the morality of the matter. But it is not the question of morality that is at issue here but rather that of practicality; and I say here that we Jews cannot undertake this ... this can only be done by the British government if it so wishes' (Protocol of the joint meeting of the JAE and the Political Committee of the Zionist Actions Committee, 12 June 1938, p. 25/6009).
   In other words, Ussishkin views the transfer of *some* Arabs *by the British authorities* (*not*

two meetings not involve any lengthy debate of the transfer idea, but they *did not* discuss the subject *at all*!

But even if Morris had given an accurate description of these meetings – which he certainly did not – still this would not have established his (mis)claim that the transfer idea 'had a basis in mainstream Jewish thinking, if not actual planning, from the late 1930s and 1940s'. Five days in the life of a national movement can scarcely provide proof of long-standing trends or ideologies, especially since these meetings were called in response to a specific agenda forced upon the Zionist movement by the British government. In order to prove that the transfer idea had a life beyond the Peel Commission, Morris should have gone systematically through *all* JAE meetings between the mid-1930s and the late 1940s, among other archival sources, rather than randomly pick the odd meeting and hinge on it an entire historical construction. Needless to say, the four-and-a-half pages devoted by Morris to the transfer idea show no trace whatsoever of such an investigation.

by the Zionist movement) as a direct consequence of the Peel Partition Plan – to which he was adamantly opposed in the first place – rather than an ideal to be aspired to; its morality being in his eyes a corollary of the expropriation of 90 per cent of the Land of Israel from its rightful owners. Had the Royal Commission not made this particular proposal, there would have been no need for the 'sweetener' of transfer. As Ussishkin put it when asked by one of the participants what he proposed to do if the Zionist movement were offered the entire country: 'We will not accept the state today in the whole of the Land of Israel before we possess most of the land and a large part of the Yishuv ... We hope that with the passage of time we will become the majority [through immigration] and possess the lands and then there will be a Jewish State in which we will be our own masters' (ibid., p. 27/6011).

Similarly, Morris misrepresents Ben-Gurion as supporting the morality of compulsory transfer as such at a time when a) Ben-Gurion's perception of the idea and its implementation was identical to that of Ussishkin (despite their differences over the issue of partition); b) Ben-Gurion was categorically opposed to compulsory transfer as a concrete policy option. Morris cites Ben-Gurion as saying: 'I support compulsory transfer. I don't see in it anything immoral' (*The Birth*, p. 27). The meeting's protocol reads as follows: 'I saw in the Peel Plan two positive things: the ideas of a state and compulsory transfer ... I support compulsory transfer. I don't see in it anything immoral, but compulsory transfer can only be effected by England and not by the Jews ... Not only is it inconceivable for us to carry it out, but it is also inconceivable for us to propose it' (pp. 8a-9a/6029-30). Hence the Woodhead Commission's above-noted comment that 'on behalf of the Jews it was made clear to us that Jewish opinion was opposed to the exercise of any degree of compulsion'.

To sum up, in contemporary Zionist thinking transfer was an integral part of the Peel Partition Plan. It was suggested by the Commission, was to be executed by the British government, and derived its legitimacy from the parallel reduction of the prospective Jewish State to a tiny fraction of the Land of Israel. No Peel Plan – no transfer.

Yet this superficial eclecticism is the least of Morris's professional flaws. In his endeavour to prove the unprovable and to create history in an image of his own devising he does not shrink from distortion of evidence, to the point that few are the documents that Morris relies on without twisting and misleading, either by a 'creative rewriting' of the original text, or by taking things out of context, or by truncating texts and thereby distorting their original meaning.

REWRITING BEN-GURION

Take for example the JAE meeting of 7 June 1938. Morris writes:

> Ben-Gurion put it clearly at a meeting of the Jewish Agency Executive in June 1938: 'The starting point for a solution of the Arab problem in the Jewish State' was the conclusion of *an agreement with the Arab States that would pave the way for a transfer of the Arabs out of the Jewish State to the Arab countries*. Ben-Gurion supported the establishment of a Jewish State on a small part of Palestine 'not because he is satisfied with part of the country, but on the basis of the assumption that after we constitute a large force following the establishment of the state – we will cancel the partition of the country [between Jews and Arabs] and we will expand throughout the Land of Israel.' When one of the participants asked him whether he contemplated *such a population transfer* and expansion 'by force,' Ben-Gurion said: '[No]. Through mutual understanding and JewishArab agreement ... [But] the state is only a stage in the realization of Zionism and it must prepare the ground for our expansion throughout the whole country through a Jewish–Arab agreement'.[13]

13   Morris, *The Birth*, p. 24 (emphasis added).

The key passage here is the mention of 'an agreement with the Arab States that would pave the way for a transfer of the Arabs out of the Jewish State to the Arab countries'. The trouble is, nothing of this sort is found in the actual text of the meeting protocol, which reads as follows:

> Mr. Ben-Gurion: The starting point for a solution of the question of the Arabs in the Jewish State is, in his view, the need to prepare the ground for an Arab–Jewish agreement; he supports [the establishment of] the Jewish State [on a small part of Palestine], not because he is satisfied with part of the country, but on the basis of the assumption that after we constitute a large force following the establishment of the state – we will cancel the partition [of the country between Jews and Arabs] and we will expand throughout the Land of Israel.

> Mr. Shapira [a JAE member]: By force as well?

> Mr. Ben-Gurion: [No]. Through mutual understanding and Jewish–Arab agreement. So long as we are weak and few the Arabs have neither the need nor the interest to conclude an alliance with us. So long as it would seem to the Arabs that they can stop our growth and leave us as a small minority – they will try to do so. He does not imagine Arab agreement to mass Jewish immigration – so long as the Jews are weak and few. Only when we become a major power – and the [establishment of a Jewish] state will help this more than anything else – will the Arabs recognize the need to reach an agreement with us. And since the state is only a stage in the realization of Zionism and it must prepare the ground for our expansion throughout the whole country through Jewish–Arab agreement – we are obliged to run the

state in such a way that will win us the friendship of the Arabs both within and outside the state. Hence the question of the Arabs in the Jewish State is not an ordinary minority question – but one of the fundamental questions of our Zionist policy. The state will of course have to enforce order and security and will do this not only by moralizing and preaching 'sermons on the mount' but also by machine guns should the need arise. But the Arab policy of the Jewish State must be aimed not only at full equality for the Arabs but at their cultural, social, and economic *equalization*, namely, at raising their standard of living to that of the Jews.[14]

As is clearly borne out by the original text, Ben-Gurion made no mention whatsoever of the need to transfer the Palestine Arabs and *ipso facto* he could not have been asked by one of the participants whether such a transfer would be effected by force. All that Ben-Gurion suggested was that the

14 Protocol of the meeting of the Jewish Agency Executive of 7 June 1938, pp. 11–12 (emphasis in the original).

   To Morris's 'credit', it should be noted that Nur Masalha, in his propagandist *The Expulsion of the Palestinians* (Washington: Institute for Palestine Studies, 1992), goes much further in falsifying the proceedings of the same JAE meeting. The list of distortions is infinite. For example Masalha claims that Ben-Gurion 'never considered the possibility of an Arab minority as an integral part of a Jewish State requiring long-term plans for integration' – a blatant distortion given the fact that most of Ben-Gurion's presentation on the Arab question during the meeting was devoted to their integration in the prospective Jewish State rather than their expulsion. He then replicates Morris's falsification above that 'the starting point for a solution of the Arab problem in the Jewish State was the negotiation of an agreement' with neighbouring countries that would ensure the removal of the Arabs from the Jewish state, with the added distortion of Ben-Gurion's negative reply to Shapira's question whether Jewish expansion (but not transfer!) should be carried out by force, before moving *inter alia* to distort Ben-Gurion's reference to the enforcement of law and order. As Masalha put it: '… the state, however, must enforce order and security and it will do this not by moralizing and preaching "sermons on the mount", but by machine guns, which we will need' (pp. 107–8). The real citation, as we have already seen, is not only fundamentally different from Masalha's distortion but also demolishes his (mis)claim that Ben-Gurion 'never considered the possibility of an Arab minority as an integral part of a Jewish state': 'The state will of course have to enforce order and security and will do this not only by moralizing and preaching 'sermons on the mount' but also by machine guns should the need arise. But the Arab policy of the Jewish State should be aimed not only at full equality for the Arabs but at their cultural, social, and economic *equalization*, namely, at raising their standard of living to that of the Jews'.

question of the Arabs in the prospective Jewish State should be resolved by peaceful means through an 'Arab–Jewish agreement' – *not* an agreement between Israel and the Arab States, and certainly not one that 'would pave the way for a transfer of the Arabs out of the Jewish State to the Arab countries' – the words falsely put in his mouth by Morris. Had Ben-Gurion really suggested the eviction of the Palestine Arabs (which he did not) he would not have dwelt on the need to win the friendship of the Arab citizens of the Jewish State and to improve their social, cultural and economic lot. After all, if one presses Morris's (mis)claim to its logical conclusion, Arab citizens would not remain for this purpose!

But Morris is not the person to be troubled by such niceties. His is the *idée fixe* of Ben-Gurion's commitment to the transfer idea that has to be proven come what may; and if this requires a good measure of textual acrobatics, so be it. As Morris put it:

> Ben-Gurion understood that few, if any, of the Arabs would uproot themselves voluntarily; the compulsory provision would have to be put into effect. 'We must expel Arabs and take their places … and if we have to use force not to dispossess the Arabs of the Negev and Transjordan, but to guarantee our own right to settle in those places – then we have force at our disposal,' he wrote to his son Amos, contemplating the implementation of the transfer recommendation of the Peel Commission report.[15]

This passage is incompletely cited from Shabtai Teveth's study of Ben-Gurion's attitude towards the Palestinian Arabs. Teveth's original text reads as follows:

15 Morris, *The Birth*, p. 25.

In reflecting on the transfer provision of the Peel Commission's recommendations, Ben-Gurion planned his next step: 'We must expel Arabs and take their places.' *He did not wish to do so, for 'all our aspiration is built on the assumption – proven throughout all our activity – that there is enough room for ourselves and the Arabs in Palestine.'* But if the Arabs did not accept that assumption, 'and if we have to use force – not to dispossess the Arabs of the Negev and Transjordan, but to guarantee our own right to settle in those places – then we have force at our disposal'.[16]

Teveth claimed that Ben-Gurion *did not wish* to expel the Palestinians since his fundamental article of faith was 'that there is enough room for ourselves and the Arabs in Palestine'; in Morris's truncated text, Ben-Gurion wished to do precisely that. Again, Morris has taken liberty with his evidence; this time not by putting his own words into other people's mouths but by deleting key sentences from the original text in a way that turns its real meaning upside down.

Now Morris may deem Teveth's judgement to be impaired so as not to merit serious consideration; but a minimum scholarly obligation, and the decent thing to do, would have been to cite sources accurately, to give one's evaluation of them, and to let the readers form their own judgement. This is the foundation of *bona fide* scholarly research of which Morris's 'honour-bound' historian surely must be aware.

But there is a more complex and serious side to the ledger. The elementary rule of historical investigation is to rely on original sources whenever possible, not their citation by other authors (or, in the jargon of historians, on primary rather than secondary sources); and this rule applies with far greater force to the self-styled 'new historians', whose claim to 'newness'

16 Shabtai Teveth, *Ben-Gurion and the Palestine Arabs* (New York: Oxford University Press, 1985), p. 189 (emphasis added).

is predicated on access to archival materials that were not available to earlier generations of historians. Yet instead of consulting the original document in the archive, Morris has chosen to base an important part of his 'incriminating evidence' against Ben-Gurion on a secondary source (albeit not without distorting it in the process); and not just an ordinary secondary source but an archetypal 'old historian', whose scholarly credentials have repeatedly been derided by Morris himself.[17]

That the first part of Ben-Gurion's statement in Morris's truncated account ('We must expel Arabs and take their places') appears to contradict its second part ('if we have to use force – not to dispossess the Arabs of the Negev and Transjordan, but to guarantee our own right to settle in those places') makes it all the more important to consult the original document. This contradiction is further sharpened if one considers the part of the citation omitted by Morris: 'all our aspiration is built on the assumption – proven throughout all our activity – that there is enough room for ourselves and the Arabs in Palestine'. For if Ben-Gurion believed that there was enough room in Palestine for Arabs and Jews and did not wish to dispossess the Arabs, why did he ostensibly feel obliged to expel them?

Indeed, an examination of Ben-Gurion's original letter (in handwriting), sheds important light on this apparent contradiction. In the letter, written to his son Amos on 5 October 1937 from London, Ben-Gurion defended his decision to support the Peel Commission partition proposal. 'I do not dream of and do not love war', he wrote

> And I still believe – more than before the possibility
> of a state was created – that after we become numer-
> ous and strong in the country, the Arabs will under-

17 See, for example, Benny Morris, 'The Eel and History: A Reply to Shabtai Teveth', *Tikkun*, January–February 1990.

stand that it is best for them to strike an alliance with us, and to benefit from our help, provided they allow us, in good will, to settle in all parts of Palestine … the Jews can be equal allies, true friends, and not occupiers and oppressors.

[But] let us assume that the Negev will not be included in the Jewish State. It will then remain barren [since] the Arabs are not capable of nor need to develop and build it. They have their fair share of deserts – and they lack the human resources, the money, and the initiative [for such an enterprise]. And it is very likely that in exchange for our financial, military, organizational and scientific assistance, the Arabs will agree that we develop and build the Negev. It is also possible that they will not agree. A people does not always behave according to logic, common sense, and best interest. Just like you [i.e., Amos] feel a contradiction between your mind and your heart, so it is possible that the Arabs will act according to sterile nationalist emotion and will tell us: 'We want neither your honey nor your sting. It is better for the Negev to remain barren than to be populated by Jews'. And then we will have to talk to them in a different language. And we will have a different language, which we will not have unless we have a state. Because we cannot stand to see large areas of unsettled land capable of absorbing dozens of thousands of Jews remain empty, or see Jews not returning to their country because the Arabs choose that neither we nor they will have the place.

A: And then we will have to use force and will use it without hesitation though only when we have no other choice. We do not wish and do not need to expel Arabs and take their place ['ein anu rotsim ve-ein anu tsrihim legaresh aravim ve-lakahat mekomam']. All our aspiration is built on the assumption – proven throughout all our activity in the Land [of Israel] – that there is enough room in the country for ourselves and the Arabs. *B: But if we have to use force – not to dispossess the Arabs of the Negev and Transjordan, but to guarantee our own right to settle in those places – then we have force at our disposal.*

This text makes two points clear:

- Ben-Gurion made no mention whatsoever of the Arab population of the prospective Jewish State; hence he could not have intended its expulsion from that State. Rather, he talked about the possibility of Jewish settlement in the Negev (and Transjordan) despite the exclusion of these areas from the territory of the Jewish State-to-be; and he made it abundantly clear that he had no intention of dispossessing any Arabs from these areas. On the contrary, he viewed Jewish settlement in these sparsely populated areas, specifically the Negev, as contributing to their development in general, and to the collective good of their Arab population in particular. Were force to be used, *as a means of last resort*, it would be to ensure the Jewish right to settle in those areas – *not* to expel Arabs.
- The sentence 'we need to [or 'must' as translated by Teveth] expel Arabs and take their place' appears to result from hasty writing, not political intention. In the process of writing the letter, Ben-Gurion apparently realized he had repeated himself on the question of the use of force; or he decided to rephrase this sentence. In any case, he crossed out the emphasized words in sentence A above, rewriting them in a slightly different form as sentence B above. In so doing, most probably due to an abrupt brush of the pen, he erased the critical words 'do not' ('ve-ein') leaving the sentence as 'we need' ('anu tsrihim') rather than as 'we do not need' ('ve-ein anu tsrihim'). As a result a momentary,

fleeting typographical oversight has become a pointed weapon in the hands of future detractors, though only if this sentence is taken out of context and presented in a truncated form.[18]

But even if Morris does not accept this interpretation, which is the only bona fide way to resolve the glaring contradiction in the above citation, he has certainly failed his own test of 'gather[ing] and present[ing] his facts accurately'. Had he taken the trouble to read the original letter, he would easily have realized that a) Ben-Gurion did not refer at all to the Arabs of the prospective Jewish State, let alone to their expulsion, and b) the sentence 'we need to expel Arabs and take their place' is totally out of place not only in the paragraph in which it appears, but in the entire letter which makes no mention whatsoever of the transfer idea.

But then, having got away with distorting Teveth's citation, Morris accuses Teveth of foul play. In a recent Hebrew article, Morris accepts the veracity of the sentence 'We do not wish and do not need to expel Arabs', claiming even that the critical words 'do not' were erased by somebody other than Ben-Gurion.[19] To which one can only say, paraphrasing Prophet Nathan's words to King David: 'Hast thou falsified and then moralised?'

FABRICATING PROTOCOLS

Having established himself as an accomplished practitioner of the strange craft of rewriting historical documents, to use

18 Jerome Slater (of the State University of New York) carries the distortion of this sentence a step further than Morris: 'We will [rather than the original 'need to'] expel the Arabs [rather than 'Arabs'] and take their place ... with the force at our disposal'. He adds insult to injury by presenting this truncated sentence, which in the first place never meant what he attributes to it, and which was written in a unique context in 1937, as 'proof' of Zionist disingenuousness in accepting the UN Partition Resolution of November 1947, as if nothing had changed during this momentous decade. See, Jerome Slater, 'Lost Opportunities for Peace: Reassessing the Arab–Israeli Conflict', *Tikkun*, 10, 2 (May/June 1995), p. 61.
19 Benny Morris, 'A New Look on Central Zionist Documents', *Alpayim*, 12 (1996), pp.76–7.

his own words,[20] Morris proceeds with his distorted picture. As he put it:

> The Jewish Agency Executive, the 'government' of the Yishuv, in June 1938, against the backdrop of the Woodhead Commission's review of possible solutions to the conflict, debated at length various aspects of the transfer idea. Ben-Gurion proposed 'Lines of Action' for the Jewish State-to-be: 'The Jewish State will discuss with the neighbouring Arab States the matter of voluntarily transferring Arab tenant-farmers, labourers and *fellahin* from the Jewish State to the neighbouring states.' Such a transfer and the concomitant encouragement of Jewish immigration to the state 'were not tantamount to discrimination,' he said.[21]

This time Morris does not plant words in Ben-Gurion's mouth: he 'only' twists them in a way that distorts their real context. First he creates the false impression that Ben-Gurion proposed his 'Lines of Action' in the midst of a lengthy discussion of the transfer idea and that these lines revolved *ipso facto* around that idea. They did not. As we shall see shortly, there was *no* discussion of transfer at that meeting, and only one of the 28 'Lines of Action' proposed by Ben-Gurion dealt with the *voluntary* transfer of *some* Arabs who, *of their free will*, would choose to leave the prospective Jewish State.[22] About half of these Lines did not deal with the Arab

---

20 Benny Morris, 'Falsifying the Record: A Fresh Look at Zionist Documentation of 1948', *Journal of Palestine Studies*, XXIV, 1 (Spring 1995), p. 44.

21 Morris, *The Birth*, pp. 25–6.

22 Writing on this proposal, Nur Masalha makes the absurd claim that 'the term "voluntary" did not mean a free choice for the individual transferees; rather it referred to an agreement with neighbouring Arab countries'. Masalha, *Expulsion*, p. 107.

Alas, the word voluntary means precisely that, namely, something that is done of one's free will, which is how it appeared in the original Hebrew (*Haavara Be-ratson* – transfer of free will). But if Masalha still cannot bring himself to admit the self-evident fact that when Ben-Gurion spoke of 'the voluntary transfer of Arab tenant-farmers, labourers and *fellahin* from the Jewish State to the neighbouring states' (Line of Action

question at all and those that did were based on the assumption that most Arabs would stay in the Jewish State-to-be as equal citizens, rather than be expelled. Second, the concomitance of Jewish immigration and the voluntary transfer of (some) Arabs attributed to Ben-Gurion by Morris is patently false. What Ben-Gurion actually said was that neither of these two distinct issues contradicted the commitment of the Jewish State-to-be to complete non-discrimination on grounds of ethnicity, religion, sex, or class: not that they were linked in any way, shape or form.[23]

The agenda of the JAE meeting of 7 June 1938, in which Ben-Gurion proposed his 'Lines of Action', included eight items, of which the question of the Arabs in the prospective Jewish State – *not* their transfer from that State – ranked sixth on the list.[24] Already in his opening remarks asking Ben-Gurion to introduce the discussion on the Arab question, Werner David Senator, a JAE member, said that, to his understanding, the transfer idea was not on the agenda.[25] Indeed, of the 18 packed pages of the meeting's protocol, only four lines referred to the transfer idea, namely the above noted possibility of the voluntary transfer of some Arab tenant-farmers, labourers and *fellahin*, whose resettlement costs, incidentally, would be fully incurred by the Jewish State.[26]

18) he meant the transfer of *only* those who chose of their free will to do so, he is advised to examine Line of Action 23 which proves beyond a shadow of doubt that this was indeed Ben-Gurion's intention: 'The state's handling of the transfer of Arabs to the neighbouring Arab countries *of the transferees' free will (mi-toch retsonam ha-hofshi shel ha-mu'avarim)* (emphasis added). But then Masalha translated this sentence as 'the state engagement in transferring the Arabs [rather than Arabs as in the original!] to neighbouring Arab States voluntarily' and denied that the word voluntarily means 'of the transferees' free will' as written in the original Hebrew.

23 Protocol of the meeting of the Jewish Agency Executive of 7 June 1938, p. 16, Line of Action 23.

24 The agenda included the following items: minutes of the JAE meeting of 29 May 1938; possible appeal to the British authorities for clemency for Jewish underground caught bearing arms; the state of Austrian Jewry; financial report by a special committee on certain issues; commemoration of the late Professor Otto Warburg; the position of the Arabs in the Jewish State-to-be; a committee for examination of religious questions in the Jewish State-to-be; the directorship of the department for agricultural settlement.

25 Protocol of the meeting of the Jewish Agency Executive of 7 June 1938.

26 Ibid., p. 14, Line of Action 14.

Yet there is no doubt that this is not the agreement 'that would pave the way for a transfer of the Arabs out of the Jewish State-to-be to the Arab countries', falsely attributed to Ben-Gurion by Morris. For one thing, Ben-Gurion did not talk about the transfer of the Arab population as a whole but rather of those of them who, *of their free will*, would prefer not to become citizens of the Jewish State-to-be but to emigrate to one of the neighbouring Arab States.[27] For another thing, his presentation was dedicated almost exclusively to the position of the Arab population *in* the prospective Jewish State; and his proposed 'Lines of Action' were aimed at incorporating this community into the state as full and equal citizens, including the adoption of the necessary affirmative action to this end, not at their mass eviction as implied by Morris. Within this framework, Ben-Gurion suggested that,

> 1.   'The constitution of the Jewish State will be based on the general voting right of all its adult citizens regardless of their religion, race, sex, or class ...' (Line of Action 19).[28]

> 2.   'The Jewish State will protect the rights of the religious and national minorities and will ensure the freedom of worship and conscience of all communities and citizens' (Line of Action 21).

> 3.   'Every religious community will enjoy complete freedom to make its own practising arrangements, without undermining public order and the foundations of morality. Holy days of each religious community will be recognized as official resting days of this community' (Line of Action 22).

27   Ibid., p. 16, Lines of Action 20, 23.
28   Initially Ben-Gurion envisaged this constitution to enter into force 'after the consolidation of peace and public security in the state', until which time political power would reside with the Jewish Agency, but he backed down in light of his colleagues' scepticism.

4. 'There will be no discrimination among citizens of the Jewish State on the basis of race, religion, sex, or class ...' (Line of Action 23).

5. 'Hebrew will be the state language. But every national minority will be given full freedom to use its own language in educating its children and in managing the rest of its internal needs' (Line of Action 24).

6. 'The Arab minority will be able to use the Arabic language not only in its own educational, religious, and communal institutions, but also in its contacts with all state institutions. In every district, town, or village, where Arabs form a majority, all government announcements will be published in Arabic as well' (Line of Action 25).

7. 'The Jewish State will not content itself with full legal equality of all its citizens but will make deliberate graduated efforts to bring the quality of life of the Arab minority to the cultural, social, and economic level of the Jewish majority – through compulsory education to all children, medical and sanitary services, special legislation to protect industrial and agricultural workers, and the cultivation of general trade unionism and market cooperation with no ethnic discrimination among Jewish and Arab workers, peasants, members of the free professions, industrialists, and merchants' (Line of Action 26).

8. 'Until the barriers between the standards of living of the Jewish majority and the Arab minority will have been blurred – the state will ensure a fair percentage of its working places and services to Arab civil servants and workers at equal salaries to Jewish

civil servants and workers. In addition, Arab representatives will be ensured a fair percentage in the
state's elected institutions, without institutionalizing
sectarian elections' (Line of Action 27).

9.   'In tandem with its effective protection of minority
rights in all economic, political, and cultural walks of
life – the state will endeavour to root among all its
citizens a mutual awareness of their being members
of the same state and will cultivate any action and
organization aimed at destroying barriers between
ethnic groups and religions in all official spheres'
(Line of Action 28).[29]

This, in a nutshell, was Ben-Gurion's vision of Jewish–Arab
coexistence in the Jewish State-to-be: a far cry from the brutish
world-view attributed to him by the 'new historiography'
in general, and from the desire to transfer 'the Arabs out of
the Jewish State to the Arab countries' in particular. If anything, these 'Lines of Action' represent a progressive socio-
economic-political programme that would not shame any
Western social-democratic party. Recognition of minority
religious holy days as official resting days, to mention one
example, is something that many minorities do not enjoy in
some of the most advanced Western democracies even today.

That this progressive vision of Jewish–Arab coexistence
was not confined to Ben-Gurion is clearly borne out by the
minutes of the JAE meeting of 9 June, which was exclusively
devoted to the question of the Arab minority in the Jewish
State-to-be. Like its precursor of two days earlier, there was
no discussion whatsoever of the transfer idea; hence Morris's
claim that 'there was a consensus in favour of implementing
the proposed transfer, though an argument raged about its
scale and about whether it was to be accomplished with

29   Ibid., pp. 15–17.

or without Britain' is a complete figment of his imagination.[30]

It is true that there were two brief references to transfer during the meeting, but both were in passing and none kindled any discussion. At the beginning of the session Ben-Gurion read a letter from Fischel Rottenstreich, a JAE member who could not attend the meeting, suggesting the Peel Commission's recommendation of transfer be endorsed, should the Woodhead Commission force the Arab question on the Jewish Agency, which he thought would be ill-advised in the first place;[31] but this suggestion generated no response from the participants, only a brief comment by Ben-Gurion that:

a) In the Jewish State there will be several minorities as follows: Armenian, German, Christian-Arab, Druze, Mutawallis, Bahais etc. The largest minority are the Muslim Arabs;

b) The question of the Arabs in the Jewish State is not just a question of minority. It is a central political question, that of the Jewish State's relations with the Arab World. The question of the Arab minority is not akin to the question of the Germans in Czechoslovakia. Hypothetically, Czechoslovakia can forego good relations with Germany if it enjoys a secure alliance with other great powers such as Britain, France, and Russia, while for the Jewish State, relations with the neighbouring Arab countries will constitute the first and central question of its foreign relations, and the question of the Arab minority is an organic part of this problem.[32]

In no way does this comment imply any endorsement of the transfer idea. If anything, it reflects Ben-Gurion's perception

30   Morris, *The Birth*, p. 26.
31   Protocol of the meeting of the Jewish Agency Executive of 9 June 1938, pp. 1–2.
32   Ibid., pp. 2–3.

of the Arab minority as a bridge between the prospective
Jewish State and its Arab neighbours; hence his belief,
expressed already at the 7 June meeting, that the Jewish State
had to be ruled 'in such a way that will win us the friendship
of the Arabs both within and outside the State'. This belief, as
we shall see shortly, ran like a thread in Ben-Gurion's strategic
thinking at least until the outbreak of the 1947–49 War; and
none of the participants of the 9 June meeting questioned its
validity. Far from discussing the implementation of the transfer idea, the meeting focused on the affirmative action that
had to be taken on behalf of the Arab minority, and the dis-
agreements between participants revolved around the extent
to which the prospective State would be able to afford the
financial and economic costs of such action without undermining the well-being of the Jewish majority. 'If the prospective Jewish State will not be able to maintain full and real
equality it will be unable to survive, as demonstrated by the
experiences in the world', argued Werner David Senator. 'If
Zionism will not be able to solve the question of Jewish–Arab
coexistence in the state, he [Senator] will personally consider
it the failure of Zionism to fulfil its moral promises to the
Jewish people'. 'There is of course another solution, namely,
the transfer of the Arabs as suggested by the Peel Commission', he said. 'Had this been feasible – he [Senator] would
have supported it; otherwise – we have no other way but to
observe real equality between Jews and Arabs in the Jewish
State ... If we will not do everything to give the Arabs real
equality we will bring disaster on the Jewish State ... He
cannot imagine any Jewish government that will not include
representatives of the Arab minority, which is a substantial
minority'.[33]

This was the second allusion to transfer in the meeting,
and, as noted earlier, it was neither made in the context of a
discussion of the idea, nor generated any such discussion, nor

33   Ibid., pp. 9–11.

even suggested that the idea be discussed. To the contrary, a careful examination of Senator's full comments would easily reveal his acquiescence in the idea of a binational state, which is scarcely surprising given his position as a representative of the a-Zionists in the Jewish Agency Executive, and his membership in Brit Shalom which advocated the binational ideal.

Be that as it may, by no stretch of imagination can these two brief allusions constitute the imaginary 'consensus in favour of implementing the proposed transfer' attributed by Morris to the meeting. As a matter of fact, the only consensus reached at the meeting was to form a special committee to study the minorities question and to discuss the matter at a later date.[34]

THE FINAL INSULT

But this is not the last of Morris's falsifications. In his eagerness to invent Israeli history, he stretches the alleged Zionist interest in the idea of transfer as a political option up to the outbreak of the 1947–49 War. In this case he bases his 'proof' on two sources: a JAE meeting on 2 November 1947, and Ben-Gurion's speech to Mapai supporters early in December 1947; and as with his use of earlier documents, Morris does not shrink from blatant distortion of evidence to suit his needs. According to Morris:

> In early November 1947, the Jewish Agency Executive discussed various proposals for giving the prospective Jewish State's Arab minority citizenship in the neighbouring prospective Palestine Arab State. The consensus was for giving as many of the Arab minority in the Jewish State citizenship of Arab Palestine rather than Jewish State citizenship. In the

34 Ibid., p. 11.

event of war between the two Palestine states, said Ben-Gurion, the Arab minority in the Jewish State would be 'a Fifth Column.' Hence, it was best that they be citizens of the Palestine Arab State so that, if hostile, they 'could be expelled' to the Palestine Arab State. But if they were citizens of the Jewish State, 'it would only be possible to imprison them, and it would be better to expel them than to imprison them.' There was no explicit mention of the collective transfer idea.[35]

This time Morris had the decency to concede that 'the collective transfer idea' was not discussed during the meeting, though leaving the impression that its spirit hovered over the discussion. It did not. Most of the meeting was devoted to issues that had nothing to do with the 'Arab question', such as the appointment of a director-general to the education department; internal security in the Yishuv; the murder of a Zionist activist in the Austrian town of Insbruck etc.

Morris furthermore distorts the essence of the part of the meeting devoted to the Arabs and the positions of the personae involved. First, contrary to his claim, the meeting did not discuss 'various proposals' – only one proposal made by the US Government. Second, this proposal did *not* suggest giving 'the prospective Jewish State's Arab minority citizenship in the neighbouring prospective Palestine Arab State', but rather obliging Arabs in the prospective Jewish State, as well as Jews in the Arab State-to-be, who chose not to take the citizenship of the respective State in which they resided, to leave this State after some time.[36] Initially Ben-Gurion opposed this proposal – partly because he did not want the departure of the Jewish residents of the prospective Arab State from their place of residence; partly because he thought that,

35   Morris, *The Birth*, p. 28.
36   Protocol of the Jewish Agency Executive meeting of 2 November 1947, p. 3.

as foreign nationals, citizens of the Arab State residing in the Jewish State would be less involved in its internal affairs; and partly because of the reason cited by Morris. Contrary to Morris's narration, however, Ben-Gurion's view as cited above was not amenable to most participants in the meeting; indeed, after listening to his colleagues Ben-Gurion changed his mind and endorsed the American proposal. True to nature, Morris fails to note this change which renders the above citation totally irrelevant for the simple reason that it represented Ben-Gurion's view at one point in the discussion rather than his final position.[37]

But this all-too-common act of historical distortion pales into insignificance in comparison to Morris's tampering with Ben-Gurion's speech of 13 December 1947. Yes, Morris concedes that in testifying before the United Nations Special Commission on Palestine (UNSCOP) in July 1947, Ben-Gurion 'went out of his way to reject the 1945 British Labour Party platform "International Post-war Settlement" which supported the encouragement of the movement of the Palestine Arabs to the neighbouring countries to make room for Jews'.[38] Yet Morris insinuates that Ben-Gurion was anything but sincere and that in his heart of hearts he still subscribed to the transfer idea as late as the beginning of the 1947–49 War (in Israeli parlance, the War of Independence). Donning the mind-reader's mantle Morris writes:

> However, there was perhaps a hint of the idea in Ben-Gurion's speech to Mapai's supporters four days after the UN Partition resolution, just as Arab–Jewish hostilities were getting under way. Ben-Gurion starkly outlined the emergent Jewish State's main problem – its prospective population of 520,000 Jews and 350,000 Arabs. Including Jerusalem, the state would

37   Ibid., pp. 4–5.
38   Morris, *The Birth*, p. 28.

have a population of about one million, 40% of which would be non-Jews. 'This fact must be viewed in all its clarity and sharpness. With such a [population] composition, there cannot even be complete certainty that the government will be held by a Jewish majority ... There can be no stable and strong Jewish State so long as it has a Jewish majority of only 60%.' The Yishuv's situation and fate, he went on, compelled the adoption of 'a new approach ... [new] habits of mind' to 'suit our new future. We must think like a state.'[39]

On this note Morris chose to end the chapter, leaving his readers with the clear impression that Ben-Gurion believed that transfer alone would resolve the problem of a substantial Arab minority in the Jewish State.

Incidentally, the insinuation that this prospective ratio between Arabs and Jews in the Jewish State-to-be could have pushed the Zionist leadership towards the 'transfer solution' has become an integral part of the 'new historiography'. In the words of Ilan Pappé:

> Moreover, one is tempted to point to the possibility of a certain link between the Jewish expulsion activities against the Palestinians, and the demographic situation in the Jewish State as delineated by UNSCOP. The UN suggested a binational state of 1.1 million citizens of whom 45 per cent would be Arabs: only the a-Zionist Jews in Palestine were reconciled to binationalism, all other political groups regarded such a state as the shattering of the Zionist dream. However, the evidence that the demographic situation

---

39   Ibid. Morris traces the speech to 3 December 1947, as is done in the secondary source from which he borrowed it. In the original source, however, the date given is 13 December 1947.

engendered the decision to expel the Arabs of Palestine is merely circumstantial.[40]

As is well known, both the majority proposal of UNSCOP and the subsequent UN Partition Resolution of 29 November 1947 called for the establishment of two states in the territory of Mandatory Palestine – one Jewish and one Arab: not a bi-national state. But even if one were to accept Pappé's bizarre assertion, then the Zionist movement, given its jubilant response to the UNSCOP proposal, must have been unknowingly a-Zionist. So must have been the hundreds of thousands of Jews dancing in the streets after the UN vote on partition, apparently unperturbed by the 'shattering of the Zionist dream'. If one pressed Pappé's (mis)claim to its logical conclusion, there would have been no need whatsoever to expel the Palestinian Arabs since the Jewish community in Mandatory Palestine was unwittingly a-Zionist.

But going back to Morris's earlier citation, is his mind-reading of Ben-Gurion correct? Was there really a hint of the transfer idea in the speech? A quick glance at the text from which Morris took his citation will start disentangling the riddle:

> In the territory allotted to the Jewish State there are now above 520,000 Jews (apart from the Jerusalem Jews who will also be citizens of the state) and about 350,000 non-Jews, almost all of whom are Arabs. Including the Jerusalem Jews, the state would have at birth a population of about one million, nearly 40

40 Ilan Pappé, *The Making of the Arab–Israeli Conflict*, p. 98. See also Shlaim, *Collusion*, pp. 117–19: 'No less anomalous and scarcely more viable was the demographic structure of the proposed Jewish State ... the proposed Jewish State would have had a total population of 1,008,800, consisting of 509,780 Arabs and 499,020 Jews. In other words, from the very beginning the proposed Jewish State would have had an Arab majority'. Not only does Shlaim uncritically take both this argument and these figures from the partisan Walid Khalidi, but he also 'forgets' to include in his figures the 100,000-strong Jewish community of Jerusalem which, despite the city's exclusion from the Jewish State due to its internationalization, would have been citizens of that State as noted by Ben-Gurion (whereas the Jerusalem Arabs would have probably been citizens of the Arab State).

per cent of which would be non-Jews. This [population] composition does not constitute a solid basis for a Jewish State; and this fact must be viewed in all its clarity and sharpness. In such composition there cannot even be complete certainty that the government will be held by a Jewish majority ... There can be no stable and strong Jewish State so long as it has a Jewish majority of only 60 per cent, *and so long as this majority consists of only 600,000 Jews* ...

We have been confronted with a new destiny – we are about to become masters of our own fate. This requires a new approach to all our questions of life. We must reexamine all our habits of mind, all our systems of operation to see to what extent they suit our new future. *We must think in terms of a state, in terms of independence, in terms of full responsibility for ourselves – and for others* ...[41]

In what seems to have become second nature, Morris has twisted his evidence. Leaving aside the small distortions created by his tendentious reconstruction of Ben-Gurion's speech, three points are of critical importance. First, Morris creates the false impression that Ben-Gurion's call for a 'new approach ... [new] habits of mind' applied to the Arab minority problem, with the implicit aim of transfer, at a time when it actually applied to the formidable challenges attending the transition from a community under colonial domination to national self-determination and the consequent need for reorganization of Zionist institutions. Second, Morris omits Ben-Gurion's emphasis on the need to take 'full responsibility for ourselves – and for others ...'. Who are these others but the non-Jewish minority of the Jewish State? Finally, and most importantly, Morris omits Ben-Gurion's statement that there can be no stable and strong Jewish State so long as its Jewish

41   Ben-Gurion, *Yoman Ha-milhama*, vol. I, p. 22 (emphasis added).

majority 'consists of only 600,000 Jews'. Morris distorts Ben-Gurion's intention by narrowing the picture to a preoccupation with the 60–40 per cent ratio, when its real scope was a concern for the absolute size of the Jewish population. The original text makes clear the alternative solution to this problem: *aliya* (or Jewish immigration).

These acts of omission and commission are serious enough as they are, but the story does not end here. As in the case of Shabtai Teveth, Morris chose to rely on a secondary source (again, in a twisted form) rather than to consult the primary document; and yet again this secondary source comes from among the ranks of the much-maligned 'old historians'. Elhannan Orren, one of the two editors of Ben-Gurion's war diary, from where the above citation is borrowed, has been personally castigated by Morris as one of the most prominent 'falsifiers' of the history of Israel's War of Independence.[42] Yet surprisingly enough, Morris repeatedly turns to such 'unreliable witnesses' as Orren and Teveth to further his (mis)claim. Had this happened only once, it could have been excused by a more lenient observer as sloppiness; as things are, the recurrence of this phenomenon points to a clear pattern in which Morris, who takes such great pride in his documentary 'discoveries', seems to avoid the archives like a plague whenever the use of the original document can put his fictitious historical edifice at peril. To prove this contention and dispel once and for all the cloud of innuendo with which Morris surrounds Ben-Gurion's speech of 13 December 1947, let me cite the speech from the *primary* source:

> In the territory allotted to the Jewish State there are now above 520,000 Jews (apart from the Jerusalem Jews who will also be citizens of the state) and about 350,000 non-Jews, almost all of whom are Arabs. Including the Jerusalem Jews, the state would have

42   See, for example, Morris, *1948 and After*, p. 3.

at birth a population of about one million, nearly 40 per cent of which would be non-Jews. This [population] composition does not constitute a solid basis for a Jewish State; and this fact must be viewed in all its clarity and sharpness. In such composition there cannot even be complete certainty that the government will be held by a Jewish majority ... There can be no stable and strong Jewish State so long as it has a Jewish majority of only 60 percent, and so long as this majority consists of only 600,000 Jews.

From here stems the first and principal conclusion. The creation of the state is not the formal imple-mentation process discussed by the UN General Assembly ... *In order to ensure not only the establishment of the Jewish State but its existence and destiny as well – we must bring a million-and-a-half Jews to the country and root them there. It is only when there will be at least two million Jews in the country – that the state will be truly established.* This aliya and settlement enterprise may require as many as ten years – and these ten years should be viewed as the implementation and the actual creation of the state. A Jewish government whose concerns and actions will not be predominantly geared to the enterprise of aliya and settlement that will increase our number in the Land of Israel to two million in the shortest period of time – will betray its foremost responsibility and will endanger the great historical achievement gained by our generation.[43]

Thus, there is not a shred of a hint in Ben-Gurion's speech of the transfer idea. His long-term solution to the 60–40 per cent ratio between the Jewish majority and non-Jewish minority is clear and unequivocal: mass Jewish immigration. As for the

---

43   Ben-Gurion, *Ba-ma'araha*, vol. IV, 2, pp. 258–9 (emphasis added).

position of the Arabs in the Jewish State, Ben-Gurion could not be clearer:

> We must think in terms of a state, in terms of independence, in terms of full responsibility for ourselves – and for others. In our state there will be non-Jews as well – and all of them will be equal citizens; equal in everything without any exception; that is: *the state will be their state as well.* ... The attitude of the Jewish State to its Arab citizens will be an important factor – though not the only one – in building good neighbourly relations with the Arab States. If the Arab citizen will feel at home in our state, and if his status will not be in the least different from that of the Jew, and perhaps better than the status of the Arab in an Arab state, and if the state will help him in a truthful and dedicated way to reach the economic, social, and cultural level of the Jewish community, then Arab distrust will accordingly subside and a bridge to a Semitic, Jewish–Arab alliance, will be built ... The striving for a Jewish–Arab alliance necessitates us to fulfil several obligations, which we are obliged to do in any event: full and real equality, de jure and de facto, of all the state's citizens; graduated equalization of the economic, social, and cultural standard of living of the Arab community with that of the Jewish community; recognition of the Arabic language as the language of the Arab citizens in the administration, courts of justice, and above all – schools; municipal autonomy in villages and cities etc.[44]

This is how Ben-Gurion envisaged Jewish–Arab relations in the prospective Jewish State and in the wider Middle East. Not 'transfer' of the Arab population from the Jewish State

44 Ibid., pp. 260, 265, 266 (emphasis added).

but a true partnership among equal citizens; not 'fortress Israel', a besieged European island in an ocean of Arab hostility but a Jewish–Arab semitic alliance. One can easily see where Shimon Peres, Ben-Gurion's foremost self-professed disciple, has drawn his ideas of a 'New Middle East'. Why Benny Morris has chosen to truncate, twist and distort Ben-Gurion's real vision of Jewish–Arab relations, or for that matter the Zionist position on the question of transfer, is for him to say. After all, as Morris himself said, the historian 'must remain honour-bound to gather and present his facts accurately'.

3 The Collusion that Never Was

> The facts of history do not exist for any historian
> till he creates them.
>
> CARL BECKER

One of the central myths propagated by the 'new historiography' is that 'in 1947 an explicit agreement was reached between the Hashemites and the Zionists on the carving up of Palestine following the termination of the British mandate, and that this agreement laid the foundation for mutual restraint during 1948 and for continuing collaboration in the aftermath of war'.[1] According to this myth, the alleged agreement was reached in a secret meeting on 17 November 1947 between the Acting Head of the Jewish Agency's Political Department, Golda Meir, and King Abdullah of Transjordan, and was 'consciously and deliberately intended to frustrate the will of the international community, as expressed through the United Nations General Assembly, in favour of creating an independent Arab States in part of Palestine'.[2] 'The common ground for the agreement was a mutual objection to the creation of a Palestinian state', runs the myth. 'The Jewish Agency in particular abhorred such a possibility, asserting that the creation of a Palestinian state would perpetuate the ideological conflict in Palestine'.[3]

Most forcefully articulated by Avi Shlaim's *Collusion Across*

---

1 Shlaim, *Collusion*, p. 1.
2 Shlaim, *The Politics of Partition*, p. viii.
3 Pappé, *The Making of the Arab–Israeli Conflict*, p. 118.

the Jordan, this myth is predicated on the single episode approach, namely, the identification of an allegedly critical event which has supposedly affected the course of history in a profound way – in this particular case the course of the Israeli–Palestinian conflict, if not of the Arab–Israeli conflict. While ostensibly dealing with the 30-year-long record of intermittent covert contacts between Transjordan's King Abdullah and the Zionist movement, Shlaim's book effectively focuses on the short period between the run-up to the 1947–49 War and its immediate aftermath. More specifically he traces the clinching of the alleged 'collusion' to the Meir–Abdullah conversation.

In an abridged paperback edition published two years later, Shlaim watered down the nature of the alleged Zionist–Hashemite understanding to 'a clear and explicit if not necessarily binding agreement ... on bypassing the Palestinians and peacefully dividing the territory of the British mandate between themselves'. He also removed the pejorative 'collusion' from the book's title, though insisting that the alleged agreement 'did involve at least some of the elements associated with collusion'.[4] In an article published in 1995, Shlaim watered down the nature of the alleged deal still further to an 'unwritten agreement', while praising it as 'a reasonable and realistic strategy for both sides'. Yet he expressed regret for changing the title of the paperback edition. 'Collusion is as good a word as any to describe the traffic between the Hashemite king and the Zionist movement during the period 1921–51', he stated, 'forgetting' that his thesis unequivocally traced the alleged collusion to the Abdullah–Meir meeting, and not to the intermittent Hashemite–Zionist contacts as a whole.[5]

Needless to say, the notion of an agreement that is 'not necessarily binding' constitutes a contradiction in terms

---

4   Shlaim, *The Politics of Partition*, pp. viii, 99.
5   Shlaim, 'The Debate', pp. 296, 298–9.

which renders Shlaim's collusion thesis hollow. There cannot be half an agreement. Either there is one or there is none. The essence of an agreement, both at the personal and at the collective levels, is an understanding that binds all involved parties in one form or another and is considered by them as such, even if the agreement has not yet received full legal formalization. Whether formal or informal, explicit or tacit, written or unwritten, an agreement is always binding in the minds of its makers; otherwise it would not have been reached in the first place.

But leaving aside this contradiction, a careful examination of the very two documents used by Shlaim to substantiate the claim of 'collusion' – reports by Ezra Danin and Eliyahu Sasson, two Zionist officials who attended the meeting – will easily reveal that Meir's response to Abdullah's territorial ambitions was far less committal than Shlaim lets us believe. Moreover Meir's own verbal report on the conversation, which Shlaim fails to bring in his book despite his keen awareness of its existence (he cites the part of this report which does not address the November 1947 meeting), proves beyond a shadow of doubt that Palestine was *not* divided on 17 November 1947.

Last but not least, the Jewish Agency with which Abdullah allegedly struck the deal on the 'division of Palestine' was totally unaware of the existence of any such deal for months after its alleged conclusion: it did not authorize Meir to 'divide Palestine' with the Hashemite King, and it did not approve any such action *post factum*. In fact, Meir's conversation with Abdullah was never discussed by the Jewish Agency Executive. If Meir reached 'a clear and explicit if not necessarily binding agreement with King Abdullah on bypassing the Palestinians and peacefully dividing the territory of the British mandate between themselves'[6] – which she did not – she also bypassed her own movement.

6 Shlaim, *The Politics of Partition*, p. 99.

Before examining whether Shlaim's own evidence sub-
stantiates the existence of his alleged 'collusion', let alone in
the way he portrays it, two methodological observations are
in order.

LOOKING IN THE WRONG DIRECTION

To paint the Hashemite–Zionist 'collusion' (even in its positive
depiction as 'a reasonable and realistic strategy') as the main
culprit for the abortion of the UN Partition Resolution of 29
November 1947 is to look for the keys under the street-light
rather than where they were actually lost. If anything it
was the categorical rejection of partition by the fragmented
Palestinian leadership and the Arab States (with the qualified
exception of King Abdullah of Transjordan), and their resort
to armed force to prevent its materialization, which, together
with the cold shoulder given to the idea by Britain and its
adamant refusal to help its implementation, which made the
Partition Resolution stillborn. As Foreign Secretary Bevin
assessed, upon advising the British Cabinet to disengage from
Palestine rather than help enforce the majority proposal of
the UN Special Commission on Palestine (UNSCOP) to partition the land, such disengagement might well be 'effected at
the cost of a period of bloodshed and chaos in the country' in
which 'some or all of the Arab States would probably become
involved in the resulting disorder; they might even quarrel
among themselves over the country's future'.[7] That this self-
fulfilling prophecy was vindicated well beyond Bevin's wildest
dreams is evidenced by the fact that it was not until four decades later, in 1988, that the Palestinian mainstream body politic
reconciled itself to the idea of partition, and not insignificant
parts of the 'Arab masses' remain opposed to the idea to date.
Unfortunate as this rejectionism has been for both Arabs

7 'Palestine – Memorandum by the Secretary of the State for Foreign Affairs', 18 September
1947, CAB 129/21, C.P. (47) 259.

and Jews, it is not difficult to comprehend. Viewing Palestine as Arab patrimony, 'the very idea of partition was abhorrent to the Arabs of Palestine' and UNSCOP's partition plan was seen as 'Zionist in inspiration, Zionist in principle, Zionist in substance, and Zionist in most details', to use Walid Khalidi's words.[8] This prognosis is not that misconceived. Since the late 1930s the Zionist movement had been gradually reconciling itself to the impossibility of materializing the Zionist dream in its full scope and the consequent inevitability of dividing the Land of Israel between Arabs and Jews. This awareness gained considerable momentum in the wake of the Second World War and was reflected not only in tireless Zionist attempts to convince the international community of the merits of partition but also in their exertions towards the Arab States in this respect. Since all Zionist efforts during the 1930s to reach an understanding with the Palestinian leadership came to nought,[9] and since there was no 'Palestinian option' in the late 1940s – as Shlaim aptly notes[10] – due to the extreme fragmentation of Palestinian society and the intransigence of its leadership, the Zionists sought to win over whatever Arab partners they could find to the cause of partition. King Abdullah figured prominently in these efforts given his informal contacts with the Zionist movement since the early 1930s, but he was by no means the only one.

As Shlaim records in his book, in 1946 the Zionists managed to convince the Egyptian Prime Minister, Ismail Sidqi, to persuade the Arab world in the desirability of partition, though this success was aborted by Sidqi's fall from power in the autumn of 1946.[11] Shlaim also mentions a last-minute desperate attempt to convince the Arab world of the desirability of partition, made in a secret meeting in London on 15 September

8 Cited in Shlaim, *Collusion*, p. 120.
9 The most comprehensive account of these contacts is Neil Caplan's *Futile Diplomacy* (London: Frank Cass). See also Avraham Sela, 'Talks and Contacts between Zionist Leaders and Palestinian–Arab Leaders, 1933–1939', *Ha-mizrah Ha-hadash*, 22, 4 (1972), pp. 401–23 (I); 23, 1 (1973), pp. 1–21 (II).
10 Shlaim, 'The Debate', p. 298.
11 Shlaim, *Collusion*, pp. 76, 80–81.

1947 between Aubrey (Abba) Eban and David Horowitz, the
Jewish Agency's liaison officers with UNSCOP, and Abd al-
Rahman Azzam, Secretary-General of the Arab League. The
two tried to convince Azzam that 'once agreement had been
reached on a practical compromise such as that suggested by
UNSCOP, it should not be difficult to convince the Arab world
that it had nothing to fear from Jewish development, and that
no threat of Jewish expansion would exist'; and by way of
allaying Arab fears of Jewish expansionism they expressed
readiness 'to offer a Jewish guarantee, and to accept the
guarantees of the Arab League and the United Nations,
against any encroachments by the Jews upon the boundaries
of other states'. They also tried to convince Azzam that 'the
Palestine conflict was uselessly absorbing the best energies of
the Arab League, diverting it from the constructive purposes
to which it might otherwise address itself'; that both Arabs
and Jews would greatly benefit 'from active policies of
cooperation and development'; and that the Jewish State-to-
be was keenly interested in being integrated into processes of
regional development, and in certain conditions would not
even be averse 'to joining with the Arab States in a single
League'.

Their arguments were to no avail. Azzam remained
unmoved. 'No Middle Eastern League based on diversity
could in any way be considered', he said. 'The Arabs were not
afraid of [Jewish] expansion. They resented [Zionism's] very
presence as an alien organism, which had come without their
consent, and which refused to be assimilated to their way of
life.' Astonished by his interlocutors' attribution of realism to
the Arab peoples which, like all other peoples, were animated
by strong historic emotions, Azzam said:

> For me you may be a fact, but for them you are not a
> fact at all – you are a temporary phenomenon. Cen-
> turies ago the Crusaders established themselves in
> our midst against our will, and in 200 years we ejected

them. This was because we never made the mistake
of accepting them as a fact.

'The Arab world is not at all in a compromising mood', he
continued:

> You will achieve nothing with talk of compromise or
> peace. You may perhaps achieve something by force
> of your arms. We will try to rout you. I am not sure
> we will succeed, but we will try. We succeeded in
> expelling the Crusaders, but lost Spain and Persia,
> and may lose Palestine. But it is too late for a
> peaceable solution … You speak of the Middle East.
> For us there is no such concept; for us there is only
> the concept of the Arab world. Nationalism is the
> great force that moves us. We do not need economic
> development. For us there is only one test, the test of
> strength. If I were a Zionist leader, perhaps I would
> behave as you do. You have no choice. In any case,
> the problem is likely to be solved only by force of
> arms.[12]

Yet another emotional plea to Azzam to accept the idea of
partition and to forego the recourse to violence was made on
5 December 1947 in a personal letter from Eliyahu (Elias)
Sasson, the Damascus-born Director of the Arab Section of
the Jewish Agency's Political Department. The General
Assembly's Partition Resolution of the previous week had
triggered a wave of Arab violence (Azzam himself promised
an Arab invasion of Palestine following the British departure),
which the Zionists were anxious to contain before things got
out of hand. 'You and us stand today at the crossroads of
history', Sasson wrote,

12 Caplan, *Futile Diplomacy*, pp. 274–6, citing Eban's account; Cohen, *Israel and the Arab
World*, p. 381, citing Horowitz's account.

It depends on you whether you are going to hamper our path or to accept us as we ask to be accepted, as sons of the East returning after centuries of an enforced exile to the Land of our Fathers. I am not going to indulge in prophecies, but I should like to say to you who, I believe, has an eye for historic perspectives, that these returning sons of Israel may become a source of great blessing to the Middle East as a whole. They were driven out against their will and they have given a great deal to the lands of their adoption. They are now returning laden with the treasures of that unique experience of an Eastern people in Western lands, to find here what no other land can give them – roots in the soil, peace, security, a home. Their efforts will be concentrated on that task alone and on this land alone, but it is inevitable that what they achieve here will beneficially affect also their neighbours and will help in that general revival of the Middle East on which the peace, the security and the prosperity of all that dwell therein essentially depend. Such, indeed, is our hope which we maintain in spite of what is being inflicted on us in these days. During the past week, while a deliberate effort was made to embroil us in trouble and goad us into reprisals, our people maintained self-restraint and our leaders continued to hold out the hand of peace and cooperation to our Arab neighbours. Our work of reconstruction will proceed whether our neighbours wish it or not, but it depends on them what part our new Commonwealth will take in the revival of the Middle East. The choice is theirs. Let me end by quoting a passage from our Holy Bible: 'I have set before thee life and death, blessing and cursing: therefore choose life, that both thou and thy seed may live'.[13]

13 Gedalia Yogev et al., eds, *Teudot Mediniot Ve-diplomatiot, December 1947 – May 1948* (Political and Diplomatic Documents, December 1947 – May 1948) (Jerusalem: Israel State Archives & Central Zionist Archives, 1979) p. 30 (hereafter – *Teudot*).

No response ever came from Azzam.

Against this backdrop of assiduous Zionist attempts to bring about international acceptance of partition and relentless Arab rejection of the idea, Shlaim's collusion theory is totally flawed. The Hashemite–Zionist 'connection' may well be 'one of the most fascinating and vital strands in the generally tragic encounter between Arab and Jewish nationalism', as he claims,[14] but the key to the failure of partition in 1947–49 lies elsewhere, namely, in the 'uncompromising mood' of the Arab world, to use Azzam's handy quip. In this respect, Shlaim's book looks completely in the wrong direction.

MISCOMPREHENSION OF THE DECISION-MAKING PROCESS

If anything Shlaim's single episode approach reflects a fundamental lack of understanding of the nature of foreign policy-making in general and of the Zionist decision-making process in particular. Whether regular or irregular, direct or indirect, overt or covert, political relations among nations are routinely maintained through foreign policy establishments – diplomats, officials, and politicians – without necessarily informing the State's ruling institutions (be it a Cabinet or a 'Revolutionary Command Council' of sorts) on every single twist and turn; yet, on the whole, they operate within the broad lines set by the State leadership. Resourceful bureaucrats, can of course, find ways and means to influence their ministers, just as powerful foreign secretaries can sidestep their own officialdom and manipulate, even deceive the Cabinet; conversely, heads of State can, and at times do, circumvent their foreign policy establishments. Yet in democratic societies there are clear limits to what the most powerful foreign secretaries or even heads of state can do without Cabinet, or at times parliamentary

14   Shlaim, *Collusion*, p. 2.

approval: they cannot commit their countries to binding agreements in the course of a single conversation, let alone to such far-reaching undertakings as the making of war and peace, or the division of foreign lands.

This state of affairs was fully applicable to the Zionist movement. The lion's share of its covert contacts with King Abdullah, among other Arab leaders, was maintained by the Jewish Agency's Political Department, headed since 1933 by Moshe Sharett, and more concretely by the department's Arab Section, headed since the 1930s by Eliyahu Sasson. In this way the Political Department enjoyed a wide latitude, but it nevertheless remained bound by the policy guidelines set by the Zionist movement's governing bodies and institutions.

Indeed the main source of strength of the Jewish national movement had been its ability to organize itself from an early stage as a 'State in the making' based on democratic-parliamentary principles: 'It was all there, set up and running, within a year or two of the calling of the first Congress of Zionists in 1897: free elections on a constituency basis; universal suffrage (i.e. men and women voting and members of the Congress itself); a fully representative assembly; a political leadership responsible to that assembly; open debate on all major issues; and, before long, what might usefully be called a loyal opposition too'.[15] As Jewish presence in Mandatory Palestine grew rapidly during the 1930s and the centre of gravity of Zionist activities shifted from Europe to Mandatory Palestine, the Jewish Agency Executive (JAE) evolved into the foremost decision-making body of the Zionist movement and the *de facto* 'government' of the Yishuv, managing its affairs, from the more mundane aspects of daily life to the critical political issues of the day, such as the various British proposals on the future of Palestine, Jewish–Arab relations in the prospective Jewish State, etc.

---

15   David Vital, 'Some of the Forks in the Road', in Efraim Karsh and Gregory Mahler, eds, *Israel at the Crossroads* (London: British Academic Press, 1994), pp. 9–10.

It is inconceivable, therefore, for the Zionist movement to have reached any binding agreement with Abdullah, let alone such a far-reaching understanding on the division of Palestine and the incorporation of its Arab parts into Transjordan, without the matter being thoroughly discussed and approved by the JAE; this is all the more pertinent to this specific case since the alleged deal would have run counter to the Jewish Agency's own contemporary efforts to bring about a UN resolution on partition. That Meir's conversation with Abdullah was not discussed at any of the JAE's meetings – either prior to its occurrence or in its aftermath – indicates that it involved no binding agreement of the sort alleged by Shlaim. During the six fateful months between November 1947 and May 1948, when it was superseded by a 13-member Provisional State Council, the JAE discussed numerous critical issues pertaining to the Yishuv's ability to weather both the war unleashed by the Palestinians following the UN Partition Resolution, and the general Arab attack that was bound to come if a Jewish State were to be proclaimed upon the end of the Mandate. The alleged Meir–Abdullah agreement was not one of them. On the contrary, as we shall see shortly, the isolated references to Abdullah reflected deep uncertainty as to the king's future agenda.[16]

Meir did not report to her colleagues upon returning from the meeting, thus reflecting her conviction that there was nothing concrete to report about. One must conclude therefore that for all its significance, the meeting was both a part of the above-mentioned Zionist effort to weaken Arab opposition to partition and to prevent the outbreak of an Arab–Jewish war, as well as a link in the long chain of Jewish–Hashemite secret contacts aimed at forging the widest possible common denominator between the two parties. While it is reasonable to assume that Meir would not have

16 See, for example, protocols of the Zionist Agency Executive meetings of 2, 9, 16, 23, 30 November 1947, 7, 9 December 1947.

gone to see Abdullah without the approval of the JAE
Chairman, David Ben-Gurion, it is equally clear that he could
not, and would not have single-handedly committed the
Zionist movement to a definitive agreement on an issue of
such magnitude. Interestingly enough, Shlaim indirectly
contradicts his own conspiracy theory by accusing Ben-
Gurion of aborting the prospects of peace with the Arab
States, specifically Syria, in the wake of the 1947–49 War by
refusing to personally meet the Syrian ruler Husni Zaim
during the latter's brief spell in power (30 March–14 August
1949).[17] But the entire edifice of the 'Collusion Across the
Jordan' thesis is predicated on precisely the opposite assumption, namely, that lower-level officials could and did commit
the Zionist movement to far-reaching undertakings. Shlaim
therefore has to make up his mind: either critical foreign
policy decisions can be taken by other officials than heads of
State, which means that Ben-Gurion did not abort Husni
Zaim's flimsy peace feelers since he was fully prepared to send
senior Israeli officials to meet the Syrian leader[18] or they
cannot be taken by lower officials, which means that Golda
Meir could not have single-handedly committed the Zionist
movement to the 'division of Palestine' with Abdullah.

The truth of the matter of course is that both of Shlaim's
contentions are equally misconceived, not least because of his
above-mentioned lack of understanding of the foreign policy
process. International agreements, let alone those related to
peace and/or demarcation of international boundaries, are
not reached in a single conversation, not even between heads
of State. Rather, they are the culmination of a prolonged and
painstaking negotiation process by government officials, the
relevant ministers, and third-party mediators, among others.
Moreover, even summit meetings, not least between heads of

17   Avi Shlaim, 'Husni Zaim and the Plan to Resettle Palestinian Refugees in Syria', *Journal
of Palestine Studies*, 20, 1 (Summer 1986), pp. 68–80.
18   See, for example, Ben-Gurion, *Yoman Ha-milhama*, 9 July 1949, vol. III, pp. 993–4; 'Ben-
Gurion's Diary' (Ben-Gurion's Archive, Sede-Boker), 30 April 1949 (hereafter BGA).

enemy States, are a delicate matter that needs thorough and extended preparation. It required a string of Israeli secret overtures through King Hasan of Morocco and Romanian President Nikolai Ceausescu to arrange a secret meeting between Israeli Foreign Minister Moshe Dayan and Egyptian Deputy Premier Hasan al-Tuhami in Morocco, which in turn led to Anwar Sadat's historic visit to Jerusalem in November 1977; and it required an additional year-and-a-half of tough negotiations to reach contractual peace between Israel and Egypt; even then the two parties remained locked for years in a legal fight over the tiny piece of land in Taba. Similarly, it took years of open talks in Washington and months of secret negotiations in the Norwegian capital of Oslo before Israeli Premier Yitzhak Rabin and PLO Chairman Yasser Arafat could shake hands on the White House lawn on 13 September 1993 and sign the Declaration of Principles on Palestinian Interim Self-Government Arrangements (DOP); and at least five more years will have passed before the conclusion of final peace agreements between Israel and the Palestinians.

Incidentally, since the convocation of the Madrid Peace Conference some five years ago, Syria and Israel have been engaged in peace negotiations under American auspices. During this prolonged period, the Syrians have adamantly refused to move to direct talks without American mediation, or to upgrade the level of the negotiators, not to mention a summit meeting between President Asad and his Israeli counterparts. Why have the 'new historians' and their ilk not questioned the sincerity of Syria's professed interest in peace? Perhaps they reckon that as far as Damascus is concerned, foreign policy decision-making can be a protracted and tortuous process.

In a recent book on the history of Syrian–Israeli relations, Moshe Ma'oz, though not a recognized member of the 'new historiographical' club, unquestioningly accepts Shlaim's misinterpretation of the Zaim episode, while failing to press this acceptance to its logical conclusion and claim that Asad may not be that interested in peace. Quite the reverse in fact; to Ma'oz, Asad is the paragon of virtue whose peaceful intentions should be accepted at face value. Surely Ben-Gurion's willingness to send his foremost advisers to meet Zaim face to face indicates that he was no less interested in peace than Asad who has not even been willing to authorize direct negotiations with Israel after so many years of American-mediated talks.[19]

The intermittent contacts between the Jewish Agency and Abdullah prior to the 1947–49 War could scarcely qualify as a negotiation process. There was a meeting between Abdullah and Sasson on 12 August 1946, defined by Shlaim as 'a preliminary reconnaissance mission to appraise the king's thinking and dispositions';[20] this was followed a week later by yet another meeting between the two. In Shlaim's view, 'the two meetings in Shuneh were useful in identifying at least some common ground between Abdullah and the Zionists and in providing a basis for future cooperation between them'.[21] A year later, on 21 August 1947, Danin met the king for yet another conversation, to be followed by the 17 November 1947 Abdullah–Meir meeting. To claim that one of these conversations, or even all of them as a whole, contained a bilateral agreement between the Jewish Agency and Abdullah is the same as to suggest that the chief Israeli negotiator in Oslo, Uri Savir, committed his government to a binding agreement in one of his many talks with his Palestinian interlocutors – and at least Savir was engaged in an official process of negotiations, something that applied to neither Danin, nor Sasson, nor Meir. All that they were doing, to use Shlaim's words, was to attempt to identify some common ground between Abdullah and the Zionist movement so as to provide a basis for future co-operation between them. Nothing more, nothing less.

19   Moshe Ma'oz, *Syria and Israel: From War to Peace-Making* (Oxford: Clarendon Press, 1995), especially Chapter 2.
20   Shlaim, *Collusion*, pp. 78–9.
21   Ibid., p. 83.

The same applied to Ben-Gurion's response to Zaim's dubious overture. At the time he learned about Zaim's alleged interest in peace with Israel, the two countries were engaged in negotiations on an armistice agreement. Though suspecting a ploy by Zaim to gain a better deal in the ongoing talks, Ben-Gurion was prepared to send his most seasoned personal emissaries to Damascus including Eliyahu Sasson and Reuben Shiloah (Zaslani) and even Foreign Minister Moshe Sharett to gauge the seriousness of Zaim's ideas, while on the other hand insisting that Syria continue its armistice negotiations in good faith. Shlaim claims that 'Ben-Gurion, as his diary reveals, considered that the armistice agreements with the neighbouring Arab States met Israel's essential needs for recognition, security and stability. He knew that for formal peace agreements Israel would have to pay by yielding substantial tracts of territory and by permitting the return of a substantial number of Palestinian refugees, and he did not consider this a price worth paying'.[22] Yet the entries in Ben-Gurion's diary mentioned by Shlaim prove the precise opposite of his ill-conceived claim:

> 16 June 1949: [Mordechai] Maklef and [Joshua] Palmon spoke to Zaim's representatives without the participation of the UN. The Syrians offered separate peace with Israel, cooperation and joint army ... but they want a border rectification – half of the Sea of Galilee ... I told them to inform the Syrians in clear terms that first of all – an armistice agreement on the basis of the previous international line. And then – discussion of peace and alliance. We will be prepared for maximum cooperation.

> 9 July 1949: ... The representatives of the refugees pressure the Arabs to make peace and thus resolve their problem. But no state would like to be the first

22 Shlaim, 'The Debate', p. 301.

one [to do so], and there is no recognition [of Israel] either. Only Zaim stated in a conversation with a Swiss writer that he wanted peace with Israel.

In my opinion [i.e., Ben-Gurion's] we should cling to this statement. The fact that Zaim is prepared for an armistice that involves complete withdrawal to the international border proves that for one reason or another he wants good relations with us. Is it because of the conflict with Iraq? Also, the interest of France – Zaim's friend – requires peace between Syria and Israel. If the armistice agreement between ourselves and Syria will be signed this week, as Maklef believes, it is desirable that Sasson will go to Damascus to check the ground.[23]

In other words, contrary to Shlaim's contention, Ben-Gurion did not dismiss Zaim's feelers out of hand but was rather keen to 'cling' to them despite some sceptical assessments of Zaim's character and motivations. On July 18, for example, American journalist Kenneth Bilby briefed Ben-Gurion on a tour he had just completed in Transjordan, Syria, and Lebanon. Bilby's impression from his conversations with Arabs was that they would not accept Israel: 'The humiliation over their defeat is deep – and they will wait until they can exact their revenge.'

'Why then did Zaim declare his interest in peace?' Ben-Gurion queried.

'Because he needs time and wants to make a good impression in the world, and feels strong enough to say whatever he wants.'[24]

23 Ben-Gurion, *Yoman Ha-milhama*, vol. III, p. 993.
24 BGA, 18 July 1949, p. 2791 059. Taking the last sentence of Ben-Gurion's conversation with Bilby out of context, Shlaim brings it as 'proof' of Ben-Gurion's lack of interest in reaching peace in the immediate future. As he cites Ben-Gurion: 'I am prepared to get up in the middle of the night in order to sign a peace agreement – but I am not in a hurry and I can wait ten years'. Shlaim, *Collusion*, p. 465. Morris, not surprisingly, takes his cue from Shlaim (*1948 and After*, p. 22).
      As we have just seen, both Shlaim and Morris 'forget' to mention that this sentence

In the circumstances, Ben-Gurion handled Zaim's overtures as any responsible leader in his position would have
done. He was not willing to accept Zaim's opening proposal,
as noted from his diary entry of 16 June; but then negotiations
by their very definition are a give-and-take relationship and
Ben-Gurion, who was certainly interested in exploring the
seriousness of Zaim's intentions, made it eminently clear that
Israel would be prepared for 'maximum co-operation'. More
importantly, it is clear from Ben-Gurion's diary entry of 9 July
that his declining of Zaim's opening proposal did not dam-
pen the latter's interest in peace, as he accepted the Israeli
terms for an armistice agreement and still sustained his
interest in taking the matter further.

That these peace feelers did not reach fruition, therefore, had
nothing to do with Israeli (or for that matter Syrian) intransigence but rather resulted from the simple fact that Zaim was
overthrown on 14 August 1949, after a mere four months in
power. In fact, as the next page in Ben-Gurion's diary reveals,
Zaim began retracting already before his downfall:

> Reuben [Shiloah] came to say goodbye before leaving
> for Lausanne and told me on behalf of [General
> William] Riley [Head of the UN observers] that he had
> the clear impression that Zaim wanted peace, but he
> would like the matter to be postponed for several
> weeks; he did not wish to breach the wall of Arab
> unity. It is only if it transpires during the next several
> weeks that the Lausanne talks do not lead to peace
> that he will be prepared for direct peace negotiations
> with us, hence we should not prod him now.[25]

was said in response to Bilby's stark prognosis that the Arabs would not be prepared
to accept Israel but would rather prefer to bide their time in anticipation of 'a second
round'. Put in its real context, therefore, Ben-Gurion's comment gets the complete
opposite meaning of that attributed to it by Shlaim and Morris, namely, 'while I am
prepared to get up in the middle of the night to sign a peace agreement – if the Arabs
are in no hurry to accept our existence, neither is the State of Israel – it can wait ten
years'.

25 Ben-Gurion, *Yoman Ha-milhama*, 26 July 1949, vol. III, p. 994.

Whether or not Zaim would have been able or willing to carry his professed interest in peace to its natural conclusion, had he remained in power, is a matter of historical speculation. What is clear, however, though not to Shlaim and his fellow 'new historians', is that peace is not achieved in a single conversation between state leaders, let alone lower-rank officials, and that summit meetings require thorough and extended preparation.

THE ABDULLAH–MEIR MEETING:
THE DANIN–SASSON REPORTS

Having established these two methodological flaws in Shlaim's thesis, let the two Zionist accounts of the meeting used by Shlaim – the reports of Ezra Danin and Eliyahu Sasson – speak for themselves. First Danin's report, as narrated by Shlaim:

> In the course of the ensuing conversation Abdullah invited his visitors *to join him in thinking aloud*: they had discussed partition in the past and he was interested to know what their current thinking was ... 'Over the past thirty years you have grown and strengthened yourselves and your achievements are many' [he said]. 'It is impossible to ignore you, and it is a duty to compromise with you. Between the Arabs and you there is no quarrel. The quarrel is between the Arabs and the British who brought you here; and between you and the British who have not kept their promises to you. Now, I am convinced that the British are leaving, and we will be left face to face. Any clash between us will be to our own disadvantage. In the past we talked about partition. *I agree to partition that will not shame me before the Arab world when I come out to defend it. My wish is to take this opportunity to suggest to you the idea, for future thought, of an independent Hebrew Republic in part of Palestine within a Transjordan*

state that would include both banks of the Jordan, with me at its head, and in which the economy, the army and the legislature will be joint'.

Noticing the unease evoked by this suggestion, Abdullah stressed that the Hebrew Republic would not be dominated by Transjordan but would simply be part of the Transjordanian monarchy. He did not press for an answer but simply explained that in the event of such a republic being formed, his kingdom could be expanded to embrace Greater Syria and even Saudi Arabia.

Mrs. Meir drew attention to the fact that the Palestine question was under consideration at the UN and that her side was hoping for a resolution that would establish two states, one Jewish and one Arab, and that they wished to speak to the king only about an agreement based on such a resolution. Abdullah said he understood and that it would be desirable to meet again immediately after the UN pronounced its decision in order to discuss how they might co-operate in the light of that decision. *At this point Abdullah asked how the Jews would regard an attempt by him to capture the Arab part of Palestine? Mrs. Meir replied that they would view such an attempt in a favourable light, especially if he did not interfere with the establishment of their state and avoided a clash between his forces and theirs and, secondly, if he could declare that his sole purpose was to maintain law and order until the UN could establish a government in that area. Now it was the king's turn to be startled and he answered sharply: 'But I want this area for myself, in order to annex it to my kingdom and do not want to create a new Arab State which would upset my plans and enable the Arabs to ride on me. I want to ride, not to be ridden!' He also brushed aside a suggestion that he might secure his objective by means of a referendum in which his influence would be decisive.*

... Asked if he [i.e., Abdullah] would be prepared to sign a written agreement in the event of a common denominator being identified in political, economic and defence matters he replied affirmatively and asked them [i.e., his Jewish interlocutors] to produce a draft. In bringing the meeting to an end he re-iterated that concrete discussions could only take place after the UN had made its decision and that they must meet again as soon as the decision was known.[26]

Sasson's report, as cited by Shlaim, reads as follows:

[Abdullah] will not allow his forces to collide with us nor co-operate with other forces against us. Belittled military power [of] Arab States. Believed would not dare break into Palestine. In case he will decide [to] invade Palestine will concentrate [on] Arab areas with a view to prevent bloodshed, keep law and order, forestall Mufti. Prepared [to] co-operate with us [in] this matter ... Believe position Mufti weakened. Not to be expected head of Arab provisional govern-ment with support [of] Arab world. Abdullah ready [to] sign written agreement with us provided we agree [to] assist attach Arab part to Transjordan. Replied we prepared [to] give every assistance within frame [of] UN Charter. Agreed meet after 25th of this month after UN decision.[27]

Between them the two reports prove the following points:

● As stated by Abdullah at the outset, the conversation was seen as a joint exercise in 'thinking aloud' about the general

26 Shlaim, *Collusion*, pp. 112–13, 115 (emphasis added).
27 Ibid., pp. 115–16.

principles of a possible Hashemite–Jewish understanding, not as one designed to reach a concrete agreement. Hence his avoiding of pressing for an answer to his preferred option; hence his concluding remarks that no concrete issues could be discussed until after the UN General Assembly had made its decision.

● In Abdullah's thinking, partition 'that will not shame me before the Arab world' meant 'an independent Hebrew Republic in part of Palestine within a Transjordan State that would include both banks of the Jordan with me at its head'. This was the basis of his acquiescence in the partition plan of the Peel Commission in 1937 and the thrust of his message to his Zionist interlocutors, both before and in the wake of the Second World War. And this was no idle talk; Abdullah truly believed that an autonomous Jewish province would greatly benefit his kingdom, mainly through the influx of Jewish funds and technological know-how. As his Prime Minister, Samir al-Rifai, told Brigadier I.N. Clayton of the British Middle East Office (BMEO) in Cairo on 11 December 1947: 'the enlarged Transjordan State with the support of Jewish economy would become the most influential State in the Arab Middle East'.[28]

It was only upon realizing that this solution was totally unacceptable to the Jews that Abdullah opted for the lesser choice of incorporating the Arab areas of Mandatory Palestine into his kingdom. But even then he did not view the borders set by the United Nations as final and never tired of trying to convince the Jews either to give him some of the territory awarded to them by the UN or even to forego the idea of an independent State, the last such attempt being made in his second meeting with Golda Meir on 11 May 1948, three days before the establishment

28 Clayton to Foreign Office, 12 December 1947, telegram 67, FO 371/62226/E11928.

of the State of Israel and its subsequent invasion by the
Arab States.

- Contrary to Shlaim's claim, Abdullah was not prepared to
'commit himself in writing' to the division of Mandatory
Palestine between himself and the Jews.[29] As shown by
Shlaim's own text above, Abdullah was *not* asked by his
Jewish interlocutors to sign an agreement on the division
of Palestine but rather an agreement in either of the
political, economic or defence spheres 'in the event of a
common denominator being identified' in any of these
matters. It would have been sheer madness, if not political
suicide for Abdullah to have committed himself in writing
to the division of Mandatory Palestine between himself
and the Jews.

- Most importantly, in no way, shape or form did Golda Meir
give Abdullah a 'green light' to annex the Arab part of
Mandatory Palestine to his kingdom. Quite the reverse in
fact. While quiescent in his possible capture – but by no
means annexation! – of this area, 'especially if he did not
interfere with the establishment of their state and avoided
a clash between his forces and theirs', she made it crystal
clear that a) she wished to speak only about an agreement
based on the imminent UN Partition Resolution; b) the
sole purpose of Transjordan's intervention in Palestine 'was
to maintain law and order until the UN could establish
a government in that area', namely, *a short-lived law-
enforcement operation aimed at facilitating the establishment of
a legitimate Palestinian government*. There is little doubt that
the Zionist movement preferred to see Abdullah at the head
of this government rather than the extremist Palestinian
leader, Hajj Amin al-Husseini, or the Mufti as he was commonly known; hence Meir's suggestion for a referendum

29   Shlaim, *Collusion*, p. 116.

that would establish Abdullah's supremacy in the Arab parts of Mandatory Palestine, both in the eyes of its Palestinian population and the world at large, and would legitimize his claim to rule this area. But the distance from this position to approval of Abdullah's annexation of this territory to his kingdom is very great indeed.

In other words it was the Jewish representative at the meeting who defended Palestinian political rights, by insisting on the ephemerality of the Transjordanian seizure of the Arab parts of Mandatory Palestine as a means to facilitate the establishment of a legitimate government there; and it was the Arab leader who insisted on annexing the area to his kingdom rather than 'create a new Arab State which would upset my plans and enable the Arabs to ride on me'.

Hence Shlaim's conclusion that 'in November 1947 the Jewish Agency succeeded in reaching a clear and explicit if not necessarily binding agreement with King Abdullah on bypassing the Palestinians and peacefully dividing the territory of the British mandate between themselves'[30] is both wrong and misleading:

- First, as shown by Shlaim's own account, it was Abdullah and not Meir who sought to bypass the Palestinians and seize their territory. The Jews, after all, were about to be granted their part of Mandatory Palestine by the United Nations within less than two weeks and had no need to receive this territory from a party who did not possess it in the first place. All they wanted was to avert an unnecessary war with this key neighbour and to coexist peacefully with whoever ruled that part of Mandatory Palestine.

30 Shlaim, *The Politics of Partition*, p. 99.

- Second, as noted above, Meir never gave her consent to the annexation of the Arab part to Transjordan but insisted on a solution concomitant with the UN Partition Resolution. In Danin's words: 'We explained that our matter was being discussed at the UN, that we hoped that it would be decided there to establish two states, one Jewish and one Arab, and that we wished to speak now about an agreement with him [i.e., Abdullah] based on these resolutions'.[31] In Sasson's words: 'Replied we prepared [to] give every assistance within [the] frame [of the] UN Charter'.[32]

- Third, the Jewish Agency could not succeed in reaching an agreement with Abdullah on the division of Palestine for the simple reason that it did not officially seek such an agreement and did not approve it. As noted earlier, Meir's meeting with Abdullah was never discussed by the JAE, and therefore she was not authorized to strike a concrete deal with Abdullah. She was not the Chairperson of the JAE but merely acting head of the Political Department, 'standing in for Moshe Sharett who was conducting the diplomatic struggle for partition at the UN's temporary headquarters in Lake Success'.[33] In this capacity she could do little more than try to convince Abdullah not to violently oppose the impending UN Partition Resolution and to acquaint him to the gist of Zionist thinking – which is precisely what she did.

- Finally, both Danin's and Sasson's reports state unequivocally that no concrete decisions were reached during the meeting. In the words of Danin: 'At the end he [Abdullah] reiterated that concrete matters could only be discussed

---

31   Ezra Danin, 'Siha Im Abdullah, 17.1.47' (Conversation with Abdullah), CZA, S25/4004.
32   Sasson to Shertok, 20 November 1947, CZA, S25/1699.
33   Shlaim, *Collusion*, p. 110.

after the UN had passed its resolution, and said that we must meet again immediately afterwards'.[34]

THE OVERLOOKED DOCUMENT:

MEIR'S VERBAL REPORT

But how did Meir herself interpret her understanding with Abdullah? She presented no official report on her conversation to the JAE at the time of the event, which indicates that she deemed that it contained no concrete agreement that needed to be discussed and approved by this highest decision-making institution of the Zionist movement. It was only six months later, on 12 May 1948, in a verbal report to the Provisional State Council on her second meeting with Abdullah (held on the previous day) in which she failed to convince him not to join the imminent Arab attack on the Jewish State, that Meir gave her own account of the November 1947 meeting:

> I do not know whether all present here are aware that several months ago, about ten days before the UN Resolution, a meeting with King Abdullah took place with the participation on our part of Sasson, Danin, and myself. The meeting was in Transjordan, though on Jewish territory, that is – he came from Amman to see us. The meeting was conducted on the basis that there was an arrangement and an understanding as to what both of us wanted and that our interests did not collide.
>
> For our part we told him then that we could not promise to help his incursion into the country [i.e., Mandatory Palestine], since we would be obliged to

34   Danin, 'Siha Im Abdullah'.

observe the UN Resolution which, as we already reckoned at the time, would provide for the establishment of two states in Palestine. We could not therefore – so we said – give active support to the violation of this resolution. If he was prepared and willing to confront the world and us with a *fait accompli* – the tradition of friendship between us would continue and we would certainly find a common language on settling those matters that were of interest to both parties.

He then promised us that his friendship towards us still existed and that there could be no confrontation between us. He spoke on his friends and on the other [Arab] states and especially on the Mufti; he dismissed the strength of the other neighbouring states and agreed with us that if we were attacked by Arabs it went without saying that we had to respond.

The meeting was conducted very amicably and without any arguments. During the conversation he said, as if by passing, two things that raised some suspicion, apprehension. But the meeting ended on the understanding that we would meet again after the UN Resolution. The two things that raised suspicion were:

a) He wanted to know what we thought about the possible inclusion of the Jewish State (the 'Jewish Republic' as he called it) within the Transjordanian Kingdom;

b) He hoped to have a partition that would not disgrace him [in front of the Arabs].

These two things raised, as already noted, our apprehension, and we thought that in due course we would discuss the matter.[35]

As is clearly evident from Meir's account, Mandatory Palestine *was not* divided in November 1947. There was mutual recognition of the lack of enthusiasm on either side for military confrontation and of the existence of a certain convergence of interests. But no definitive agreement on the future of Palestine was reached. To the contrary, as Meir saw it, Abdullah was made to understand that the decision on whether to confront the world with a *fait accompli* by annexing the Arab parts of Palestine to his kingdom was exclusively his, and that he could expect no Jewish support for such a move. This gist is also borne out by Sasson's and Danin's reports: 'Replied we prepared [to] give every assistance within [the] frame [of the] UN Charter'; 'Mrs. Meir replied that they would view such an attempt in a favourable light ... if he could declare that his sole purpose was to maintain law and order until the UN could establish a government in that area.'

Shlaim narrates the part of Meir's report relating to her second meeting with Abdullah; yet, significantly enough, he fails to mention its most critical point for his case, namely Meir's account of her November 1947 conversation in general, and her refusal to help a solution that was non-concomitant with the UN Resolution in particular. Is it because this would have pulled the rug from under his absurd claim that the Zionist movement was seeking to subvert the very UN Resolution which it was so assiduously trying to bring about?

Shlaim's abstention from using Meir's report and his exclusive reliance on Danin's and Sasson's accounts, though not without overlooking their most critical points, is all the more incomprehensible in this particular case since it was Meir after all who allegedly gave Abdullah the 'green light' to annex the

---

35 Golda Meir's verbal report at the Provisional State Council's meeting of 12 May 1948. *Minhelet Ha-am, Protokolim, 18 April – 13 May 1948* (Provisional State Council, Protocols, 18 April – 13 May 1948) (Jerusalem: Israel State Archives, 1978), vol. I, p. 40.

Arab parts of Mandatory Palestine to his kingdom. Even if Shlaim deems Meir's account of her November 1947 meeting to be unreliable, his minimum obligation still is to introduce it to his readers and to explain his reasons for discounting it. But then there is no particular reason to suspect that Meir's account, given to the Yishuv's 'government' in camera, is less reliable than that of her advisers. Indeed, not only does Shlaim not question the authenticity of Meir's report but he also lauds it as 'nowhere as unsympathetic and unflattering about Abdullah's behaviour as the account she later wrote in her memoirs'.[36] If Meir's account of her May 1948 meeting was so fair-minded, then surely the part relating to the November 1947 conversation is no less reliable. Danin who attended the meeting certainly believed so. Yet Shlaim preferred not to bring it in his book.

THE JEWISH AGENCY AND THE PARTITION IT NEVER APPROVED

If Palestine was indeed divided on 17 November 1947, which it was not, then the Jewish Agency which was an alleged party to this deal displayed no awareness of such a partition. Not only was it never discussed by the JAE, but there is no trace of its existence either in the Yishuv's military operations during the war imposed on it by the Palestinians, or in its planning for the anticipated invasion of post-Mandatory Palestine by the Arab States. To the contrary, as is clearly shown by Meir's verbal report, the meeting left her and the Zionist leadership at large deeply suspicious of Abdullah's expansionist ambitions, the precise nature of which were to be gauged in a future meeting shortly after the passing of the UN Resolution. In the event, this meeting did not take place until 11 May 1948, and Jewish suspicions of Abdullah's real

36   Shlaim, *Collusion*, p. 211.

agenda remained unabated until the Arab attack on the newly-established State of Israel, in which Transjordan's Arab Legion participated.

The Jewish Agency's distrust of Abdullah was vividly demonstrated by its vehement opposition to the presence of Transjordan's British-led Arab Legion in Mandatory Palestine and its tireless efforts to bring about its departure.[37] Thus, for example, at a JAE discussion on security issues on 16 November 1947, a day before Meir's meeting with Abdullah, Ben-Gurion warned his colleagues that the Arab Legion's presence in Palestine constituted a potential security threat. 'It is true that it is headed by a person who is not our enemy', he said, 'but we must brace ourselves for all trouble'.[38] The Abdullah–Meir meeting did nothing to allay these apprehensions. On 7 December 1947 Ben-Gurion reiterated his apprehensions of the deployment of the Arab Legion in Palestine. 'The Government claims that this is their force', he told his colleagues, alluding to a meeting he had just held with the British High Commissioner Sir Alan Cunningham in which he had protested on this point, 'but this is an Arab Legion'.[39] Two days later, Ben-Gurion expressed doubts regarding Abdullah's political standing. 'All evidence points to the fact that the Mufti has gained control over the Arab community in the country [Mandatory Palestine]', he told a JAE meeting. 'King Abdullah is isolated'.[40] In a cable to Sharett in New York he was equally puzzled about Abdullah's intentions, if slightly more optimistic: '"The King" is still defiant – does not lend a hand to the Mufti

37 See, for example, Meir's meeting with Sir Alan Cunningham, 17 December 1947, and her letter to him from the same day, *Teudot*, pp. 83–4; a meeting in London between representatives of the Jewish Agency and the Colonial Secretary, Arthur Creech-Jones, on 23 December 1947, Ibid., pp. 96–7.
38 Jewish Agency Executive meeting of 16 November 1947, p. 4 (12697).
39 Jewish Agency Executive meeting of 7 December 1947, protocol 13, p. 2 (12717), protocol 14, p. 1 (12724).
40 Protocols of the JAE meeting of 9 January 1948, p. 1 (12740). In his diary Ben-Gurion made the point in similar terms: 'Opposition [to the Mufti among the Palestine Arabs] is feeble … According to Sasson the Mufti has gained control over all the Palestine Arabs. The king is isolated and cannot be trusted'. Ben-Gurion, *Yoman Ha-milhama*, 9 December 1947, vol. I, p. 28.

or the League; it is not clear to me whether he will stay his course, but there is a chance for this'.[41]

By January 1948 this guarded optimism was all but gone. 'There have been some news recently which may change our view of the king', Ben-Gurion wrote in his diary on 1 January 1948:

> It is said that the Arab Legion will operate [in Palestine] and the neighbouring Arab States will send a symbolic force. These news may be correct. According to these news, the Legion will occupy *the whole* of Palestine, though without entering the populated areas, and will force the Jews to negotiate on the [Arab] League's terms: autonomy for the Jewish community under a single [Arab] regime for the whole country; Palestine within the League. Sasson recalled what [the King] said during the [November 1947] meeting in Naharyim: 'A partition that will not disgrace me in front of the Arabs. What do you think about a small republic [within my kingdom]?' This proves that the idea resides in the king's heart and is not of recent origin.[42]

Later that day Ben-Gurion dined with Avraham Rutenberg, in whose house the Meir–Abdullah meeting took place, and who now tried to convince Ben-Gurion to persuade the United Nations to introduce Abdullah into the Arab parts of Palestine. 'We have to examine whether this is desirable – because Abdullah means Iraq',[43] was Ben-Gurion's cautious response, reflecting the lack of any agreed deal on the partition of Palestine. Two days later he received a warning from

---

41 *Teudot*, p. 60.
42 Ben-Gurion, *Yoman Ha-milhama*, 1 January 1948, vol. I, pp. 100–1 (emphasis in the original).
43 Ibid., p. 103. As late as 16 April 1948 Ben-Gurion warned a JAE meeting that 'we should not be lured into a sense of relief, there may be various mishaps, for example if the Arab Legion will go into action' (p. 3, 12562).

Eliyahu Epstein (Eilath), the Jewish Agency's delegate in the United States, of Abdullah's intention to employ the Arab Legion in Palestine on behalf of the Arab League. 'In the entire country?', the puzzled Ben-Gurion jotted to himself. 'In the Arab area?'[44]

This scepticism was not confined to the leader of the Zionist movement. Contemporary documents are replete with deep-seated suspicions of Abdullah both by Zionist officialdom and by such 'moderate' leaders as Moshe Sharett, all of whom were totally mindless of any agreement with the King on the division of Mandatory Palestine. Early in January 1948 Sharett opined that if it transpired that Abdullah was capable of gaining control over the Arab parts of Palestine, either directly or by proxy, then the Zionist movement should make serious efforts to support him. Yet he profoundly feared that 'the King will deceive and cheat us'.[45] In other words, two months after Meir's meeting with Abdullah, her direct superior and the head of the department which had maintained covert contacts with the king for well over a decade was unaware of any deal to divide Mandatory Palestine, despite receiving Sasson's report on the conversation three days after its occurrence.

Even Sasson who participated in the Meir–Abdullah meeting did not behave as if there was any firm agreement with the king. To the contrary, as Palestinian–Jewish fighting intensified, he increasingly lost trust in Abdullah's ability to stay his course. On 9 February 1948 he told Ben-Gurion that the king would most probably have to play along the Arab League's plan; Sasson still believed in Abdullah's sincerity, but he was dependent on the British, his power was limited, and he could not be relied upon.[46] A month later Sasson told Ben-Gurion of the need to establish a secret dialogue with the

---

44 Ibid., 3 January 1948, p. 107.
45 E. Danin to E. Sasson, 4 January 1948, *Teudot*, p. 127. In the same cable Danin also reported David Horowitz's great fear that Abdullah 'will cheat and fail us'.
46 Ben-Gurion, *Yoman Ha-milhama*, 9 February 1948, vol. I, pp. 224–5.

governments of Egypt, Lebanon and Syria in an attempt to reach an understanding that would prevent an all-out war. 'Have you despaired of your King?' Ben-Gurion asked, apparently surprised at Abdullah's glaring absence from this list. 'No, but he is helpless', Sasson answered. 'I despaired of the King since the British had surrendered him', said Reuben Shiloah who attended the meeting.[47]

If anything, one need not look further than Sasson's above-cited appeal to Azzam on 5 December 1947 to realize that no such deal had been struck; had Palestine actually been divided between the king and the Zionist movement on 17 November, then there would have been no need for such an appeal in the first place. That the Zionist movement sought a mutually-agreed solution with the Arab League, which Abdullah so detested, three weeks after his meeting with Meir, indicated that as far as it was concerned all options were open.

TRANSJORDANIAN ANNEXATION OR AN INDEPENDENT PALESTINIAN STATE?

Indeed the Zionists' unquestioned preference of Abdullah over the Mufti as their direct neighbour did not *ipso facto* preclude the possibility of an independent Palestinian State that would not be headed by this arch enemy of the Jewish national cause. As far as the Zionist movement was concerned, a Jewish State was to be established in part of Mandatory Palestine; what happened to the rest of the country, as noted by Moshe Sharett, 'is not for us but rather for them [the Arabs] to decide, whether it would be merged [with Transjordan] or separated'.[48]

That the Zionist movement was not averse to the possibility of a Palestinian State was also evidenced by Meir's

---

47   Ibid., 7 March 1948, p. 284.
48   Shertok to Sasson, 18 August 1946, CZA, S25/10015.

refusal to condone Abdullah's annexation of the Arab parts of Palestine and her insistence on the temporary nature of Transjordan's occupation 'until the UN could establish a government in that area'. It was further underscored on 8 August 1948 by a telegram by Foreign Minister Moshe Sharett to Bechor Shalom Shitrit, Minister of Police and Minorities in the Israeli Government:

> We should strive for contact and mutual under-standing with people and circles among our opponents who carry weight in Arab public life and who are today prepared for cooperation with us, whether on the basis of recognizing the State of Israel within its borders or in order to establish independent rule in the Arab part of Western Palestine.
>
> Without being able to totally remove from the agenda the possibility of the annexation of the Arab part of Western Palestine to Transjordan, we must prefer the establishment of an independent Arab State within Western Palestine. In any event we must endeavour to explore this possibility and to underscore its desirability in our eyes over the annexation proposal.[49]

Similarly, in a conversation in early December 1948 with the British Ambassador to Transjordan, Sir Alec Kirkbride, Ralph Bunche, the UN Mediator for Palestine, claimed that

> the Jews had practically abandoned their original idea of insisting on the Arab areas of Palestine being formed into an independent state because he, Bunche, had convinced them that it was as likely as not to fall under the influence of Haj Amin el

---

49 Sharett to Shitrit, 8 August 1948, in Yehoshua Freindlich, ed., *Teudot Mediniot Ve-diplomatiot, May–September 1948* (Documents on the Foreign Policy of Israel, May–September 1948) (Jerusalem: Israel State Archives, 1981), p. 498.

Husseini and to be an endless source of friction and disorder.[50]

In other words, more than a year after Palestine had been allegedly divided by Abdullah and Meir, Israeli leaders still needed to be convinced of the merits of Abdullah's permanent (as opposed to temporary) occupation of the Arab parts of Palestine. Even a cursory examination of Ben-Gurion's war diary of the time would easily reveal divergencies within the Israeli leadership over the future status of the Arab areas of Palestine: an independent state or part of Transjordan.[51] It is true that Bunche was probably somewhat over self-complimentary in crediting himself with this attitudinal change. On the one hand, the Zionists hardly needed reminding of the hazards of a Mufti-dominated State, and were painfully aware of the slim prospects of the emergence of a viable, moderate Palestinian leadership. On the other hand, Bunche did not succeed in converting the Israeli leadership to the 'Transjordanian option' as he wrongly believed. While Sasson was disposed to Transjordan's annexation of the Arab parts of Palestine (though not necessarily due to Bunche's influence),[52] Ben-Gurion subscribed to Sharett's above-noted prognosis. 'While we may still expect two more [military] operations, our main objective now is peace', he said at a meeting with foreign policy officials and experts on Arab affairs on 18 December 1948:

> There is too much drunkenness with victory. Aliya requires the end of war, our future necessitates peace and friendship with Arabs. Therefore I support talking to Abdullah, though I doubt to what extent the British will allow him to make peace [as we shall see in Chapter 6, this scepticism was fully justified since

50 Kirkbride to B.A.B. Burrows, 10 December 1948, FO 371/68603/E16265.
51 See, for example, Ben-Gurion, *Yoman Ha-milhama*, 29 December 1948, vol. III, p. 910.
52 Ibid., 30 December 1948, p. 913.

Britain was bent upon preventing a separate Israeli–Transjordanian agreement – E.K.]. But we should clarify [to Abdullah] from the outset that, apart from a truce, there is not yet any agreement between us, and that the discussion is on the basis of *tabula rasa*. *We will not be able to agree lightly to the annexation of [the Arab] parts of Palestine to Transjordan*, because of 1) Israel's security: *an Arab State in Western Palestine is less dangerous than a state that is tied to Transjordan, and tomorrow – probably to Iraq*; 2) Why should we vainly antagonize the Russians? 3) Why should we do this [i.e., agree to Transjordan's annexation of Western Palestine] against the [wishes of the] rest of the Arab States? This does not mean that we might not agree under any circumstances – but only in the context of a general arrangement.[53]

In line with this view, Ben-Gurion instructed the Israeli delegation to the truce talks with Transjordan 'to remain non-committal for the time being, while avoiding [outright] objection; to explain the difficulties (England, the Arab States, Russia); to express sympathy; to say that there is not yet a government decision on this issue'.[54]

OLD HAT, 'REVISIONIST' FEATHERS

Not surprisingly, Shlaim's distortion of Meir's reply to Abdullah has been unanimously endorsed by his fellow 'new historians'. Benny Morris, without doing any original research on the subject, warmly endorsed the thesis that the Yishuv and the Hashemites 'had conspired from 1946 to early 1948 to nip the impending UN partition resolution in the bud',[55]

53   Ibid., 18 December 1948, p. 885 (emphasis added).
54   Ibid., 4 January 1949, p. 927.
55   Morris, *1948 and After*, p. 10.

totally 'forgetting' that until February 1947 Britain was the
Mandatory Power for Palestine; that until UNSCOP's majority
recommendation on partition was published on 31 August 1947,
a solution in this vein was by no means a foregone conclusion;
that until the General Assembly passed the Partition Resolution on 29 November 1947, there was no absolute certainty
that UNSCOP's recommendation would be adopted by the
United Nations; and that, above all, this Partition Resolution
was what the Zionist movement had been consistently
fighting for.

For his part, Ilan Pappé goes further than Shlaim in misrepresenting the record. While Shlaim at least brings Danin's
and Sasson's reports more or less in their entirety (though
keeping away Meir's own report), Pappé makes no mention
of the most significant part in Meir's reply, namely her objection to any agreement non-concomitant with the UN Partition
Resolution, and her insistence on the ephemerality of Transjordan's occupation of the Arab parts in Palestine until the
establishment of a legal government there. As Pappé put it:

> In November 1947, King Abdullah met the head of
> the Political Department of the Jewish Agency, Golda
> Meyerson (Meir), and offered the Jews an independent
> Jewish republic as part of a Hashemite monarchy
> covering Transjordan and ex-mandatory Palestine.
> When this was rejected, he asked for the Jewish
> Agency's consent to his annexing the territories
> allotted to the Arabs in the UN partition plan. The
> Jewish Agency representative gave her consent in
> return for the king's promise not to attack the future
> Jewish State.[56]

> For that purpose in November 1947 a meeting took
> place between Golda Meyerson (Meir), the acting

---

56 Ilan Pappé, *Britain and the Arab–Israeli Conflict, 1948–51* (London: Macmillan, 1988),
    p. 10.

head of the Political Department of the Jewish Agency, and King Abdullah. At this meeting Abdullah presented a new vision of Palestine in which a Jewish republic would be integrated into a newly-formed Hashemite kingdom – consisting of Transjordan and Palestine [as shown earlier, this was not 'a new vision' but rather Abdullah's long-standing solution to the Palestine problem – E.K]. When, not surprisingly, this was rejected out of hand by the other side, Abdullah asked for Jewish consent to the annexation to Transjordan of the UN-defined Arab States. To this the Jewish Agency representative did give her assent, in return for the king's promise not to attack the Jewish State in the event of a war breaking out.[57]

That the 'new historians' have distorted Meir's reply to Abdullah is scarcely surprising; the interesting point is that 'old historians' have preceded them in doing so. For example, while citing Meir's insistence on the ephemerality of the Transjordanian seizure of the Arab parts of Palestine, Aharon Klieman has been captive of the same misconception as Shlaim and Pappé. 'Thus', he wrote in his study of Hashemite–Zionist relations published two years before Shlaim's book, 'an authorized representative of the [Jewish] Agency and on Ben-Gurion's behalf gave a clear and rather explicit agreement to the Hashemite leader's occupation of the "Arab part" of Western Palestine according to the partition principle, on condition that he would not obstruct the establishment of the Jewish State'.[58]

According to Morris, 'Shlaim's description of the Yishuv–Hashemite relations down to 1951, including the premise of tacit Israeli–Jordanian agreement during 1948' has been by

57 Pappé, *The Making of the Arab–Israeli Conflict*, p. 119.
58 Klieman, *Du Kium*, pp. 129–30.

Fabricating Israeli History

and large accepted by 'the Israeli historiographic community'.[59] The truth of the matter, as shown by Klieman's above citation, is that it is Shlaim who has been following in the footsteps of 'the Israeli historiographic community' rather than the other way round.[60]

Interestingly enough, Klieman, the quintessential 'Zionist' historian, even goes further than Shlaim in censuring the Hashemite–Jewish 'connection'. While Shlaim views this connection as a 'reasonable and realistic strategy for both sides' Klieman deems it politically imprudent but avoids the pious high moral ground taken by Shlaim. This provides further proof, if such were at all needed, that the difference between 'old' and 'new' historians has nothing to do with access to new facts, and not necessarily even with their interpretation: for in this case both 'old' and 'new' historians have (mis)interpreted a specific historical episode in precisely the same way.

True, there have been a handful of historians who have highlighted the restrictive nature of Meir's response to Abdullah.[61] But even they fail to recognize that a) decisions of such magnitude cannot be made in the course of a single conversation; b) that Meir was not authorized to make a decision of this kind; c) that no agreement that bound the Zionist movement could conceivably be reached without the authorization of the JAE – which was never given; d) that the Jewish Agency showed no awareness of the existence of any such agreement and that Zionist distrust of Abdullah remained unabated for a long time after the Meir–Abdullah meeting; and that e) the Jewish Agency remained undecided between the two options – an independent Palestinian State or Transjordan's annexation of Western Palestine – well after the Meir–

59 Morris, *1948 and After*, p. 39.
60 For other scholars who have preceded the 'new historians' on the issue of Hashemite–Zionist relations see Chapter 1 fn.19.
61 See, for example, Yoav Gelber, *The Alliance of Bars Sinister: Jewish–Transjordanian Relations, 1921–1948* (London: Frank Cass, forthcoming); Ron Pundik, *The Struggle for Sovereignty: Relations between Great Britain and Jordan, 1946–1951* (Oxford: Blackwell, 1994).

Abdullah meeting, with its most influential leaders, David Ben-Gurion and Moshe Sharett, disposed to the former option. Not least, even these more careful historians have overlooked Meir's own account of the meeting, focusing instead on Danin's report.

This in turn brings us back to the conclusion that on this particular historical episode both 'old' and 'new' Israeli historians have unquestioningly been recycling an old and familiar myth, whose broad contours were delineated already 30 years ago, while ignoring the only first-hand account of the person involved. Shlaim is not even 'new' in being wrong.

4 The Warning That Whitehall Never Gave

It is much easier to be critical than to be correct.

BENJAMIN DISRAELI

The second leg of the 'collusion' myth is that 'Britain knew and approved of th[e] secret Hashemite–Zionist agreement to divide up Palestine between themselves, not along the lines of the UN partition plan'.[1] According to Avi Shlaim

> At a secret meeting in London on 7 February 1948, [British Foreign Secretary Ernest] Bevin gave Tawfiq Abul Huda, [Trans]jordan's Prime Minister, the green light to send the Arab Legion into Palestine immediately following the departure of the British forces. But Bevin also warned [Trans]jordan not to invade the area allocated by the U.N. to the Jews. An attack on Jewish State territory, he said, would compel Britain to withdraw her subsidy and officers from the Arab Legion.[2]

And Ilan Pappé put it in similarly unequivocal terms:

1 Shlaim, 'The Debate', p. 297.
2 Ibid., p. 293.

Thus, in February 1948, a delegation headed by the Prime Minister, Tawfiq Abu'l-Huda, went to Britain to discuss the future of Palestine as well as the revision of the [Anglo–Transjordanian] treaty. In the course of those talks, the Transjordanians revealed to their British interlocutors the scope and content of their negotiations with the Jews and it was then that the king obtained Britain's blessing for the tacit understanding he had reached with the Jewish Agency about the partitioning of post-mandatory Palestine.[3]

'Bevin's meeting with Abul Huda was a major turning-point in Britain's policy towards the Middle East', Shlaim claims:

Up to this point Britain had declined to enforce the UN partition plan but had failed to develop a clear strategy for defending her position in the area following the end of the mandate. There was a pro-Hashemite school which advocated an enlarged Transjordan as the principal bulwark of British power and influence in the Middle East. But there was also opposition to this line of argument inside the Foreign

3 Pappé, *The Making of the Arab–Israeli Conflict*, p. 120. See also idem, *Britain and the Arab–Israeli Conflict*, pp. 9, 11. Pappé bases this claim on two sources:
   a) A brief prepared for Bevin's meeting with Abul Huda by Michael Wright of the Eastern Department: as shown in this chapter, this brief makes no mention whatsoever of Transjordanian–Jewish contacts, let alone of an existing tacit understanding between the two parties.
   b) Shlaim's *Collusion Across the Jordan*. But Shlaim's claim that 'it was not the first time that Britain had heard about Abdullah's contacts with the Jewish Agency, but it was the first time that the Transjordanian government had asked for British advice on this matter' (p. 139) is a near-verbatim citation from Pappé's earlier work (*Britain and the Arab–Israeli Conflict*, p. 9), which provides no reference whatsoever in support of this (false) claim!
   Pappé is also misleading in implying that the main task of the Transjordanian delegation was 'to discuss the future of Palestine'. It was not. A quick glance at the minutes of the delegation's discussions will easily reveal that they focused almost exclusively on the revision of the Anglo-Transjordanian treaty. It was only in Abul Huda's meeting with Bevin that the Palestine issue was really raised, and this meeting was kept secret from the other members of the delegation, not least the Transjordanian foreign minister.

Office, on the grounds that siding with Abdullah against the rest of the Arab countries could lead to the destruction of the Arab League. Abul Huda helped to persuade Bevin that the Transjordanians could be relied upon to act discreetly and moderately and that the proposed course of action would be to Britain's advantage. The keystone of British policy swung into place. From this point on Britain worked in close co-operation with Abdullah to secure the expansion of his kingdom over most of Arab Palestine.

In effect [Shlaim continued], Britain now became a party to an attempt to frustrate the UN partition plan and divide up Palestine instead between Abdullah and the Jews. This was the solution urged by the Jews on Abdullah and the basis of his agreement with Golda Meir at Naharayim. It was not the first time that Britain had heard about Abdullah's contacts with the Jewish Agency, but it was the first time that the Transjordanian government had asked for British advice on this matter.

Significantly, the only word of warning appended by Bevin to his acceptance of the Transjordanian plan was to refrain from invading the areas allotted to the Jews. Thus Bevin, who is portrayed by Zionist historians as irreconcilably opposed to the establishment of a Jewish State, appears, by February 1948, to be resigned to the inevitable emergence of a Jewish State but intent on frustrating the emergence of a Palestinian Arab state. It is hardly an exaggeration to say that he colluded directly with the Transjordanians and indirectly with the Jews to abort the birth of a Palestinian Arab state.[4]

4   Shlaim, *Collusion*, pp. 138–9.

However intriguing, this thesis is totally misconceived. In fact, one need go no further than Shlaim's concluding chapter to belie this fantastic claim:

> Britain was careful not to get involved in active collusion with Abdullah in frustrating the United Nations partition scheme and gave only implicit agreement to Abdullah's plan. The point of the agreement was not to prevent the birth of a Palestinian state, since by that time it was clear that the Palestinian leaders were not prepared to set up a state in part of Palestine, but to prevent the Jews from occupying the whole of Palestine.[5]

As this citation proves, Shlaim does not believe his own claim that Britain 'became a party to an attempt to frustrate the UN partition plan' or that it 'colluded directly with the Trans-jordanians and indirectly with the Jews to abort the birth of a Palestinian Arab State'. Rather, he aptly notes that Britain tacitly collaborated with Transjordan against the Jews, although his claim that it did so 'to prevent the Jews from occupying the whole of Palestine' is as far from the truth as the 'collusion' myth itself.[6]

GETTING THE PICTURE WRONG

But leaving aside this self-contradiction, Shlaim's and Pappé's conspiracy theory is flawed in three critical respects:

---

5 Ibid., p. 618.
6 Contemporary British documents unequivocally show that policy-makers in London believed that the end of the Palestine Mandate would lead to an Arab attack on the prospective Jewish State rather than the other way round. Similarly, in a conversation with Kirkbride a few days after the passing of the UN Partition Resolution, Transjordan's Prime Minister Samir al-Rifai 'made no prophecy as to what form of administration would fill the vacuum in the Arab part of Palestine when British left, but he did not expect Jews to march into it'. Kirkbride to Bevin, 3 December 1947, telegram 359, FO 816/111.

- Contrary to their claim, Britain *did not know* of the alleged 'secret Hashemite–Zionist agreement to divide up Palestine between themselves', not least because this agreement did not exist; nor did Abul Huda make any mention whatsoever of 'Abdullah's contacts with the Jewish Agency' during the meeting, let alone of their 'scope and content'. Hence Bevin was not asked for 'advice on this matter' and *ipso facto* could not give 'Britain's blessing' for the alleged Hashemite–Zionist deal.

The Foreign Office knew of Abdullah's desire to incorporate the Arab parts of Palestine, if not the entire country into his kingdom; they also had second-hand knowledge of Zionist preference of Abdullah over the Mufti as a future neighbour.[7] Yet they were not (and could not be) aware of any concrete Hashemite–Zionist deal to divide Mandatory Palestine, an idea to which they were ill-disposed in the first place. Nor were they even aware of the real scope of Abdullah's contacts with the Jewish Agency as the king was very careful to keep his cards close to his chest.

On 17 November 1947, the same day when Abdullah and Meir held their secret conversation, Ambassador Kirkbride responded to a memorandum by Bevin on possible courses of action in the light of the impending UN vote on partition, in which the Foreign Secretary mooted *inter alia* the hypothetical possibility of a Hashemite–Jewish agreement that would lead to Transjordan's annexation of the Arab areas of Palestine. Totally unaware of the meeting that took place that very day, Kirkbride wrote:

> I submit that prior formal agreement between King Abdullah and the Jews would be dangerous in that secrecy would be impossible[.] [I]t would

---

7   Kirkbride to Foreign Office, 19 December 1947, telegram 582, FO 371/61583/E12092, reporting a conversation with Avraham Rutenberg.

act as a focus for the anger of the other Arab States against the King and alienate the Palestinian Arabs. It might in any case be difficult to secure in the time available.[8]

This view was shared by Harold Beeley, Bevin's chief adviser on Palestine who, like Kirkbride, did not know of any Hashemite–Jewish agreement. Writing on 20 January 1948, about two weeks before the Foreign Secretary's meeting with Abul Huda, he stated:

> I think there can be little doubt that the Jewish Agency are trying to tempt Abdullah into accepting as an addition to the Kingdom of Transjordan, those parts of Palestine awarded to the Arabs by the United Nations. We have not so far had any evidence that Abdullah is falling for this, and I think he would be very unwise to do so.[9]

And a brief prepared for Bevin by Michael Wright of the Eastern Department a day before his meeting with Abul Huda showed no awareness of the existence of any Hashemite–Zionist agreement on the division of Palestine, though envisaging such an eventuality at some future time as a result of the Transjordanian intervention in Palestine:

> It seems likely that the Prime Minister may wish to put forward the idea of action by Transjordan in Palestine which would lead to eventual

8   Kirkbride to Bevin, 17 November 1947, telegram 342, FO 816/89. For Bevin's cable see: Bevin to Kirkbride, 11 November 1947, telegram 493, ibid. In his memoirs, Kirkbride downplays the secrecy of the meeting, thus creating the false impression that it was common knowledge at the time: 'The date was on November 10th 1947. No particular pains were taken up to keep the occasion secret and there was no violent reaction in the other Arab countries when the occurrence became known'. Sir Alec Kirkbride, *From the Wings: Amman Memoirs 1947–1951* (London: Frank Cass, 1976), p. 4.

9   A personal and secret letter from Beeley, Eastern Department, Foreign Office, to T.E. Bromley, 20 January 1948, FO 371/68403/E1877.

agreement with the Jews. This might take the form of occupation by the Arab Legion after May 15th of some or all of the areas allotted to the Arabs by the United Nations, but without the occupation of any areas allotted to the Jews. Then after a suitable lapse of time, King Abdullah would come to a *de facto* agreement with the Jews that they would not encroach on each other's territory in return perhaps for a share of Jewish customs revenue.[10]

Indeed, as late as March 1949, a year-and-a-half after the alleged division of Palestine between Abdullah and Meir, Wright still believed that 'the idea that there is any deep plot between King Abdullah and the Jews, of which we have knowledge, is mistaken'.[11]

- Contrary to Shlaim's and Pappé's claim, Bevin *did not* warn '[Trans]jordan not to invade the area allocated by the UN to the Jews'. The territorial scope of the 'Arab' and 'Jewish' parts of Mandatory Palestine remained oblique in the wake of the meeting, with Bevin and some of his key foreign policy advisers clearly favouring Transjordan's annexation of substantial territories allocated to the prospective Jewish State, most notably the Negev or parts of it (the rest being earmarked for Egypt).

- Last but not least, Bevin never asked for Cabinet approval for his alleged deal with Abul Huda. Hence Shlaim's statement that 'from this point on Britain worked in close

10 Michael Wright, 'Brief for Conversation with Transjordan Prime Minister on Palestine', 6 February 1948, FO 371/68367/E1980G. See also a memorandum on the same subject by Christopher Pirie-Gordon of the British legation in Transjordan: 'I have no knowledge of what the Prime Minister proposes to say if the interview he has requested should be granted, but I strongly suspect that he has made the move in response to direct orders from King Abdullah, and that he may well be contemplating the suggestion of some course of action in which an *eventual understanding* with the Jews is envisaged' (emphasis added). Pirie-Gordon to Burrows, 28 January 1948, 371/68366/E1730.
11 Wright to Campbell, 30 March 1949, FO 371/75064.

co-operation with Abdullah to secure the expansion of his kingdom over most of Arab Palestine' could not be further removed from the truth. The most that can be argued is that Bevin and his advisers turned a blind eye to Abdullah's intention to invade Palestine and allowed themselves and the unwitting Cabinet to be swayed in this direction; but even they did not actively collaborate with Abdullah, let alone sanctify the alleged Zionist–Hashemite partition of Palestine. On the contrary, until Transjordan's attack on the newly-born State of Israel in mid-May 1948 the Foreign Office remained in the dark over Abdullah's real intentions; even the influential Kirkbride failed to see the true substance of the king's thinking.

WHAT BEVIN SAID AND DID NOT SAY
TO ABUL HUDA

Where did Shlaim and Pappé derive their misconceptions? As noted earlier, it was Glubb Pasha who first claimed that Bevin gave Abul Huda the approval to invade the Arab, but not the Jewish parts of Mandatory Palestine after the British withdrawal. His account has Abul Huda treating Bevin to a lengthy exposition of the situation in Palestine and the widespread support for Abdullah among the Palestinians before suggesting 'to send the Arab Legion across the Jordan when the British Mandate ended, and to occupy that part of Palestine awarded to the Arabs which was contiguous with the frontier of Transjordan'. To this Bevin reportedly responded by repeating his reply twice: 'It seems the obvious thing to do … it seems the obvious thing to do … but do not go and invade the areas allotted to the Jews'. At the end of the talk Bevin thanked his guest for his frank exposition of the Transjordanian position and reportedly reiterated his agreement with the plans put before him.[12]

12   Glubb, *A Soldier with the Arabs*, pp. 63–6.

But does Glubb's account stand the test of the declassi-fication of British documents 30 years later? The official record of the meeting, sent by Bevin to Kirkbride on 9 February, suggests not. It reads as follows:

Shortly after his arrival here the Transjordan Prime Minister expressed the wish to have a private con-versation with me on Palestine in which his Minister for Foreign Affairs would not participate. He stated that he wished to put before me certain considera-tions which might not be acceptable to the Foreign Minister, who represented the younger and more nationalist elements in Transjordan. It was accordingly arranged for Tawfik Pasha Abul Huda to see me on 7th February without the Foreign Minister. Brigadier Glubb Pasha interpreted. Mr. [Christopher] Pirie-Gordon [of the British Legation in Amman] was also present.

Future of the Arab Legion in Palestine

2.   Tawfik Pasha said that he knew he was not entitled to speak to me officially or to enter into any negotia-tions about Palestine but he would like us to know the point of view of King Abdullah without expecting us necessarily to make any comment or reply. It was expected that difficulties might arise immediately after 15th May either from Jewish action against Arabs or from the activities of unorganised gangs of Arabs. Transjordan was unwilling to encourage dis-turbances or anarchy in Palestine because this would adversely affect the Palestine Arabs and would also react on Transjordan. The Arab Legion who were now in Palestine had made a good impression by their discipline and behaviour. Their presence would also be beneficial in the more chaotic situation which would arise after 15th May. It was well understood

that the Arab Legion would have to leave Palestine before 15th May as part of the evacuation of British forces, but after that date, when the Legion would be controlled solely by the Transjordan Government and would not be in any way under British command, it would be to the public benefit if it returned to the Arab areas of Palestine to maintain law and order.

3.   Tawfik Pasha appreciated that His Majesty's Government might be held morally responsible vis-à-vis the United Nations and world opinion for what the Arab Legion might do, on account of our subsidy payments, and that this would cause us embarrassment if the Arab Legion attacked any part of the civil population. If, however, the United Nations saw that the Arab Legion were reducing bloodshed, they would be grateful rather than critical of its activities.

4.   Transjordan did not intend to act on these lines simply for its own advantage but because it was convinced that the Arabs of Palestine could not effectively set up a Government of their own, whereas Transjordan could ensure stability. The presence of the Arab Legion in Palestine would not prevent the execution of any United Nations decision which might ultimately be taken, but would enable such a decision to be more easily enforced. If, as his Excellency hoped, some solution was ultimately adopted involving a modification of the present arrangements in favour of the Arabs, the Arab Legion would be able to help enforce such a solution. Even if, on the other hand, the United Nations tried to enforce the present decision, the presence of the Arab Legion would limit the ensuing chaos and not increase it. Tawfik Pasha thought it was possible that

the Jews would find that they had opened their mouths too wide and that the United Nations would come to a similar conclusion, but, however this might be, the Arab Legion could not wait for the prior permission of the United Nations to enter the Arab areas of Palestine.

5.   In conclusion Tawfik Pasha repeated his assurance that he did not desire to create difficulties for His Majesty's Government or to involve them in respon- sibility. Any action which might be taken would be purely on Transjordan's responsibility. He recog- nised that Transjordan must also study the position in relation to the other Arab Governments and that it would be undesirable if her position became too isolated.

6.   I asked his Excellency whether, when he spoke of the Arab Legion entering Palestine, he referred to the Arab areas as laid down in the United Nations' decision or whether he thought it would also enter the Jewish areas. Tawfiq Pasha replied that the Arab Legion would not enter Jewish areas unless the Jews invaded Arab areas. He saw that the entry of the Arab Legion into Jewish areas would create such strenu- ous United Nations opposition as to cause great difficulty for Transjordan.

7.   I said that I would study the statements which his Excellency had made. Tawfik Pasha repeated that he did not want any reply. If as a result of my study we wished to pursue the discussion he would be glad to do so, but otherwise he would not expect us to refer to the matter again.[13]

13   Bevin to Kirkbride, 'Conversation with the Transjordan Prime Minister', 9 February 1948, FO 371/68366/E1916/G.

As is clear from the above report, Bevin neither encouraged Abul Huda to invade the Arab parts of Palestine as 'the obvious thing to do' nor warned him off invading the Jewish areas. All he did was to ask for a clarification of the territorial scope of the envisaged Jordanian intervention following Abul Huda's bluster about the Jews discovering 'that they had opened their mouths too wide'; but this amounted to no warning against invading the Jewish areas. Had Bevin been genuinely concerned about such an eventuality, here was the perfect opportunity to fend it off. For all the Foreign Secretary's many weaknesses, timidity was not one of them; even a cursory examination of his conversations with Arab leaders during the same period would easily reveal that he never shied away from speaking his mind. Moreover, Bevin had no reason to strike this warning off the report. Quite the reverse. Given his overwhelming preoccupation with American foreign policy in general, and towards the Palestine Question in particular, and his conviction that President Harry Truman was very much under the Zionist spell, Bevin now had a golden opportunity to disprove his image as an implacable enemy of the Jewish national movement. If anything, the alleged warning against invading the Jewish areas was more likely to appear in the report – even if it had not been made – rather than disappear from it despite its utterance. As things were, it was not there.

Nor was there any trace of such a warning in a second report of the meeting of which Shlaim seems to be totally unaware. Prepared by Bevin on 10 February and cabled to Kirkbride the following morning, it briefly highlighted the main points made in the Foreign Secretary's above-cited report, which was apparently dispatched to Amman by diplomatic mail. Again, there was no mention of Bevin's alleged encouragement of Transjordan's occupation of the Arab parts of Palestine while keeping away from the Jewish areas. On the contrary, Bevin informed Kirkbride that 'opportunity was taken in a subsequent conversation between

Tawfik Pasha and a member of the staff of this Department to convey to him the warning suggested in paragraph 1(c) of my telegram No. 559 of December 11th 1947 and to make sure that he realized that we should in the event of aggressive action by the Arab Legion be under serious pressure with regard to the payment of the subsidy and the presence of British Officers'.[14] Had Bevin given Abul Huda any specific warning, there would have been no need whatsoever for this further communication by a civil servant, whose word was bound to carry far smaller weight than that of his minister.

But what precisely did this lower-ranking official tell Abul Huda? Did he specifically warn against invading the Jewish areas? The key to this riddle lies in paragraph 1(c) of Bevin's telegram No. 559 to Kirkbride of 11 December 1947, which reads as follows:

> If King Abdullah asks you what would be our attitude if after the end of the British civil administration in Palestine the Arab Legion returned there and became involved in hostilities, you should say that while we would expect to be under very strong pressure to cease, while hostilities continued, all payment to Transjordan and to withdraw British officers, we would propose to leave this question over for decision in the light of all the circumstances at the time. If King Abdullah does not raise this point you need not do so at this stage.[15]

This paragraph makes no specific mention of the Jewish areas of Mandatory Palestine, let alone threatens the severance of British subsidy and the withdrawal of advisers from the Arab Legion if it invaded this territory. It only states that, in the event of Transjordan's involvement in hostilities, Britain

14 Bevin to Kirkbride, 10 February 1948, telegram 87, FO 371/68818/E1788G.
15 Bevin to Kirkbride, 11 December 1947, telegram 559, FO 816/111. I am grateful to the Foreign Office for agreeing to release this file, as well as other files of correspondence between Whitehall and the Amman Legation, originally classified until 2023.

might come under severe international pressure to make such a move for the duration of hostilities. But far from constituting an ultimatum, this prognosis was presented as a friendly reminder by a senior ally to his junior partner of certain potential constraints attending the latter's anticipated move; the general tenor of the message makes it eminently clear that Bevin did not welcome this international pressure and hoped to be able to resist it. Hence his reluctance to raise this point with Abdullah unless it was first raised by the king; hence his suggestion to advise Abdullah 'to leave this question over for decision in the light of all the circumstances at the time', thereby keeping both Britain's and Transjordan's options open. Not only was Abul Huda *not* threatened with British retaliation if Transjordan invaded the Jewish areas but during his visit the Foreign Office started to plan for 'the possibility of circumventing any future demands in the international sphere that we should cut off all supplies to the Arab Legion'.[16] Indeed, when in the spring of 1948, Britain imposed an arms embargo of sorts on the Arab States in an attempt to prevent the lifting of an American embargo which in turn would have allowed the Yishuv to obtain weapons in the United States, the Arab Legion was not only spared of this measure but even received arms deliveries at an *accelerated* pace. That this was not related to any Transjordanian undertaking to avoid coming to blows with the Jews was evidenced by the continuation of these arms supplies after Transjordan's attack on Israel on 15 May 1948, when Whitehall acquiesced in a request by Glubb Pasha to provide the Arab Legion with an additional 30 days' worth of ammunition.[17]

Keenly aware that Bevin's detailed report demolishes his thesis of British sanctification of the alleged Hashemite–Zionist deal, Shlaim twists this historical document in order

---

16   Pirie-Gordon to Burrows, 10 March 1948, FO 816/112.
17   Amitzur Ilan, *Embargo, Otzma Ve-hachra'a Be-milhemet Tashakh* (Embargo, Power, and Military Decision in the 1948 Palestine War) (Tel-Aviv: Ma'arachot, 1995), p. 133. For further discussion of the British embargo and its underlying logic see below pp.164–76.

to prove its concomitance with Glubb's claim. 'When Glubb's account is taken in conjunction with the briefs prepared for Bevin', he writes, 'it appears highly probable that the latter in fact used the opportunity to warn Abul Huda against attempting to seize any of the Jewish areas'.[18]

Leaving aside the irony of a 'new historian' attempting to superimpose an old and partisan second-hand account on a newly-released official document, there is absolutely no need for the elaborate detective techniques used by Shlaim for the simple reason that Bevin's two reports of the meeting are perfectly clear as they stand: he *did not* tell Abul Huda that invading the Arab parts of Palestine was 'the obvious thing to do' and he *did not* warn him off invading the Jewish areas. All he said was that he 'would study the statements which his Excellency had made'.

To Shlaim's credit it must be admitted that at least he performs elaborate textual acrobatics in order to bridge the gap between Bevin's original report and Glubb's partisan account. Other historians have not even taken the trouble to do this. William Roger Louis (of the University of Texas), for one, fails to mention the existence of Bevin's reports, relying instead on Glubb's account exclusively.[19] Similarly, in his sympathetic biography of Ernest Bevin, Alan Bullock uncritically adopts Glubb's partisan version of the meeting without informing his readers of the discrepancy between this account and Bevin's report. He also misrepresents the contents of the Foreign Secretary's report by claiming that 'Bevin was satisfied with Tawfiq's assurances on this point [i.e., not to invade the Jewish areas] and it was understood that Abdullah would come to an agreement with the Jews not to encroach on each other's territory'. As we have just seen, no such things were ever said during the meeting.[20]

18 Shlaim, *Collusion*, pp. 137–8.
19 Wm. Roger Louis, *The British Empire in the Middle East 1945–1951: Arab Nationalism, the United States, and Postwar Imperialism* (Oxford: Clarendon Press, 1984), p. 372.
20 Alan Bullock, *Ernest Bevin: Foreign Secretary, 1945–1951* (London: Heinemann, 1983) p. 509. The only allusion to the possibility that 'Abdullah would come to an agreement

But leaving Glubb aside, even if we read Bevin's reports in conjunction with the briefs prepared for him by his advisers, Shlaim's conspiracy theory does not stand. There were two such briefs, the most important of them being written by Michael Wright a day before Bevin's meeting with Abul Huda. In Wright's opinion, Transjordan's occupation of the Arab parts of Palestine 'would not upset the United Nations, but unless handled very carefully indeed, would create very serious trouble with the other Arab States and thus possibly endanger King Abdullah's position'. He therefore advised Bevin to reserve comment on the Transjordanian ideas; indeed, 'Tawfiq Pasha realises the difficulty of our position and will almost certainly not expect the Secretary of State to make any reply to the statement which he may make'. However, *'if it seems impossible to avoid giving some reply'*, then 'it is essential that the Secretary of State should take this opportunity to give a confidential warning that if Transjordan became involved in hostilities against a Jewish State or [acted] blatantly contrary to the United Nations, we should be under strong pressure to suspend the subsidy and to consider the position of British officers seconded to the Arab Legion'.[21]

In citing Wright's report Shlaim significantly omits the key words 'if it seems impossible to avoid giving some reply', thus misrepresenting the thrust of the latter's recommendation.[22] While Wright advised against any comment on Abul Huda's ideas unless it was absolutely necessary, Shlaim creates the false impression that he suggested warning the Prime Minister against excessive behaviour. But even if Wright's first choice would have been to warn Abul Huda of some risks attending

with the Jews not to encroach on each other's territory' was made in Michael Wright's above-cited memorandum, which estimated that 'after a suitable lapse of time, King Abdullah would come to a *de facto* agreement with the Jews that they would not encroach on each other's territory in return perhaps for a share of Jewish customs revenue'. However, this issue never came up in the talks. Furthermore, Wright referred to the possibility of a *future* Jewish–Hashemite agreement that would result from Transjordan's intervention in Palestine: not to a *prior* agreement that would lead to such an intervention.

21 Wright, 'Brief for Conversation with Transjordan Prime Minister' (emphasis added).
22 Shlaim, *Collusion*, p. 135.

an invasion of the Jewish areas (not from the slightest concern for Jewish interests but because of the detrimental effects of such a move on Abdullah's position), which is not the same as warning against such an invasion altogether, then, as is clearly borne out by Bevin's reports, his advice was not acted upon. In actual fact, Bevin did follow Wright's advice by refraining from commenting on Abul Huda's proposed line of action.

The second brief, written by Christopher Pirie-Gordon on 23 January 1948, identified the nature of the dilemma posed by Abdullah's territorial ambitions in Palestine. Were the king to occupy those areas awarded to the Arabs by the United Nations, 'he would in effect be helping the United Nations to implement their plan, against which the whole Arab world has protested. This course would therefore expose him to condemnation as a quisling, and might even cost him his throne in Transjordan'. If, on the other hand, Abdullah chose 'to disregard the frontier drawn by the United Nations, and to occupy, if not the whole country, at least those areas which are permanently Arab in population', then he would 'run the same risk of sanctions against him as any other Arab Government which intervened openly in defiance of the United Nations'.

The only conceivable way to avoid both dangers, in Pirie-Gordon's view, was for the Arab Legion to participate 'in the Arab resistance in Palestine, on the understanding that it would not itself transgress the frontiers drawn by the United Nations, but would collaborate with other Arab forces operating in the Jewish areas'. However,

> since it is impossible to suggest this course of action to the Transjordan Government, it is recommended that the Secretary of State should again speak on the lines of his message to King Abdullah, emphasizing the embarrassment which would be caused to His Majesty's Government if their ally, Transjordan,

were to fall foul of the United Nations, or to become isolated from the other Arab States, with all of whom we desire to be in close and friendly relations.[23]

In other words, both briefs advised Bevin against giving any encouragement to Transjordan's intervention in Mandatory Palestine, either in the Arab areas of the country or in its Jewish parts – advice followed orthodoxically by the Foreign Secretary.

Bevin, of course, needed no reminder from his subordinates of the difficulty of squaring the Transjordanian circle, as indicated by his inclination 'to leave this question over for decision in the light of all the circumstances at the time'.[24] Not that he had the slightest concern for Jewish interests, or for that matter for the aspirations of the Palestine Arabs, who at the time were admittedly far from being a cohesive national society: as early as July 1946 he had suggested to the Cabinet that most of the Arab areas of Palestine be assimilated in Transjordan and Lebanon.[25] Rather, Bevin was keen to avoid any damage to British interests which was bound to accrue in one form or another following Abdullah's intervention. 'For your own information', he wrote to Kirkbride less than a month before his meeting with Abul Huda,

> you should know that we hope (a) to see the trouble in Palestine localised and over as soon as possible; (b) that no situation will arise which might call for Security Council action (where it is very unlikely that

23 Christopher Pirie-Gordon, 'Palestine', 23 January 1948, FO 371/68817/E1458. In a report on a conversation with the Palestinian dignitary Musa Alami, B.A.B. Burrows, Head of the Eastern Department, wrote: 'Musa el-Alami thought it was just possible that an occupation of parts of Palestine by King Abdullah might be accepted by other Arabs, provided that he secured a considerable reduction of the Jewish areas as compared with the United Nations boundaries. If he merely occupied the Arab areas as defined by the United Nations he would be finished with the Arabs'. Burrows, 'Conversation with Musa el-Alami', 6 December 1947, FO 371/61585/E11764.

24 Bevin to Kirkbride, 11 December 1947, telegram 559, FO 816/111.

25 CAB 128/6, C.M. 67 (46), 11 July 1946.

we should feel able to use our veto to protect an Arab aggressor); (c) that King Abdullah will take no action that might isolate him from the other Arab States and thus give rise to the accusation that we are using him to engineer our re-entry into Palestine and to the possibility that he might unite the rest of the Arab world against him.

So far as we can see at present [Bevin continued], it should be possible to satisfy (a) & (b) above, if King Abdullah occupied certain Arab areas of Palestine and refrained from sending the Arab Legion into the areas allotted to the Jewish State by the United Nations. This would however not satisfy (c) above, and it is hardly possible at present to think of any course of action which would satisfy all three requirements.[26]

Contrary to Shlaim's claim, Bevin's meeting with Abul Huda did little to allay British concerns over these irreconcilable implications of Transjordan's intervention in Palestine. Minuting the Foreign Secretary's report of the conversation, Beeley found Abul Huda's admission of the importance of preventing Transjordan's isolation in the Arab world 'rather perfunctory'.[27] On 12 February, five days after the meeting, the British delegation to the United Nations cabled London for instructions. They had just been told by their American counterpart that Abdullah might absorb the Arab parts of Palestine not under the control of the Jewish State and that 'the idea has certain attractions for the American mind'. What would the Foreign Office like them to do? The reply was a near-verbatim reiteration of the dilemma expressed in Bevin's above letter to Kirkbride:

26   Bevin to Kirkbride, telegram 11 of 10 January 1948, FO 371/62226.
27   'Palestine: Transjordan Attitude', FO 371/68366/E1916.

For your own secret information, we too see certain
advantages in the idea, but there are also obvious and
important difficulties and dangers. The chief of these
is that it would be most embarrassing to us if Abdullah
either came into conflict with the United Nations or
took up an entirely isolated position in regard to the
other Arab States, *and it is rather difficult to see how he
can steer between these two dangers.*[28]

Nor did the British Cabinet ever discuss the Bevin–Abul Huda
conversation and its possible implications, let alone give its
blessing to the alleged Hashemite–Zionist deal to divide
Mandatory Palestine. Bevin circulated his detailed report on
the meeting among the Cabinet members, but never brought
it up for discussion. In the Cabinet meeting of 5 February, two
days before Bevin's meeting with Abul Huda, the ministers
weighed their response to UN requests for assistance in the
implementation of partition. This was the time and the place
for the Foreign Secretary to inform his colleagues of such an
important matter as the (alleged) Hashemite–Jewish agreement of November 1947, and to seek advice for his imminent
meeting with Abul Huda; yet there is no inkling in the minutes
to indicate that he did anything of the sort.[29] On 11 March 1948
the Cabinet approved Bevin's proposal 'to authorise our
representative at Amman to sign the revised Treaty of Alliance
between the United Kingdom and Transjordan';[30] the alleged
deal with Abul Huda was not mentioned.

It was only in its meeting of 22 March 1948 that the Cabinet
decided that 'although there should be no change in the date
(15th May) fixed for the surrender of the Mandate, the British
civil and military authorities in Palestine should make no
effort to oppose the setting up of a Jewish State or a move into

28 New York to Foreign Office, telegram 462 of 12 February 1948; Foreign Office to New
    York, telegram 816 of 21 February 1948, FO 371/68648/E2205/1048/c (emphasis added).
29 CAB, 128/12, CM(48), 12th Conclusions, 5 February 1948.
30 Ibid., 12th Conclusions, 11 March 1948, p. 146.

Palestine from Transjordan'. But this decision had nothing whatsoever to do with Bevin's (alleged) approval of the (alleged) Hashemite–Jewish deal. Rather, it reflected British fears of a sharp deterioration in the Middle East situation following the US Administration's withdrawal of support from partition and its suggestion that Palestine would be placed under international trusteeship. In the view of the British Cabinet, the American proposal was not only bound to be rejected by Arabs and Jews alike but 'it might well be that in the new situation the Jews would seek to establish a Jewish State covering such parts of the area allotted to them in the partition plan as they might reasonably expect to be able to defend; and the King of Transjordan might seek to assume control of other parts of Palestine'. Yet far from welcoming the king's intervention, the Cabinet deemed it as likely to 'stir up trouble among the other Arab States in addition to the disturbance which it would create in Palestine itself';[31] its decision not to resist this development by force of arms was therefore exclusively related to its eagerness to complete the British withdrawal from Palestine as quickly and painlessly as possible: not to its approval of a non-existent Hashemite–Jewish agreement on the partition of Palestine. As Sir Alan Cunningham bitterly put it to the Colonial Secretary, Arthur Creech-Jones: 'It appears to me that H.M.G.'s policy is now simply to get out of Palestine as quickly as possible without regard to the consequences in Palestine'.[32]

---

31   Ibid., 24th Conclusions, 22 March 1948.
32   Cunningham to Creech-Jones, 25 March 1948, telegram 761, Cunningham Papers, III/2. Turning the Cabinet's decision upside down Ilan Pappé writes: 'The cabinet in London, if somewhat late in the day, supported its representative in Palestine by deciding that it would oppose by force both a large-scale Arab intervention and a premature Jewish declaration of independence' (*The Making of the Arab-Israeli Conflict*, p. 100). It is not at all clear where Pappé has derived this bizarre misrepresentation: he gives no reference to any Cabinet meeting, only to a telegram by Cunningham to Creech-Jones which predates the Cabinet's decision by more than a month and which in any event does not address the possibility of an intervention in Palestine by Transjordan, let alone by other Arab States, but rather the incursion of 'armed and organised bands' into the country (4 February 1948, telegram 288, FO 371/68366/E1785). As we have just seen, both the Cabinet's decision and Cunningham's response were the complete opposite from that alleged by Pappé.

All this further underscores the absurdity of Shlaim's rewriting of Bevin's report of his meeting with Abul Huda on the basis of the old partisan account of the far-from-reliable Glubb Pasha. That Bevin did not encourage Abul Huda to invade the Arab areas of Mandatory Palestine indicates that he did not deem this to be 'the obvious thing to do'; that he failed to warn the Prime Minister against invading the Jewish areas proves that he did not preclude this course of action altogether. These abstentions reflected the Foreign Office's muddled and indecisive state of mind and their inability to determine which course of action was best for their client, and indeed for themselves – to limit Abdullah's intervention to the Arab parts of Palestine and let him be damned in Arab eyes for ever, or to encourage him to invade the Jewish areas and run the risk of a harsh international response.[33] Following the meeting the Foreign Office started to brace itself for both eventualities by simultaneously seeking the acquiescence of Abdullah's arch enemy, Ibn Saud, in Transjordan's occupation of the Arab parts of Palestine (however ill-defined), and of the US Administration in Transjordan's possible transgression of the UN assigned boundaries.[34]

Though no two historical events can be fully identical, the Bevin–Abul Huda meeting is strikingly reminiscent of the tragic conversation between the American Ambassador to Iraq, April Glaspie, and Iraq's President Saddam Hussein on 25 July 1990, shortly before Iraq's invasion of Kuwait. In both meetings the Middle Eastern interlocutors sought to harness great-power support to their political designs; and in both instances great-power failure to set clear limits to the small State's ambitions was interpreted by the latter as acquiescence in its position; only Glaspie did a good deal of (ill-conceived) talking while Bevin hardly said a word. Nevertheless, the end result of both

33 For a similar interpretation of the Bevin–Abul Huda meeting see Pundik, *The Struggle for Sovereignty*, pp. 74–5.
34 See, for example, the memorandum by B.A.B. Burrows, 9 February 1948, FO 371/68368/E296, approved by Bevin for discussion with the US Department of State.

meetings was identical: the indecisive great power found itself trailing the lead of the single-minded small power.

By reserving judgement on Abul Huda's ideas, in line with his advisers' recommendation, Bevin presumably hoped to keep British and Arab options open so as to allow them the greatest flexibility in accordance with the vicissitudes in the Palestine crisis. In fact his aloofness was construed by Abul Huda as acquiescence in his sovereign's territorial ambitions in Palestine, and not necessarily in the purely Arab areas. 'Today I had a personal meeting with Mr. Bevin in my capacity as Minister of Defence and pure military questions were discussed', he telegraphed home. 'I am very pleased at the results and am proud to say that it is due to His Majesty that these results have been attained'.[35]

In one important respect Abul Huda's upbeat mood was well-placed. Bevin had not warned him off any intervention in post-mandatory Palestine, thus tacitly condoning the use of violence by a key British Middle Eastern client. Since the British Foreign Secretary was not aware of any (non-existent) Hashemite–Jewish agreement to divide Palestine between themselves, his implicit approval of Transjordan's military foray into Palestine could not preclude the possibility of a direct confrontation between the two parties. Whether the British believed that this incursion was to be exclusively designed 'to prevent the Jews from occupying the whole of Palestine',[36] as Shlaim claims, or to expand Abdullah's kingdom at the Jews' expense, as contemporary British documents unequivocally show, Bevin's failure to dissuade Abul Huda from this option in the first place can by no stretch of imagination be considered 'indirect collusion' with the Zionist movement. Whatever 'collusion' Whitehall hatched with Abdullah, the Jewish Agency, and latterly the State of Israel, were not part of it.

35 Abul Huda (London) to the Rais of the Diwan (Amman), 8 February 1948, FO 816/112.
36 Shlaim, *Collusion*, p. 618.

THE WARNING THAT BEVIN NEVER GAVE

As we shall see in the next chapter, Bevin and his advisers were keen to reduce the size of the Jewish State well beyond that awarded to it by the UN Partition Resolution, *ipso facto* they could not care less whether or not Abdullah transgressed Jewish territory. Their main reason for avoiding a direct recommendation in this vein during the Bevin–Abul Huda meeting was the above-mentioned fear that this course of action would expose Abdullah to harsh international retaliation that would greatly embarrass Britain on account of its Treaty of Alliance with Transjordan. Were a way to neutralize this risk to be found, Whitehall had nothing against the occupation of Jewish territory by the Arab States, first and foremost Transjordan.

As early as 11 November 1947, Bevin saw the main attraction of the possible annexation of the Arab parts of Mandatory Palestine to Transjordan in the 'probability that in virtue of the Anglo–Transjordan Treaty we should maintain our strategic facilities in a fairly large part of Palestine *including presumably an outlet to the Mediterranean*' (i.e., keeping the Negev outside the territory of the prospective Jewish State).[37] And while this view was expressed shortly before the passing of the UN Partition Resolution, when the territory of this state had not yet been defined, there is little doubt that it guided Bevin's tacit approval of Transjordan's intervention in

---

37 Bevin to Kirkbride, 11 November 1947, telegram 493, FO 816/89 (emphasis added). Another potential advantage of this suggestion, according to Bevin, was that 'it would provide the only way of avoiding major bloodshed in Palestine on our withdrawal (on the assumption that King Abdullah would reach prior agreement with the Jews before entering Palestine)' (Kirkbride, as we have already seen, was vehemently opposed to such an agrement). In contrast, the disadvantages of such a scheme were as follows: '(a) The existence of a Jewish State with presumably unlimited immigration would be a factor of instability leading sooner or later to trouble with the neighbouring Arab States; (b) some if not all of the other Arab States would presumably be violently incensed against King Abdullah (this might however have the countervailing advantage of making him more dependent upon us); (c) we should be thought to have engineered the whole scheme and to have merely pretended to evacuate Palestine in order to secure our military requirements there'.

Palestine after the British departure, irrespective of the boundaries set by the United Nations. On 7 February 1948, just after his conversation with Abul Huda, Bevin spoke to his advisers on the possible entry of Transjordanian forces into the Arab areas of Palestine, following which B.A.B. Burrows, Head of the Eastern Department, circulated a top secret memorandum. 'It is tempting to think that Transjordan might *transgress the boundaries of the United Nations Jewish State* to the extent of establishing a corridor across the Southern Negeb [i.e., Negev] joining the existing Transjordan territory to the Mediterranean and Gaza', he wrote:

> This would have immense strategic advantages for us, both in cutting the Jewish State, and therefore Communist influence, off from the Red Sea and by extending up to the Mediterranean the area in which our military and political influence is predominant by providing a means of sending necessary military equipment etc. into Transjordan other than by the circuitous route through Aqaba. It would of course be infinitely more difficult to obtain Jewish agreement for a move of this kind than for the occupation of United Nations Arab areas by the Arab Legion, which the Jews would probably welcome. The Jews would probably be to some extent satisfied if they received compensation in W. Galilee – but this raises almost insuperable difficulties on the Arab side.[38]

This memorandum, the substance of which was amenable to Bevin, proves beyond a shadow of doubt that the Foreign Secretary could not have unequivocally warned Abul Huda not to invade the Jewish areas of Mandatory Palestine (as indeed he did not) for the simple reason that he was perfectly prepared to see a significant transgression of the boundaries

---

38 Memorandum by B.A.B. Burrows, 9 February 1948, FO 371/68368/E296 (emphasis added).

of the prospective Jewish State as set by the United Nations.[39] So were his advisers. 'Whatever method is adopted by the Arabs [to abort the UN Partition Resolution], it is likely to result in a form of partition less favourable to the Jews than that proposed by the General Assembly', wrote Harold Beeley in December 1947. 'It is not clear that one form of partition would be more or less advantageous from the point of view of British interests than another. But our interests in the Middle East generally certainly make it inadvisable for us to play any part in preventing the Arabs from obtaining a settlement in Palestine more satisfactory to themselves than that proposed by the United Nations'.[40] Within this context Beeley, perhaps the most sceptical among Bevin's advisers regarding the prudence of Abdullah's occupation of the Arab parts of Mandatory Palestine, was perfectly disposed to the Legion's encroachment on Jewish territory. 'As in earlier telegrams it is not clear what Samir Pasha means by the "Arab area" and the "Jewish area"', he minuted on a conversation between the Transjordanian Prime Minister and Brigadier Clayton on the possibility of Transjordan's intervention in Palestine. 'In a period of one or two years the Jews are likely to grow stronger, and the Arab Legion would probably find it advisable to extend their occupation at the outset into part of the proposed Jewish State.'[41] And M.T. Walker of the Eastern Department, commenting on the same conversation, was equally prepared to violate the boundaries of the UN-proposed Jewish State. 'I can see no possible means of filling

39   Apparently referring to this memorandum, Bullock writes that 'In a note of 9 February 1948 Bevin is reported as speculating on the strategic advantages to Britain if a corridor could be maintained across the Negev providing direct communication from the Mediterranean at Gaza to Transjordan and the oilfields in Iraq and Iran'. Yet he fails to acknowledge that this suggestion involves the *conscious* transgression of the boundaries of the United Nations Jewish State in a major way (i.e., the severance of the Negev from its territory), which, in turn, casts serious doubt on Glubb's account of the Bevin–Abul Huda meeting to which Bullock subscribes. Bullock, *Ernest Bevin*, p. 509.

40   Harold Beeley, 'Possible Forms of Arab Resistance to the Decision of the United Nations', 22 December 1947, FO 371/68364/E11504.

41   'Relations Between H.M.G. and Transjordan', comments by Bevin's advisers on Clayton's conversation with Samir Pasha on 11 December 1948 (Cairo telegram 67 of 12 December 1948), FO 371/62226/E11928.

the vacuum in the large Arab area of Palestine, including the Negeb except the Arab Legion', he wrote.[42]

In fact Walker was far more 'generous' than that. Following the Bevin–Abul Huda meeting he was willing to avail parts of Mandatory Palestine to *other* Arab States apart from Transjordan. 'It is obvious that the Arab Legion cannot hope to control all the Arab areas', he minuted. 'The assistance of Iraq and Syria would therefore be essential and the northern areas of Palestine might well be their responsibility'.[43] That he did not view the 'Arab areas of Palestine' as necessarily identical to those laid down by the United Nations is borne out by a later memorandum by him: 'I think from the talk with the Transjordan Prime Minister recorded in E1916/11/G that King Abdullah is determined to acquire the Arab areas of Palestine, *either as defined by the United Nations or those areas with an Arab majority, except perhaps the north-west corner.* Whatever reason may be given for the return of the Arab Legion to Palestine, the ultimate intention will be to obtain new territory for King Abdullah'.[44]

The lack of any Anglo–Transjordanian understanding not to invade the Jewish areas of Palestine is also evidenced from contemporary British correspondence. The Foreign Office files burst at the seams with traffic between Whitehall and its legations in the Middle East and the United States, not to mention countless internal memoranda and working papers, indicating not only that British foreign policy officials had no clue of Abdullah's real intentions after the termination of the

42 Ibid.
43 Comments by foreign policy officials on telegram 90 from Kirkbride, dated 13 February 1948 on 'Plans for Transjordan Occupation of Arab Parts of Palestine', FO 371/68367/E2163/G. In his telegram Kirkbride reported that 'of late, King Abdullah has been talking loosely about assuming the duty of protecting the Holy Places of Jerusalem after the termination of the Mandate until some other arrangement is made'. Yet he believed that this intention, which ran counter to the UN Partition Resolution which had provided for the internationalization of Jerusalem, 'should not be taken seriously if reported, as strength of Arab Legion is quite inadequate for such a task in addition to other commitments in Arab areas'. Kirkbride was of course completely wrong.
44 M.T. Walker, 'Arab Legion after May 15th', FO 371/38366/E1916/G, 3 March 1948 (emphasis added).

Palestine Mandate on 15 May 1948, but that they clearly envisaged, if not expected and welcomed, Transjordan's infringement of the prospective Jewish State.

'We shall be grateful for up to date appreciation of King Abdullah's intentions with regard to Palestine', the Foreign Office cabled Kirkbride on 10 April. 'Do you think that he still proposes to send the Arab Legion into Palestine after the 15th May? Has he any understanding on this subject with the Committee of the Arab League which is directing opera-tions in Palestine?'[45] Kirkbride's reply was not much better informed. 'As far as I am aware the intentions of the Trans-jordanian authorities with regard to the Arab area adjacent to Palestine after 15th May are unchanged but plans for their execution are still somewhat fluid', he cabled London on 13 April:

> General idea seems to be to establish units of Arab Legion at Hebron, Ramallah and Nablus as a first step, and then to decide further moves in the light of events. It is realised that Jerusalem presents too big a problem for the Arab Legion to deal with alone, and that Galilee is too remote with communications through a Jewish area ... Present intention is to avoid a clash with the Jews but whether or not this will be possible remains to be seen.[46]

As late as 8 May, a week before the Arab States' attack on the newly born State of Israel, Kirkbride still deemed the occu-pation of the Arab areas of Palestine and the exclusion of Jerusalem from the fighting to be Transjordan's most probable course of action; he did not rule out the possibility of 'open warfare between the Jews and regular Arab forces' but believed that this may be reduced to 'minor incidents or clashes' in the Arab areas. His greatest fear, though, was 'that

45   Foreign Office to Amman, 10 April 1948, telegram 220, FO 371/68852/E4625.
46   Amman to Foreign Office, 13 April 1948, telegrams 224 & 225, FO 371/68852/E4681 & FO 371/68852/4687.

some unforeseen incident will at the crucial moment bring about a general battle which neither side wants'.[47]

Two conclusions can be drawn from Kirkbride's cables. First, for all his intimacy and influence with Abdullah he failed to grasp the essence of the king's intentions: Jerusalem was Abdullah's primary political-strategic target – not 'too big a problem' that had to be avoided like wild fire. Second, while emphasizing Abdullah's intention 'to avoid a clash with the Jews', Kirkbride dismissed neither such an eventuality nor the possibility of the Arab Legion taking 'further moves in the light of events', namely transgressing Jewish territory. Indeed Lancelot Pyman, Assistant Head of the Eastern Department, was sufficiently alarmed by Kirkbride's reply to suggest that the cable should not be distributed outside the Foreign Office.

Sir Alan Cunningham, the British High Commissioner for Palestine, was not much better informed than Kirkbride. 'A good Arab source', he reported on 20 April, 'states that King Abdullah affirmed that he had decided on military intervention in Palestine with the entire Arab Legion immediately after 15th May. First objective would be firmly to secure Haifa, Jaffa and Gaza. He intended to approach G.O.C. [General Commanding Officer] so as to ensure that there would be no clash with British troops'.[48]

Notwithstanding their ignorance of the real thrust of Abdullah's plans, Kirkbride's and Cunningham's assessment that the Arab Legion might well come to blows with the Jews and, moreover, might invade the prospective Jewish State, was widely shared by the Eastern Department. 'On current form it seems reasonable to assume', read a memorandum of 3 May 1948 to the British delegation in the United Nations,

... that on the 16th a Jewish State in Palestine will be

47   Amman to Foreign Office, 8 May 1948, telegram 302, FO 371/68852/E6008.
48   From Palestine (Gen. Sir Alan Cunningham) to the Secretary of State for the Colonies, FO 371/68852/E5167.

proclaimed by certain Jews and an Arab State in Palestine will be proclaimed by certain Arabs.

It may then happen that the so-called Arab State will invite the Transjordan Government to send members of the Arab Legion into the part of the territory which is now known as Palestine. Or that Transjordanians may just send them in without any invitation. It is probable that in the first place these troops would come into that part of Palestine granted to the proposed Arab State by the United Nations Assembly. *Subsequently, however, they might move into territory designated by the United Nations Assembly as belonging to the Jewish State.*

Fighting between the Arab Legion and Jews could thus take place in one of several ways:

(a) On territory which according to the Assembly should belong to the United Nations Arab State or

(b) *On territory belonging to the United Nations Jewish State.*[49]

That the Foreign Office anticipated a Transjordanian invasion of the Jewish State was also evidenced by its hectic search for ways and means to deflect the barrage of international criticism that was bound to be levelled at Britain due to its treaty relationship with Transjordan and its pervasive involvement with the Arab Legion in the form of both an annual subsidy and the deployment of British officers throughout the Legion's various echelons. Indeed, the Jewish Agency was quick to point out that, due to its treaty relations with Britain,

---

49   Draft memorandum to the British UN delegation as telegram 1323, 3 May 1948, FO 371/68852/E5523 (emphasis added).

Transjordan could not undertake offensive operations outside its own territory without consulting its ally.

It was not long before a 'magic formula' was devised to counter this accusation and to lay the legal ground for a Transjordanian, indeed an all-Arab attack on the prospective Jewish State. First, it was argued that

> Though H.B.M. is obliged under the Treaty of Alliance to give H.M. The King of Transjordan certain assistance as regards the Arab Legion, the Legion is in fact a Transjordan force and exclusively under Transjordan control. Therefore, though the spirit of the Treaty may require that Transjordan shall not engage in any hostilities, aggressive or defensive, without consulting the United Kingdom, if it does engage in hostilities, the United Kingdom cannot necessarily be held to have any responsibility.[50]

Second, and far more importantly, it was claimed that 'the United Nations Resolution of November 29th did not set up Jewish and Arab States. Various steps had first to be taken by United Nations Commission and provisional governments. Very few of these have been taken. The Jewish claim to United Nations authority for their state is therefore invalid'. This, in turn, would leave post-Mandatory Palestine as 'a sort of *res nullius*' with the following twin implications:

> a) 'Until H.M.G. recognize the Jewish "state", Article 2 of the Treaty of Alliance with Transjordan is not applicable to any hostilities between Transjordan and forces or individuals belonging to her'.

> b) 'An invasion by Arab armies without coming into conflict with the Jews is not necessarily illegal or contrary to the United Nations Charter. If these

50   Ibid.

armies cross the frontier recommended for the Jewish State in the United Nations Assembly Resolution of November 29th they would not *ipso facto* be doing anything illegal ...'

Put in a somewhat different form, this argument not only anticipated and justified an Arab attack on the prospective Jewish State but effectively invited such a move: 'If the United Nations took no further action, the people of Palestine would themselves be the only authority capable of determining their country's future when the Mandate came to an end. In these circumstances, the Jewish population of Palestine would no doubt have a right to try to establish a state in part of the country. But this right would be no better than the right of the Arabs to invite the intervention of the Arab League. The two actions would be legally on an equal footing'.[51]

Given that it was none other than the British Government that had prevented the United Nations Commission from taking those 'various steps' which, if taken, would have validated 'the Jewish claim to United Nations authority for their state', this legal sophistry anticipated, if not sanctioned, an Arab (including Transjordanian) attack on the Jewish State. Indeed, the invading Arab States lost no time in parroting Whitehall's 'legal' argument. 'There was no State there [i.e., in Palestine] recognized by any other State and there was no legal successor to the Mandatory Power', the Egyptian Prime Minister said in justifying his country's attack on Israel.[52]

As late as 14 May, a day before the Arab attack on Israel, Bevin cabled Kirkbride, clearly anticipating Transjordan's transgression of the boundaries of the newly-established State:

---

51   Ibid.; 'Palestine – Legal Position', Confidential Guidance prepared by the Information Office, British Embassy in Washington, 20 May 1948. FO 371/68651; Beeley (New York) to Burrows, 3 May 1948, FO 371/68554/E6677.
52   *Al-Sharq al-Adna* in Arabic, 17 May 1948, 'BBC Monitoring Service – Summary of World Broadcasts', III, No. 52, 27 May 1948, p. 56.

I agree that we should not order withdrawal of regular British Army officers unless and until hostilities
between Transjordan and a Jewish State break out as
a result of a Transjordanian attack on the Jewish State
within its frontiers as laid down by the Assembly. If
hostilities break out in this way, you should at once
instruct all such officers to withdraw from and remain
outside Palestine.[53]

And by way of providing further proof that Bevin never told
Abul Huda not to invade the Jewish areas – if such proof is at
all needed at this stage – let me conclude this chapter with
B.A.B. Burrows's memorandum of 7 May titled 'Palestine
After May 14'. In this memorandum Burrows assessed that

the Arab Legion would enter Palestine mainly by the
Allenby Bridge, and would attempt to occupy the
Nablus, Ramallah and Hebron areas, perhaps including Beersheba and perhaps *extending across the
southern Jewish area to Gaza* [thus severing the Negev
from the Jewish State] if the Egyptian Army had not
moved in there. *They would also no doubt secure the
narrow strip of Palestinian territory on the Gulf of Aqaba*
[awarded by the General Assembly to the Jewish
State].

It seems impossible at present to look much further
ahead. The Arab Legion could probably hold the
central Arab area fairly comfortably but might get
into considerable difficulty if it tried to do more than
this, e.g., an expedition to Jaffa or Haifa.

53 Foreign Office to Amman, 14 May 1948, telegram 382, FO 371/68852/E6327. See also M.T.
Walker's memo of 11 May on 'British Officers in the Arab Legion', anticipating a
Transjordanian attack on the Jewish State: 'We should arrange with Sir A. Kirkbride,
however, that in the event of a Transjordanian attack on the Jewish State, instructions
for the withdrawal of British officers should reach them with the least possible delay'.
FO 371/68852/E6008.

In these circumstances Burrows offered the following advice: 'tell King Abdullah very confidentially that if he feels bound to go into Palestine, we hope for his own sake and also in order to facilitate the maintenance of our close relations with him, that his forces will not go beyond clearly Arab areas and will not attack existing Jewish settlements or villages'. 'The critical point in this is what is the definition of "purely Arab areas"'. Burrows put his finger on the question to which the Foreign Office had not found an unequivocal answer during all these fateful months. He assumed that 'it is difficult to avoid suggesting that this should be interpreted for present purposes as meaning the "United Nations Arab State"'; however, he felt that *'we could in practice presumably not object to Arab Legion occupation of the Nejeb* [i.e., Negev]'.[54]

The importance of this memorandum cannot be overstated. A week before the Arab invasion of the newly established State of Israel, the Head of the Foreign Office's Eastern Department not only anticipated Transjordan's violation of Jewish territory but effectively suggested intimating to Abdullah that he occupy about half of this State, thus depriving it of a vital strategic hinterland and mortally wounding its trade and economic relations with Africa and Central and Eastern Asia. And he made this recommendation with the clear knowledge that it would be well received in Amman. As early as January 1948 King Abdullah told Kirkbride that 'he could not possibly agree to the Jewish State having access to the gulf of Aqaba and so cutting off Transjordan from Egypt'.[55]

54 B.A.B. Burrows, 'Palestine After May 14', 7 May 1948, FO 371/68554/E6778.
55 Kirkbride to Bevin, 12 January 1948, telegram 9, FO 816/115.

5 Bevin and the Jews: Guardian Angel or Nemesis?

> Harry: Men and women cannot be friends because the sex part always gets in the way.
>
> Sally: That's not true, I have a number of men friends and there is no sex involved.
>
> Harry: No you don't.
>
> Sally: Yes I do.
>
> Harry: You only think you do.
>
> Sally: You say I'm having sex with these men without my knowledge?
>
> Harry: No. What I'm saying is that they want to have sex with you.
>
> NORA EPHRON/ROB REINER,
> *When Harry Met Sally*

This dialogue from the famous 1980s film encapsulates Shlaim's and Pappé's thesis of Bevin's relations with the Zionist movement, and latterly the nascent State of Israel. For contemporary Jewish leaders Bevin and his advisers were implacable enemies, and vice versa; to Shlaim and Pappé they were all bosom friends without their own knowledge. The Zionist leaders deemed Britain's Palestine policy towards the end of the Mandate as highly detrimental to the Jewish national cause: its vehement opposition to partition (the Zionist objective for quite some time) and its relentless refusal to help the implementation of the UN Partition Resolution;[1] its prevention of Jewish immigration, the elixir of life of the Jewish State-to-be, up to the latest stages of the British presence in Palestine; its detention of dozens of thousands of Holocaust survivors in concentration camps in Cyprus, including the illegal retention of some 9,000 'able-bodied' men for nine months after the establishment of the State of Israel to prevent their possible participation in the ongoing war; its supply of weapons and technical/advisory services to the Arab armies and its lax attitude towards the flow of weapons from the neighbouring Arab States into Palestine, coupled with a tight naval blockade aimed at preventing the arrival of weapons for the Jews; its non-recognition of the newly-established State of Israel for some nine months and its vehement opposition to Israel's admission to the United Nations, etc. etc..

To Shlaim all these grave actions seem trivial compared with Bevin's alleged 'indirect collusion' with the Zionist movement to divide Palestine between Transjordan and the Jews. 'Zionist historiography, reflecting the suspicions of Zionist leaders at that time, is laden with charges of hostile plots that are alleged to have been hatched against the Yishuv during the twilight of British rule in Palestine', he writes. 'The

---

1   Within this framework, the British Cabinet prevented the United Nations Palestine Commission (UNPC), tasked with ensuring Palestine's smooth transition to independence, from entering the country in February 1948, as stipulated by the UN Partition Resolution; nor did they acquiesce in the Commission's request for a month 'overlap' with the British administration, driving the UN to condemn British policy as 'bordering on obstruction'. No less importantly, the British authorities failed to comply with the demand of the UN Partition Resolution 'that the Mandatory Power shall use its best endeavour to ensure that an area situated in the territory of the Jewish State, including a seaport and hinterland adequate to provide facilities for a substantial immigration, shall be evacuated at the earliest possible date and in any event not later than 1 February 1948'. Similarly the British obstructed the Jewish proposal for the deployment of an international force in Palestine to administer the country's peaceful transition to independence.

Having done all this, the Foreign Office developed the duplicitous argument that since the UN had not taken all the measures required by the UN Partition Resolution, the proclamation of the State of Israel on 14 May 1948 was not legally binding according to international law; *ipso facto*, its invasion was not an illegal act.

For the text of the UN Partition Resolution see Walter Laqueur, ed., *The Israel–Arab Reader* (New York: Bantam, 1968), pp. 113–22.

central charge is that Britain armed and secretly encouraged her Arab allies, and especially her client, King Abdullah of [Trans]jordan, to invade Palestine upon expiry of the British Mandate and do battle with the Jewish State as soon as it came into the world'. In his view, this charge 'represents almost the exact opposite of the historical truth as it emerges from the British, Arab, and Israeli documents'.[2] Far from being 'the great ogre who unleashed the Arab armies to strangle the Jewish State at birth', Bevin 'emerges from the documents as the guardian angel of the infant state'.[3]

This is probably the most preposterous of Shlaim's (mis)claims. It is also one which the Foreign Secretary himself would have most emphatically disputed. If anything, it is this claim that 'represents the exact opposite of the historical truth as it emerges from the British, Arab, and Israeli documents'. Shlaim has not produced a single document proving the slightest intention on the part of Bevin and his advisers to act as 'guardian angels of the Jewish State'. The only piece of 'evidence' on which he has built his house of cards is the account of the Bevin–Abul Huda meeting, the contents of which, as we have already seen, have grossly been misrepresented by Shlaim. Shlaim must have gone through the British archives with a fine-tooth comb to produce the odd document proving Bevin's favourable disposition to the Jewish cause, resisting the temptation to succumb to the overwhelming evidence to the contrary; still he has come away with practically nothing to substantiate his misconceived claim.

Moreover Shlaim cites no works of the 'Zionist historiography' claiming that Britain 'unleashed the Arab armies to strangle the Jewish State at birth'; and for a very good reason. For this 'official Zionist line' is nothing but a bogey created by the 'new historians' to facilitate their historical fabrication; in this particular instance, of Britain's Palestine policy in the twilight of the Mandate.

---

2 Shlaim, 'The Debate', pp. 292–3.   3 Shlaim, *Collusion*, p. 618.

It is true that as the expiry of the Mandate loomed large, both Jews and Arabs feared British 'dirty tricks' that would allow the declining empire to maintain some future presence in Palestine in one form or another (fears that were not wholly ungrounded, as we shall see shortly). But even then, there was no blanket 'Zionist' demonization of British policy, let alone in the vein suggested by Shlaim. 'It is no secret that [Abdullah] will look for an opening to grab off the Arab part of Palestine, and is in a strong position because of the Arab Legion', Michael Comay of the Jewish Agency delegation to the UN General Assembly wrote to a Zionist activist in Johannesburg on 3 December 1947. 'The British would, I believe, welcome this because of their military pact with Abdullah, and because the Mufti is as bitterly hostile to them as he was to us'.[4] And David Ben-Gurion had a similarly cool-headed view of British intentions. 'I find it difficult to form an accurate assessment of the [British] Government's position', he wrote Sharett on 14 December 1947:

> It seems to me that there is a tension between emotions and political aims: on the one hand, there is a wish (and an international need) to prove that as long as they are here – they enforce law and order and are in charge of security. On the other hand, they wish to be 'neutral' vis-à-vis Arabs and Jews – and they always put both of them on a par. From a third angle, there is anger over our defiance, over the blood of the murdered soldiers and policemen, and over our lack of cooperation with the Government (among many of them this is not sheer anger but rather burning hatred). From yet another direction, there would seem to be an ostensible wish for reconciliation with us before they depart. Many [Jews] think that there are also conspiracies – to turn the UN

4   Comay to B. Gering (Johannesburg), 3 December 1947, *Teudot*, p. 13.

[Partition] Resolution to a Morrison [provincial autonomy] plan, to prevent the establishment of a Jewish State, to foment disorder etc. *I cannot swear that there are no 'conspiracies' somewhere – but I do not believe very much in their existence.*[5]

Given such realistic and dispassionate appreciations of British behaviour by contemporary Zionist officials, it is scarcely surprising that writings of later Israeli historians are light years apart from the above caricature of 'Zionist historiography' invented by Shlaim. Take, for example, a 1985 essay by Gabriel Cohen of Tel-Aviv University, which paints a complex and multifaceted picture of the policy of the British during the last days of the Mandate.[6] In Shlaim's view, Cohen is a pioneer in 'revising the conventional Zionist view of British policy toward the end of the Palestine Mandate';[7] but the indisputable fact remains that Gabriel Cohen is the epitome of the 'old Zionist historian': a member the '1948 Generation' who fought for Israel's independence; Head of the History Branch of the Israel Defence Forces (IDF); founder of the Institute for the Study of Zionism at Tel-Aviv University; and a Professor of Jewish history at Tel-Aviv University. Moreover, the inclusion of Cohen's essay in a volume edited by another 'old' historian under the quintessential 'Zionist' title *Hayinu Ke-holmim*, 'We Were as Dreamers', and the use of the term 'The War of Independence' in Cohen's own title, rather than such 'politically correct' terms as the 'Palestine War', or the '1948 War', indicate Cohen's general 'Zionist' outlook. This proves once again that there is no such thing as 'Zionist historiography': only writings by Israeli historians of various colours and convictions; and that the only criteria for categorizing members of this variegated group as 'new' or

---

5 Ben-Gurion to Sharett, 14 December 1947, Ibid., pp. 60–1 (emphasis added).
6 Gabriel Cohen, 'British Policy on the Eve of the War of Independence', in Yehuda Wallach, ed., *Hayinu Ke-holmim: Kovetz Mehkarim al Milhemet Ha-komemiut* (We Were as Dreamers: Essays on the War of Independence) (Tel-Aviv: Masada, 1985), pp. 13–179.
7 Shlaim, 'The Debate', p. 289.

'old' historians is the conformity of their views to those of Shlaim, Pappé, Morris and Co.

Needless to say, Gabriel Cohen is neither the first nor the last person to have defied the bogus perception of British policy attributed by Shlaim to Israeli and pro-Israeli writers. 'So far as we could establish from extensive enquiries among all those intimately concerned, there was at no stage a formal arrangement between the British and the Arab leaders about the precise details of what should happen on the morrow of the British withdrawal', wrote Jon and David Kimche some four decades ago, long before the release of the relevant British documents. 'The only agreed and officially admitted arrangement was that King Abdullah of Transjordan should occupy those parts of Palestine not allocated to Israel'. But this, in their view, did not imply British goading of Transjordan against the Jews. On the contrary,

> the evidence of his military and political advisers, especially Glubb and Kirkbride, make it clear that Abdullah was not acting as a pawn for the British. If anything, he was setting the pace and taking the initiative for his own ends. But his ends also suited the British and he was not obstructed by them. In fact, it would be safe to conclude that he received a good deal of encouragement – at least unofficially – as well as quite official military and economic aid.[8]

Sounds familiar? No doubt, for this is but a milder version of Shlaim's claim that Bevin 'colluded directly with the Transjordanians ... to abort the birth of a Palestinian Arab state' and Pappé's thesis that 'the Anglo–Transjordanian understanding of the best solution for the question of post-mandatory Palestine served as the main guideline for the British policy towards the Arab–Israeli conflict in the years 1948–51'.[9] But

8   Jon and David Kimche, *Both Sides*, pp. 39, 60.
9   Pappé, *Britain and the Arab–Israeli Conflict*, p. 209 (see also pp. viii–ix).

while these 'old' and 'new' historians fully agree that the British 'colluded' with Abdullah with a view of expanding his kingdom, they strongly diverge on the consequences of this policy for Jewish national aspirations. In Shlaim's view, Bevin's direct 'collusion' with Abdullah was tantamount to 'indirect collusion' with the Zionist movement, though he contradicts himself by claiming that 'the point of the [Anglo-Hashemite] agreement was ... to prevent the Jews from occupying the whole of Palestine';[10] in the Kimches' opinion Israel was intended to be the victim of the Transjordanian intervention – not its beneficiary.

On the basis of their talks with contemporary British foreign policy officials they concluded that

> It was understood by Bevin's advisers that an arrange-
> ment had been reached with King Abdullah which
> provided that some areas allotted to the Jews would
> be occupied by the Arab Legion and that, as a result
> of any fighting, there would be a much smaller
> Jewish State than the United Nations had recom-
> mended. This rump of a state would then probably
> seek the protection of the British for an arrangement
> with its Arab neighbours. These plans for the morrow
> centred essentially on the future of Haifa, but they
> never achieved firm translation into either an
> agreement with Abdullah or an orderly, worked-out
> plan.[11]

Richard Crossman, Bevin's toughest critic within the Labour Party, found the Kimches' indictment of British policy 'all the more damning because it is so restrained'. In his view

> Once it had been decided ... to end the Mandate, Bevin's
> aim, apparently, was to ensure that Abdullah's Arab

10   Shlaim, *Collusion*, p. 618.
11   Kimche and Kimche, *Both Sides*, p. 39. See also p. 113.

Legion should overrun most of Palestine, leaving a
rump Jewish State, so weak that it would have to
throw itself on the mercy of the British Government.
This aim was so shameful that it was never revealed
to the Cabinet and so could not be expressed in clear
directives to the men on the spot. Hence the dreadful
impression of weakness and indecision, combined
with malignant anti-Jewish prejudice which charac-
terized British policy throughout. No wonder some
of our generals – Stockwell, for example, in Haifa –
were driven out by outraged decency to take independent decisions, which frustrated Bevin's aim and
in part saved the honour of Britain.[12]

In other words, neither the Kimches nor even Crossman have
argued that Britain sought to abort the establishment of a
Jewish State, let alone to unleash the Arab armies against the
newly-born State of Israel, as falsely attributed to 'Zionist'
writers by Shlaim. Only that Bevin and his advisers viewed
Abdullah as a key element of their Middle Eastern strategy;
that they were keen to see his kingdom expanded; and that
this territorial expansion was liable to come at the expense of
the Jews – not to their advantage.[13]

William Roger Louis states that 'the Kimches and
Crossman smelt the blood of British imperialism, but the scent
led them to conclusions that cannot be sustained by the
evidence', yet he concedes that following the Arab invasion
of the newly established State of Israel on 15 May 1948 'British
policy aimed at detaching the Negev in order to provide a
common frontier between Transjordan and Egypt. In this
sense there was truth in the charge that the British intended
to reduce the new Jewish State to a "rump"'.[14] Moreover Louis
reckons that 'it is clear from Foreign Office records as well as

12   'The Arab–Israeli War', review of *Both Sides*, *New Statesman*, 23 July 1960, p. 128.
13   See also Sharef, *Three Days*, p. 76.
14   Louis, *The British Empire*, pp. 372, 376.

from Glubb's published account [of the Bevin–Abul Huda meeting] that certain things were of such a sensitive and secret nature that Bevin did not wish to have them recorded'.[15] This in turn means, if one is to believe the veracity of Glubb's account, as Louis unquestioningly does,[16] that Bevin deliberately misled the Cabinet by giving it a false report of this conversation. But this is precisely the substance of Crossman's claim that Bevin's real agenda was 'so shameful that it was never revealed to the Cabinet and so could not be expressed in clear directives to the men on the spot'.[17] Only Crossman calls a spade a spade while Louis stops short of spelling out this self-evident conclusion.

But leaving aside the conspiratorial theories by both 'new' and 'old' historians, a serious examination of the newly released official British documents would easily reveal that:

a) Bevin and his advisers would rather not have seen an independent Jewish State in part of Mandatory Palestine; hence their vehement opposition to the idea of partition.

b) Having realized their inability to prevent partition, the Foreign Office wished to see a far smaller and weaker Jewish State than that envisaged by the UN Partition Resolution and did their utmost to bring about such an eventuality, despite their keen awareness that such a minuscule state would scarcely be viable. In fact they went so far as to try to forestall a separate Israeli–Transjordanian peace agreement which did not include the detachment of the Negev from the Israeli state.

c) The Foreign Office, indeed the British Cabinet, viewed Jewish national aspirations as detrimental to British imperial interests, and the Zionist movement as the 'bad guys' that had to be restrained – not as 'indirect accomplices'.

15   Ibid., p. 372.
16   Ibid.
17   *New Statesman*, 23 July 1960, p. 128.

BRITAIN'S QUEST FOR 'SMALLER ISRAEL'

Contrary to Louis's claim, British interest in the detachment of the Negev (or for that matter of any other parts of Mandatory Palestine) from the Jewish State *was not* an opportunistic response to the Arab attack on Israel in May 1948; rather, as shown in the previous chapter, it was the key component of British political and strategic thinking on Palestine's future at least since the country's partition by the United Nations became a distinct possibility. Suffice it to recall Burrows' suggestion of 7 May 1948 that the Foreign Office should intimate to Abdullah their acquiescence in his occupation of the Negev in order to see that Britain wished the soon-to-be-born Jewish State no good.

The war was seen by the Foreign Office as a golden opportunity to undo the UN Partition Resolution and 'cut Israel down to size'. On 20 May 1948, five days after the Arab invasion of the newly established State of Israel, Bevin wrote to the British Ambassador in Washington, Lord Inverchapel: 'I do not (repeat not) intend in the near future to recognize the Jewish State and still less to support any proposal that it should become a member of the United Nations. In this connexion I hope that even though the Americans have recognized the Jewish State *de facto* they will not commit themselves to any precise recognition of boundaries. It might well be that if the two sides ever accept a compromise it would be on the basis of boundaries differing from those recommended in the Partition Plan of the General Assembly.'[18]

That these border revisions were not conceived in terms favourable to the Jewish State was evidenced by the tireless British efforts to induce the UN Mediator, Count Folke Bernadotte, who arrived in the Middle East at the end of May 1948, to devise a solution that would reduce Israel to approximately the same size as that envisaged by the 1937 Peel Partition Plan –

18   Bevin to Lord Inverchapel, PREM 8/859, II, telegram 5459 of 20 May 1948.

about half the size allotted to the Jewish State by the 1947 UN Partition Resolution. This included *inter alia* the surrender of the Negev to Transjordan and Egypt, with all its attendant detrimental consequences for Israel's strategic and economic interests;[19] the prevention of a Jewish land corridor between the coastal plain and Jerusalem; the surrender of some territory in the eastern Galilee to Syria;[20] and the creation of a substantial ex-territorial enclave in the Haifa harbour that would serve as a 'free port' for the use of the Arab and the Western countries under the control of the UN Port Commissioner.

Apart from seriously restricting Israel's use of its primary naval outlet and expropriating some of its vital economic assets such as the oil refineries, the 'free port' plan (to which the Kimche brothers alluded) was bound to infringe on Israeli sovereignty and to constrain its transport system in another important respect by assigning agreed facilities 'for the movement of sealed trains and of transfer on specified roads between the free port and the neighbouring Arab countries including Iraq'. In other words, Israel was to avail its primary port, vital economic installations and national transport infrastructure to the strategic and economic needs of its enemies.[21]

19 For example, in a meeting with the US Ambassador to London on 25 May 1948 Bevin said, *inter alia*, that 'the inclusion of Gaza and the Negeb in the Jewish State had been a terrible mistake as there were no Jews there, and this must be righted'. 'Record of Meeting with the U.S. Ambassador to Discuss the Palestine Situation', 25 May 1948, FO 800/487.

20 On 11 September 1948 the British *chargé d'affaires* in Beirut, Trefon Evans, cabled the Foreign Office: 'Of course if Syria could also be given a share albeit small in the spoils Abdullah's position would be stronger. But practical difficulties particularly the strength of Jewish position in Houleh area would appear to exclude this possibility'. Two days later the Foreign Office relayed this idea to Sir John Troutbeck, head of the British Middle East Office (BMEO), which acted as Britain's main liaison with Bernadotte: 'I have been considering the suggestion that Syrian acquiescence in the aggrandisement of Transjordan would be more easily obtained if there could be some session of territory in Northern Palestine to Syria. The difficulty is that the north-eastern corner of Palestine, including the Huleh concession area, is a district to which the Jews are likely to attach a very great importance'. Evans to Foreign Office, telegram 670 of 11 September 1948, FO 371/68861/E11891; Foreign Office to Rhodes, telegram 95, Most Immediate – Top Secret, 13 September 1948, FO 800/487.

21 For British plans for the significant diminution of Israel's size, see, for example, 'Palestine: Memorandum by the Secretary of State for Foreign Affairs', CAB 129/29, C.P. (48) 207, 24 August 1948; CAB 128/13, C.M. (48), 57th Conclusions, 26 August 1948; Foreign Office to B.M.E.O. in Cairo, telegram 1471 of 28 August 1948; and telegram 1058 of 11 September 1948, 800/487; from Mr. Evans (Beirut) to Foreign Office, telegram 670 of 11 September 1948, FO 371/68861/E11891; Michael Wright, 'Palestine', 15 June 1848, FO 371/68650/E8409.

'The Chiefs of Staff will be aware that we are now seeking a settlement of the Palestine question which might result in the near future in the emergence of a greatly enlarged Transjordan', read a memorandum by Burrows from 24 September 1948. 'This Greater Transjordan might include the whole of the Negeb or only the northern part thereof, the southern part being given to Egypt'. What was the Chiefs of Staff's view on the risks and opportunities attending such a development? What strategic installations would Britain require to protect its interests in both peace- and war-times? Would such installations in Gaza or elsewhere in Greater Transjordan supplement, or even replace Britain's facilities in Egypt and Cyrenaica?[22]

The Chiefs of Staff's response came a month later. They did not think that installations in Greater Transjordan would fully substitute for the Egyptian and Cyrenaican facilities; yet they considered them of great operational importance:

> In the taking up of battle positions speed and develop-
> ment of our forces will be of paramount importance
> and there are, therefore, very great advantages to be
> gained by stationing some of our fighting troops in
> peacetime in the Gaza–Beersheba–Hebron area
> rather than in Cyrenaica. Troops required to expand
> the Egyptian base will also be better placed in Greater
> Transjordan as their communications to Egypt would
> be quicker and shorter – and would not entail the
> movement of large bodies of troops through main
> centres of Egyptian populations.

And regarding Israel's place in this strategic planning, the Chiefs of Staff could not be clearer:

> Whatever Israel's attitude may be, we must have
> freedom of movement through her territory at the

22   FO 371/68860/G12387/11665/G.

outset of war. Provided our troops were already in Greater Transjordan they could, if Israel was friendly, move through Palestine in a matter of hours, and, if not, would be well placed to force their way through her territory.

To M.T. Walker of the Eastern Department this strategic appreciation did not go far enough, not least because the Chiefs of Staff were reluctant to give up their naval bases in Cyrenaica in favour of ports in Greater Transjordan. 'This is particularly unfortunate', he minuted on their memorandum, 'since the development of a Transjordan port on the Mediterranean, and also perhaps on the Red Sea, appears to us essential to Transjordan's civilian economy'.[23] That the Israeli civilian economy would have been equally afflicted by the detachment of the Negev from its territory, and that Israeli security would have been seriously endangered by the deployment of British forces 'well placed to force their way through her territory' in what was after all designed to be part of the Israeli state, did not even cross Walker's mind.

Sir John Troutbeck, Head of the British Middle East Office in Cairo, tackled the issue from a different direction. Fearing a separate Transjordanian peace agreement with Israel that would leave the Negev under the latter's control he warned:

> For ourselves the prospect of a State of Israel in direct control of the greater part of Palestine including very probably the Negeb and in indirect control of Transjordan as well must surely cause the utmost anxiety. Our whole strategy in the ME is founded upon holding a secure base in Egypt, but the usefulness of the base must be gravely impaired if we cannot move out of it except through hostile country. I do not wish

23 Chiefs of Staff Committee, Joint Planning Staff, 'The Strategic Implications of the Establishment of "Greater Transjordan" – Report by the Joint Planning Staff', 26 October 1948, FO 371/68860; and Foreign Office comments, ibid.

to exaggerate the danger of Israel entering the Communist camp or to discount the possibility that the Israeli authorities may one day cease to regard and treat us as enemies. But however favourably Anglo–Israelite relations may develop, it seems inconceivable that a Government of Israel would ever be prepared to conclude with us a treaty similar to that which we have with Transjordan.[24]

Troutbeck was not the only one to hold such views. On 23 October 1948 Kirkbride reported to the Foreign Office that two days earlier Abdullah had asked the US representative in Amman to request his government to inform the Israeli authorities that Transjordan had been forced by circumstances to take part in the war, and that it would be prepared, when conditions were right, to come to a reasonable settlement with regard to Palestine. Clearly offended that the king had failed to take him into his confidence on such a critical issue, Kirkbride dismissed Abdullah's peace initiative as premature and advised the Foreign Office that 'if the United States Government seek any advice on this subject we suggest they should be asked to decline to act as a go-between or alternatively ignore the message altogether'. A message in this spirit was relayed to the US Department of State.[25]

But while Kirkbride would not spell out the reasons for the 'prematurity' of a peace settlement after five months of hostilities, Sir Hugh Dow, Acting Consul-General in Jerusalem, did not shy from arguing flatly that it was better for Britain not to have a Transjordanian–Israeli peace agreement at all if its price involved the retention of the Negev by the Jewish State. 'I admit the overwhelming necessity for Transjordan to make peace with the Jews', he wrote with the patronizing complacency

24   BMEO to Foreign Office, 28 December 1948, telegram 45, FO 141/1246.
25   Kirkbride to Foreign Office, 23 October 1948, telegram 823, FO 371/68643/E13699. Interestingly enough, journalist Jon Kimche got wind of this British disposition. In early October 1948 he reported from Paris that Britain had advised Abdullah against entering into direct talks with Israel. Haifa to Foreign Office, 12 October 1948, telegram 808, FO 371/68643/E13302.

of the White Man who knew best where the 'real interest' of his 'native' client lay,

> If however, there is uncertainty on this question of the Negeb, it appears to me to be undesirable from our point of view to allow King Abdullah to push his negotiations with the Jews to anything like a conclusive stage. As Sir J. Troutbeck has pointed out (his telegram No. 508 to you) the Negeb is of little value to the Arabs while of strategic value to us, and King Abdullah may well be content to let the Jews have it the moment he sees that he has no prospect of getting Gaza. With all the other Arab States against him, Abdullah may even see advantage in having a wedge of neutral territory between him and Egypt. With the Negeb in Jewish hands moreover, it would be difficult for us to implement our defence obligations under Anglo–Transjordan Treaty save by air or via Aqaba.[26]

If anything, the above reports vindicate contemporary Jewish suspicions that the British were no less eager to have the Negev incorporated into Transjordan than King Abdullah himself.[27] Dow's view, also shared by Troutbeck, that 'the Negeb is of little value to the Arabs while of strategic value to us' is precisely what was argued by Zeev Sharef in his autobiographical account of the 1947–49 War. Describing the thrust of Zionist thinking following the Meir–Abdullah meeting of 11 May 1948, in which Meir failed to convince the king not to attack the State of Israel at birth, but was nevertheless convinced that he did not contemplate the prospects of battle gladly or with self-confidence, Sharef wrote:

26 From Jerusalem to Foreign Office, 20 December 1948, telegram 697, FO 371/68603.
27 For example, Ben-Gurion recorded in his war diary on 6 January 1949: 'Reuben [Shiloah] returned from Jerusalem at lunchtime. Met yesterday [Abdullah al-Tall, the Transjordanian negotiator]. Discussed the Negev. Abdullah wants the Negev [as] a road to Egypt, 100,000 Bedouins who live in the Negev, strategic interests. Reuben asked: "Whose interests? Your master's [i.e., Britain] or yours?"' Ben-Gurion, *Yoman Ha-milhama*, vol. III, p. 931.

The meeting confirmed previous reports that the British Government were planning for King Abdullah to capture the area specified for the Arab State as well as the whole of the Negev. But all this was on condition that it be carried out with the consent of the Arab League. The British hoped that he would succeed, and, of course, based their plans upon this expectation. It was apparent that Abdullah wanted Jerusalem while the British were interested in the Negev. They were waiting until the Negev would fall into the hands of the Arab Legion, which would extend its authority to beyond Gaza. This is the only explanation for the fact that in the final months of the Mandate, the army camp at Rafah, half of which was on Egyptian territory and half in Palestine, was extended. The camp was apparently intended to be one of the largest British bases in the Middle East.[28]

It is true that as part of their vision of 'Smaller Israel' the British were prepared to 'tolerate' Israel's occupation of the western Galilee, awarded to the Arabs by the General Assembly. Yet they did this most reluctantly and only because a) they hoped that this territorial concession was still reversible – 'The retention of Western Galilee by the Jews would be unfortunate from the strategic point of view', commented the Minister of Defence, A.V. Alexander, at a Cabinet meeting on 26 August 1948, 'but it might be possible to modify this element of the proposals';[29] b) there was no Arab state that could dislodge Israel from this area and stake a credible claim to its effective control afterwards; c) this area was far smaller and less significant for British and Arab interests than the Negev; d) British policy-makers feared that if their vision of 'Smaller Israel' would not be promptly imposed by the United Nations on

28   Sharef, *Three Days*, p. 76.
29   CAB 128/13, C.M. (48), 57th Conclusions, 27 August 1948.

the belligerents, under the guise of a plan by the UN Mediator, the Israelis would defeat the Arab States and regain the Negev, at the time still occupied by Egypt, while retaining the western Galilee (which is of course what eventually happened). As Bevin put it to his Cabinet colleagues: 'It would no doubt be possible to improve on the Mediator's proposals in certain respects, but [US Secretary of State] Mr. [George] Marshall had already announced that the United States Government supported them and the right course seemed to be to declare forthwith that HMG accepted the report in its entirety'.[30]

Whether a Jewish Statelet along the proposed British lines (see map) – without the Negev, with no land access to its capital, with its main naval outlet severely constrained, and with key economic installations and parts of its transport system controlled by foreign powers and manipulated to the benefit of its Arab enemies – should be defined as a 'rump of a state' (or as a 'compact state' as cynically termed by Bevin) is a matter of personal taste. What is eminently clear is that this statelet would have occupied a far smaller territory than that awarded by the UN Partition Plan, which in itself is described by Shlaim as anomalous and scarcely viable;[31] hence its economic and strategic position would have been extremely precarious, something of which the Foreign Office was keenly aware. 'Musa el-Alami would for his part accept the idea of a very restricted Jewish State, limited to the coastal plain', Burrows reported following a conversation with the 'moderate' Palestinian leader. 'I fancy with the *arrière pensée* that life for the Jews in such a small State would sooner or later become intolerable and it could be eliminated altogether'.[32] But this was precisely the straightjacket in which Bevin and his advisers so tirelessly toiled to restrain Israel.

30 Ibid., 61st Conclusions, 22 September 1948, p. 20.
31 Shlaim, *Collusion*, p. 117.
32 B.A.B. Burrows, 'Conversation with Musa el-Alami', 6 December 1947, FO 371/61585/E11764.

STUNTING THE POPULATION GROWTH OF
'SMALLER ISRAEL'

Interestingly enough, the British scheme for 'Smaller Israel' did not envisage the mere diminution of the Jewish State's territory, but also the disruption of its population growth. During the 1930s the British already cowered to Arab pressures and imposed severe restrictions on Jewish immigration to Mandatory Palestine, most notably the May 1939 White Book which made the future development of the Yishuv captive to Arab whims.[33] This policy continued during the Second World War and was carried through to the post-war era, despite the fact that the genocide of European Jewry had by now become public knowledge. The White Paper restrictions were thus kept in place, and the captains of British foreign policy, first and foremost Bevin, advocated the resolution of the 'Jewish Question' by dispersing the remnants of Nazi extermination throughout Europe and the world at large. 'Should we accept the view that all the Jews or the bulk of them must leave Germany?' Bevin cabled the British Ambassador to Washington, Lord Halifax, in October 1945. 'I do not accept that view. They have gone through, it is true, the most terrible massacre and persecution, but on the other hand they have got through it and a number have survived. Now what succour and help should be brought to assist them to resettle in Germany and to help them to get over the obvious fears and nerves that arise from such treatment?'[34]

Two months later a clever-clever argument was manufactured by the Foreign Office to keep the remnants of German Jewry in the very country which had just butchered six million of their brothers, or two-thirds of all European Jewry. Dismissing an American proposal to resettle these people in Palestine,

33 Jewish immigration was to continue at a maximum rate of 15,000 for another five years, after which it was to cease altogether unless the Arabs wished it to continue. Jewish purchase of land was prohibited in some areas and restricted in others. See, Laqueur, *The Israel–Arab Reader*, pp. 64–75.
34 Bevin to Halifax, 12 October 1945, FO 371/45381/E7757.

their ancestral homeland, it was cynically commented:

> Although opening paragraph of State Department's memorandum refers to German Jews, the succeeding paragraphs and the conclusions seem entirely to lose sight of the fact that these particular persons of Jewish faith or race are in fact *in* their country of origin and have never left it, and that the terms 'repatriation' and 'return' clearly cannot apply to the movement of any person to a country in which he has never previously been.[35]

This total lack of compassion for the unprecedented Jewish tragedy, shared by Prime Minister Clement Attlee and British officialdom at large, was indicative of the real British approach to the 'Jewish Question'. Notwithstanding sporadic expressions of feigned concern, epitomized in the patronizing advice to the Jews not 'to get too much at the head of the queue' lest this trigger 'the danger of another anti-Semitic reaction through it all'[36] (as if there was not already rampant anti-Semitism in Eastern Europe), British policy-makers were far less interested in relieving the plight of the Holocaust survivors than in preventing them from emigrating *en masse* to Palestine. In August 1945 President Harry Truman endorsed the Zionist demand for the immediate admission of 100,000 displaced Jews into Palestine, and to abort this idea Bevin suggested to establish an Anglo-American Commission of Inquiry 'to examine what could be done immediately to ameliorate the position of the Jews now in Europe' and 'the possibility of relieving the position in Europe by immigration into other countries, including the United States and the Dominions'.[37] Were the Foreign Secretary genuinely interested

35 Foreign Office to Washington, 4 December, 1945, telegram 12149, FO 371/51126/WR3268.
36 Bullock, *Ernest Bevin*, pp. 181–2.
37 CAB 128/1, 38th Conclusions, 4 October 1945. Another objective of the Commission was 'to consider how much immigration into Palestine could reasonably be allowed in the immediate future'. From the phrasing of this question, the answer which Bevin had in mind is not difficult to gauge: not very much if any at all.

in relieving the humanitarian plight of these 100,000 Holocaust survivors through their settlement outside Palestine, he
could have led the way by seeking Cabinet consent for the
admission of these displaced persons, or a substantial number
of them, into the United Kingdom; after all, a few minutes
before he made the proposal to his fellow ministers, the Home
Secretary had reported of representations from the Chief
Rabbi to admit into Britain Jews who did not desire to settle
in Germany. The burden on British society would not have
been unbearable: even the total figure of 100,000 constituted
a mere 0.2 per cent of contemporary British population. But
Bevin did not give such an idea a fleeting thought. While
exempting his own country from this humanitarian task, he
would repeatedly censure the Truman administration for
failing 'to absorb any appreciable number of Jewish refugees',
thus (allegedly) aborting the resolution of the problem of European Jewry, and by extension of the 'Palestine Question'.[38]

But the United States and the Dominions were not the only
places so cavalierly volunteered by British policy-makers to
carry the can for them. They were busy trying to block the
entry of the remnants of East European Jewry to Allied-
occupied Austria and Germany, advocating their resettlement
in their countries of origin, now a mass graveyard for millions
of Jews and the site of resurgent anti-Semitism. Needless to
say, the wishes of these refugees were not given any consideration. What mattered was that they must on no account
complicate Britain's relations with its Arab clients by migrat-
ing to Palestine and strengthening the Jewish community
there and its claim for statehood. As Bevin put it in his letter
to Halifax (above): 'I think that to fly in the face of the Arabs
after all the undertakings that have been given would cause
a breakdown at the beginning'.

The British desire to prevent a substantial increase in

---

38 'Palestine – Strategic Appreciation', prepared by Bevin for Attlee, 24 May 1948, FO
371/68650/E7032. See also Bevin to Inverchapel, 22 May 1948, FO 371/68649.

Israel's population did not cease with the surrender of the Mandate to the United Nations in February 1947. As noted above, they prevented the influx of mass Jewish immigration into Palestine until the last days of their presence there, in blatant violation of the UN Partition Resolution. Moreover, even after the completion of Britain's disengagement from Palestine and the establishment of the State of Israel, the Foreign Office sought to limit the Jewish population of the newly born state over the long term. In a memorandum from 15 June 1948, detailing various options to be suggested to Bernadotte, Michael Wright of the Eastern Department expressed the wishful thinking that the diminution of Israel beyond the boundaries awarded by the UN General Assembly 'might result in the Jewish authorities themselves having to limit immigration'. He also believed that the Arab governments would never reconcile themselves to the existence of an independent Jewish State unless 'there should be international agreement to accept numbers of Jewish displaced persons elsewhere than in Israel, and conceivably also to limit immigration to Israel'.[39]

Three days later, Bevin met the US Ambassador to London, Lewis Douglas, and tried to convince him of the importance of limiting Jewish immigration to Israel. 'It seemed to us that if the Arabs were to be brought to acquiesce in the establishment of a Jewish State a factor which would weigh heavily in the balance would be immigration', he repeated before reverting to his all-too-familiar old-new idea:

> It might be necessary not only for the Jews and the Arabs to make a contribution and sacrifices to achieve this but for other Powers to join in making contributions also. If there could be some fresh international attempt or agreement, perhaps sponsored by the Security Council, for the absorption of larger numbers

39   Michael Wright, 'Palestine', 15 June 1848, FO 371/68650/E8409.

of Jewish displaced persons elsewhere than in Palestine this might have a decisive effect upon the negotiations. The numbers were not really so large if they were divided among the different countries.[40]

In the three-year period between his letter to Halifax and his meeting with Douglas, Bevin seemed to have learned nothing and forgotten nothing. Just as his 1945 proposal to settle the remnants of European Jewry anywhere else in the world apart from their ancestral homeland had failed to prevent the advent of an independent Jewish State, so its reiteration three years later did not achieve its objective: the severance of Israel from its natural human lifeline and the rendering of the Zionist dream stillborn. But while in 1945 Britain was still the Mandatory Power in Palestine which allowed Bevin to portray his machinations to prevent Jewish Statehood as a benign attempt by the White Man to dispose of his imperial burden in the most equitable fashion (in his own view), in the summer of 1948 the Foreign Secretary was effectively attempting to subvert a sovereign State, established on the basis of a UN Resolution, by seeking to dictate both its immigration policy and its future population size. Shlaim may well deem Bevin's sustained efforts to truncate the Jewish State and to stunt its population growth to be acts of a 'guardian angel'. But whether the Foreign Secretary viewed himself as such is an altogether different matter.

SAVING THE ARABS FROM THEMSELVES

Indeed it was the anxiety to prevent Israel from establishing sovereignty over the entire territory awarded to it by the United Nations which drove Britain to suggest at the end of

40 Foreign Office to the British Ambassador in Washington, 18 June 1948, FO 371/68650/E8626.

May 1948 a four-week truce, as well as the imposition of an arms embargo on the belligerents. Shlaim claims that the embargo hurt the Arabs much more than it hurt the Jews;[41] similarly Bullock interprets the British observance of the embargo, despite Arab protests, as proof of British impartiality.[42] Both of them, however, utterly miss the point. What they fail to mention is that the embargo was imposed and maintained with a view to helping the Arab war effort, both by preventing Israel from obtaining arms and by 'saving the Arabs from themselves', namely preventing them from violating the truce at the twin risks of losing further territories (first and foremost the Negev) to Israel, and of undermining Britain's efforts to secure the best deal on their behalf in the political and diplomatic arenas.

In December 1947 the US administration imposed an arms embargo on the Middle East in response to the UN appeal to all countries not to exacerbate the situation in Palestine. This move was favourably viewed by the Foreign Office, as it damaged Jewish efforts to arm themselves while having practically no impact on the Arab States – Transjordan, Egypt, and Iraq – which were armed and trained by Britain. But by the beginning of 1948 the British became alarmed lest the embargo be removed due to pressures by the American Zionists and their local supporters. 'The American Administration are under very severe pressure to raise the embargo on shipments of arms from America to the Middle East', wrote Wright in his brief for Bevin before his meeting with Abul Huda, *some four months before the imposition of the British-initiated UN embargo.*

> This would, of course, enable the Jews in Palestine to obtain arms freely from the U.S.A. We are naturally doing our best to persuade the United States Government to maintain their embargo, but it is

41 Shlaim, 'The Debate', pp. 295, 303 fn. 26.
42 Bullock, *Ernest Bevin*, p. 595.

possible that they may not be able to do so unless we
undertake to discontinue our supplies of arms to
Arab countries. We would never take this step unless
the Arab countries thought it was in their interests
that we should do so. We are under obligations to
supply arms to Transjordan, Iraq and Egypt and we
have no intention of breaking these obligations
unless the States concerned ask us to do so. In view,
however, of the possibility that it might be more to
the advantage of the Arabs that the American embargo should be maintained even at the expense of
delay in obtaining equipment for the armies of the
Arab States from the United Kingdom, we have asked
for the views of the Arab Governments. The views
so far received are conflicting.[43]

Bevin scarcely needed this reminder from his subordinate. A
week before receiving Wright's memorandum he had already
warned the British Ambassadors in the Middle East of the
possibility that 'the Jewish pressure for the lifting of the
American embargo on the purchase of arms to the Jews in
Palestine will become irresistible unless we are able to make
an intelligent statement saying that we have decided upon a
temporary suspension of deliveries of arms to the Arab States'.
It went without saying that the Foreign Office was 'prepared
to continue deliveries which we are at present under contract
to make to the Governments of Egypt and Iraq and to tell the
Americans that in view of our treaty bonds we cannot agree

43   Wright, 'Brief for Conversation with Transjordan Prime Minister on Palestine'. Thus, for
     example, the Iraqi Foreign Minister 'thought there was every advantage in [Britain's]
     imposing the embargo on arms to the Arab States'. In contrast, the vast majority of Iraqi
     officers were reportedly opposed to such a move because they only had 'sentimental
     interest in Palestine and are not prepared to sacrifice what they regard as the interests
     of their country for it.' For his part King Abdullah believed that 'the Jews would find
     means to avoid the American embargo on the export of arms or find alternative sources
     of supply. The Arabs had no such ability and would have to depend on their ally for
     supply.' Baghdad to Foreign Office, telegram 18 (42) of 31 January 1948, FO 816/115, and
     telegram 199 of 16 February 1948, FO 816/116; Amman to Foreign Office, telegram 52 of
     1 February 1948, FO 816/115.

to their suspension'. However, since it was unclear whether 'this course would be the one most advantageous to the Arabs themselves' the Ambassadors were to sound up the governments to which they accredited. For his part Bevin had no doubt that

> The advantage which the Jews would obtain from a lifting of the American embargo in their favour would be out of all proportion to any advantage which the Arabs in Palestine could derive from our shipments to the Arab States. Whether or not the Palestine Government was able to prevent the delivery of arms to the Jews before May 15th we should have no right to interfere after that date.

> The Arab Governments may therefore wish to consider whether it would not be to the advantage of the Arab cause in Palestine if our deliveries of arms were temporarily suspended (say for 6 months in the first instance) on condition that the American embargo continued to be enforced.

> If this arrangement were made it would be understood that if the U.S. Government were for any reason to find it necessary to raise the embargo or failed to enforce it we should at once resume the delivery to the Arab States. We have of course no desire to delay the delivery of arms to them except to the extent to which they agree this is desirable in their own interests. You cannot emphasise this too strongly; it is the core of our plan.[44]

This logic was sustained following the Arab attack on the newly-established State of Israel in mid-May 1948. In the

---

44   Bevin to Kirkbride, 29 January 1948, telegram 47, FO 816/115 (also addressed to Cairo, Baghdad, Jedda, Beirut, Damascus and Amman, as well as to the B.M.E.O).

initial stage of the war, when the Arabs went from strength to strength, the British collaborated with them in forestalling an immediate Security Council ceasefire resolution,[45] both because it invoked the threat of sanctions against the Arab States under Chapter 7 (Article 39) of the UN Charter, and because the Arabs seemed well poised to make further territorial gains in Palestine.

Before long, however, the British changed their mind. The Arab States had secured substantial chunks of Palestine, reducing Israel's territory to a fraction of that awarded by the UN General Assembly: the entire Negev was in Arab hands, apart from a handful of tiny Jewish pockets; the Egyptian army was parked some 40 kilometres south of Tel-Aviv on the coastal plain and penetrated the Judean Desert up to the outskirts of Jerusalem; for its part the Arab Legion occupied most of the Arab territory of Mandatory Palestine; only in the western Galilee did Israel occupy some territory awarded to the Arabs by the UN Resolution, but even there the Arabs managed to hold a sizeable enclave in the central Galilee. Were the war to stop at this point, the British goal of 'Smaller Israel' would have fully materialized.

The second factor which drove Britain to change tack was the mounting public outrage in the United States over its attitude towards the war, and the distinct possibility that the arms embargo would be shortly lifted. On 20 May, US Secretary of State George Marshall said in a press conference that 'the lifting of the embargo by the United States was under consideration',[46] and the statement rang alarm bells in London. 'I trust that the Americans will maintain their arms embargo', Bevin cabled the British Ambassador in Washington, Lord Inverchapel, on the same day. 'If they raise it I shall almost certainly be obliged to raise our own embargo on arms to the Arab States and we shall then be in the unfortunate position

---

45   Pappé, *Britain and the Arab–Israeli Conflict*, p. 34.
46   Washington to London, 20 May 1948, telegram 2382, FO 371/68649/E6687.

of one side being largely armed by the Americans and the other by ourselves'. He left it for the Ambassador to take up the matter with the Secretary of State 'so as to avoid our getting at unnecessary cross-purposes'.[47]

The response from Washington was far from encouraging. 'The apparent inequality of the battle in which the Jews are now thought to be engaged has fostered the hope that the American embargo will shortly be lifted', wrote Inverchapel.

> This step is strongly urged and fully expected by the pro-Zionists, including their usual Congressional mouthpieces. As far as the general public is concerned there is a natural predisposition to sympathise with any group seeking to establish a new nation (May 15th has been described as the Jewish equivalent of July 4th); to support an anti-Colonial cause; and, other things being equal, to cheer the efforts of the underdog. Many non-Zionist members of Congress share this general feeling but do not yet appear to have very strong views on the subject.

In these circumstances, the Ambassador warned that 'the anti-British band wagon which has stood still for so long is once more beginning to roll' and that this anti-British sentiment

> is likely to converge upon such an obvious and practical issue as the lifting of the arms embargo. As there is almost no opposition to such a step its proponents are likely to receive the support of many elements in and out of Congress who would agree that common decency demands that the United States should not deny to the infant State the tools for its self preservation. This feeling will be all the stronger because it is popularly regarded as

47   Bevin to Inverchapel, 20 May 1948, telegram 5459, FO 371/68649.

progressive and democratic republic striving to make
its way against backward greedy and reactionary
opponents.[48]

Bevin did not lose hope. In a conversation on 22 May with
Ambassador Douglas he justified the Arab attack on Israel and
accused the administration of aggravating the Palestine
conflict through its whimsical policy which antagonized the
Arab States and the Muslim World at large, and made them
feel 'that considerations of justice and fair dealing were being
subordinated to electoral pressure from the Zionists in New
York'. He then asked Douglas to implore his government to
forego their intention to invoke Article 39 and to support
instead a British ceasefire resolution, which the British
representative to the UN, Sir Alexander Cadogan, was about
to present to the Security Council; the arms embargo, needless
to say, was to be maintained.[49]

While Douglas was well-disposed to Bevin's requests,[50] the
British Embassy in Washington continued to raise the alarm.
'The mounting criticism of the British attitude', chargé d'affaires
Sir John Balfour wrote to Bevin on 22 May, 'is not by any means
confined merely to Zionists, but is now being strongly voiced
by other influential persons in the Administration, Congress,
and the press and wireless'. What was particularly disturbing
about this criticism was that, contrary to the Foreign Secretary's perception, it was not only, or even mainly influenced
by the Jewish vote but was rather voiced by 'many influential
persons who are moved not at all by considerations of the
Jewish vote, but rather by the human and moral issues which
are held here to be involved in the present conflict in Palestine,
and in the wider issue of the future of the United Nations'.
    The main thrust of this criticism was that British policy was

48   Inverchapel to Bevin, 21 May 1948, telegram 2405, FO 371/68649.
49   Bevin to Inverchapel, 22 May 1948, telegram 5553, FO 371/68649.
50   See his cable to Secretary of State Marshall on 22 May, a copy of which was given to the
     British Foreign Office. See, FO 371/68650/E6976.

hypocritical and obstructionist in several critical respects, not least its feigned interest in a truce at a time when it was extending military aid to the Arabs and sabotaging the efforts of the Security Council to secure an end to the fighting. Since this not only prevented the immediate ending of the present war in Palestine but also exposed the United Nations to the same contempt as was visited on the League of Nations in the case of the Italian invasion of Ethiopia in the mid-1930s, it was argued that the international organization had no other choice but to issue a ceasefire order and impose sanctions on any nation that refused to obey.

To stem this rapidly growing snowball before it caused further damage to already-strained Anglo–American relations, Balfour suggested an immediate public statement by the British government that would set the record straight and would convince the Americans of Britain's genuine interest in 'an effective truce which will be just to both parties'.[51]

Concern at the Washington Embassy was growing by the day. On 24 May Chaim Weizmann held a meeting with President Truman following which he stated that 'the President gave him hope that [the] United States would lift embargo on export of arms to Middle East in the not too distant future'. He said that the President did not indicate when this would be, but claimed that he agreed with him that 'the matter was urgent'.[52] Two days later representative Jacob Javits introduced a measure to the House of Representatives, in the form of an amendment to the Greek–Turkish aid programme, to authorize a $100 million loan to Israel to provide military supplies and technical assistance.[53] To make matters worse, the Senate Appropriations Committee demanded an official investigation to determine whether funds advanced to Britain were used to assist the Arab invasion of Israel, and whether US lend-lease equipment was

51 From Washington to Foreign Office, 22 May 1948, telegram 2431, FO 371/68649/E6718.
52 Washington to Foreign Office, 24 May 1948, telegram 2454, FO 371/68650.
53 Washington to Foreign Office, 28 May 1948, telegram 2509, FO 371/68650/E17132.

being used for this purpose. The Chancellor of the Exchequer told the Cabinet 'that this enquiry might cause us some embarrassment, for, when we excluded Palestine and Trans-jordan from the sterling area, we had provided them with United States dollars with which to finance their current transactions. It seemed important that difficulties of this kind should not be allowed to affect the attitude of the United States Administration towards the flow of supplies to this country under the European Recovery Programme'.[54]

By this time the Foreign Office was sufficiently frightened that it modified its truce resolution so as to bring about its immediate adoption by the Security Council. The original proposal, which called for a four-week truce accompanied by a ban on the supply of arms to the belligerents and on the introduction of fighting men into the area, was doubtless designed to harm Israel rather than its Arab enemies. For one thing, due to the American embargo and the British naval blockade of Palestine up to the Arab attack, the Jews were overwhelmingly inferior to the invading Arab forces in terms of military equipment and war matériel; were the proposed arms embargo to be strictly applied, this qualitative imbalance would be perpetuated. For another thing, the ban on the introduction of fighting men into the area was exclusively designed to prevent a large influx of Jewish immigration into Israel – a long-standing aim of British policy;[55] indeed Britain was already making its modest contribution to this objective by holding some 9,000 young Jews in concentration camps in Cyprus and by using the small military enclave it still kept in Haifa to prevent the landing of immigrants in Israel.[56] That

---

54 CAB 128/12, C.M. (48), 33rd Conclusions, 27 May 1948; 'Palestine – British Aid to Arab States', British Embassy, Washington D.C., 25 May 1948, FO 371/68651.

55 Pappé mentions the components of the proposed British resolution, but fails to identify their real motivations (*Britain and the Arab–Israeli Conflict*, pp. 34–5).

56 See, for example, Beirut to Foreign Office, 'Jewish Immigration, Haifa Area', 18 May 1948, telegram 362, and comments by the Eastern Department, FO 371/68554/E6499; from Beirut to Foreign Office, 19 May 1948, telegram 364, FO 371/68554/E6516; Secretary of State to the Minister of Defence, 24 May 1948, FO 371/68554/E6499; Foreign Office to Baghdad, 26 May 1948, telegram 557, ibid.

the invading Arab States exploited the truce to double their armies in Palestine did not seem to trouble British officialdom: after all, they did not have to deploy forces 'from outside the region'.[57]

Yet by way of circumventing a French veto, the British relented and accepted the admission of Jewish refugees into Israel provided they would not undergo military training. 'This amendment would be unpopular with the Arab States, since it contemplated the continuance of Jewish immigration', Bevin reported to the Cabinet, 'but it was hoped that, despite this, the resolution would be accepted by the Arabs'.[58]

All this proves that the proposed British truce resolution, with its corollary arms embargo, was motivated by the conviction that the merits of such a move far exceeded the damage that could be caused to the Arab war effort by the removal of the American embargo on Israel and the imposition of UN sanctions on the Arab States.

Moreover, well before the application of the arms embargo British officials had already been devising ways and means for its circumvention. 'You may remember when I was in London [during Abul Huda's visit] we discussed tentatively the possibility of circumventing any future demands in the international sphere that we should cut off all supplies to the Arab Legion by granting the two million pounds as a lump sum in April', Pirie-Gordon wrote to Burrows on 10 March 1948. 'I naturally said nothing of this suggestion to Russell Edmonds in the treasury with whom I agreed in principle on quarterly payments. However the Minister with whom I have discussed the proposal in Amman agrees with me that in view of the tricky position which will develop in May it would be of very great advantage if the Arab Legion could have the whole year's grant already in hand before the correctness of

57 For Arab reinforcement of their Palestine contingents see, for example, Glubb Pasha, 'Transjordan and Palestine, 5 October 1948', FO 371/68642/E13240; Kimche, *Seven Fallen Pillars*, pp. 250–1.
58 CAB 128/12, C.M. (48), 34th Conclusions, 31 May 1948.

their future international behaviour can be called in question'.[59]

On 25 May the British Ambassadors throughout the Middle East were instructed to convince the Arab leaders that it was in their best interest to accept the ceasefire, 'even from the point of view of influencing American opinion'.[60] Bevin, no doubt, believed that this was the right course of action. 'I am convinced that the continuance of the truce will benefit the Arabs and that its breakdown would be disastrous from their point of view', he telegraphed Kirkbride on 6 July 1948, some three weeks after the truce had come into force:

> If they were responsible or could plausibly be represented as responsible for the renewal of fighting, it would probably be impossible for H.M. Govt. as a member of the United Nations to supply them with ammunition or indeed to give them any material assistance whatsoever. At the same time the Jews would be able to raise large sums of money in the United States and to purchase armaments either there or from other sources of supply. On the other hand the conditions now prevailing under the truce must be a source of grave embarrassment to the Jewish leaders. With much of their restricted manpower under arms and with serious interruption of their foreign trade their economic situation must be increasingly precarious.[61]

When Edgar Gallad Bey, adviser to King Farouq of Egypt, protested to Bevin against the ceasefire and the attendant embargo, claiming that the Arab States 'would be better advised to continue fighting now while their armies were advancing, rather than await such results from a conference

59 Pirie-Gordon to Burrows, 10 March 1948, FO 816/112.
60 Foreign Office to Amman, 25 May 1948, telegram 441, FO 371/68650.
61 Foreign Office to Amman, telegram 647 of 6 July 1948, FO 800/487.

under the mediator', the Foreign Secretary was incensed. 'What would happen if the Arab States did not accept the cease fire, in which case the efforts he had made to prevent the raising of the arms embargo would prove in vain?', he said. *'Would the Arabs prefer military defeat to a settlement now?'*[62]

In other words, if the British-proposed truce and arms embargo turned out to hurt the Arabs more than the Jews, as claimed by Shlaim and Bullock, then it was a major blunder on Bevin's part, not the result of a deliberate decision. Hence to view Bevin as the 'guardian angel of the Jewish State' because his attempt to starve Israel of the necessary weapons for its defence turned sour is as absurd as to credit the Mufti with the same 'honour' on account of his rejection of the 1937 partition plan which would have given the Palestinians the lion's share of the country, or for that matter as absurd as to consider the maverick Israeli politician Ariel Sharon the guardian angel of both Syria and the Palestine Liberation Organization (PLO), since his ill-conceived 1982 Lebanese campaign allowed the former to complete its long-standing dream of balkanizing Lebanon and drove the latter to a political course, thereby sowing the seeds of an independent Palestinian State. Indeed, not only did the British Foreign Office hope that the truce would mortally wound the State of Israel by keeping Arab gains intact and ushering in a political settlement that would reduce Israel's territory well beyond that envisaged by the UN Resolution, but they volunteered free advice to the Arab States on how to exploit this respite for effecting this diminution of the Israeli State. 'It might be presumed that the period of truce will be utilised by the Jews to establish an effective administration not only in those parts of their November State which are behind the military lines, but also in the Arab areas which they have occupied, such as the Central and Northern Galilee', the Foreign Office cabled the British Ambassador to Egypt, Sir Ronald Campbell,

---

62   'Record of Conversation between the Secretary of State and Edgar Gallad Bey at 11.30 a.m. on May 26th, 1948', FO 800/487 (emphasis added).

If the Arabs are to be in a position to bargain on equal terms, it is essential that they should also establish some real authority in the areas behind the lines occupied by their forces. This is particularly important in the area to the south of the Egyptian front line. The greater part of this area was awarded to the Jews last November and the Jewish settlements there are still holding out and presumably maintaining contact with Tel-Aviv. We shall have great difficulty in supporting the Arab claim to retain this part of Palestine unless it can be shown that it is in fact and not in name only under Arab administration during the truce …

Having implied the urgency of eradicating the Jewish settlements in the Negev in one form or another, the cable concluded:

If [such] administration is not operating in practice and especially if there are no traces of its presence in Southern Palestine, I should also welcome suggestions to how the Arabs can be stimulated to lay a firmer foundation for the territorial claims which we hope the United Nations will eventually endorse.[63]

BRITAIN AND THE ARABS: PARTNERS IN ADVERSITY

There was nothing more abhorrent to the Foreign Secretary than the triumph of the Zionist movement, and latterly the newly established State of Israel, over its Arab foes, and he did his best to prevent this from happening. Three of the invading Arab States – Transjordan, Egypt and Iraq – were tied to Britain by special treaties of alliance and the British felt

63   Foreign Office to Cairo, 22 July 1948, telegram 1267, FO 371/68641.

obliged to ensure their success: when it appeared that Israel was about to transgress Transjordanian territory, the British sent a military force to Aqaba and stated their readiness to fend off such an incursion; the rest of the warring Arab States, notably Saudi Arabia, occupied an important place in British imperial interests. In fact, it would be no exaggeration to say that throughout the Palestine crisis, from the surrender of the British Mandate to the UN in February 1947 to the end of the 1947–49 War, Bevin and his advisers, and by extension the British Cabinet, identified with the Arab cause to the extent of viewing its failure as their own.

In his defence of the Cabinet's decision to surrender the Palestine Mandate to the United Nations, Bevin claimed in the House of Commons that 'we really cannot make two viable States of Palestine, however we may try. We can make one viable State, and, so far as I can see, or as far as any student of the map could see, the only thing we could do would be to transfer the rest to one of the Arab States, but I ask what trouble is that going to cause in the whole of the Arab world?'[64] Seven months later, in September 1947, Bevin defined UNSCOP's majority proposal to partition Palestine as 'so manifestly unjust to the Arabs that it is difficult to see how, in Sir [Alexander] Cadogan's [the British Ambassador to the UN] words "we could reconcile it with our conscience"'.[65]

Burrows trailed his Foreign Secretary's line. 'As it is all our efforts have been taken since the end of the Mandate in repairing the situation produced by so manifestly unjust solution', he wrote on 5 June 1948. 'We cannot of course openly play a leading part in the negotiations, but we shall have considerable opportunities for giving advice to the Arab States for discussion with the Americans and for informally putting ideas into the Mediator's head'.[66] And Troutbeck put it in more

---

64 'Palestine', *House of Commons* (Government Policy), 25 February 1947, PREM 8/627, pt. 6.

65 'Palestine: Memorandum by the Secretary of State for Foreign Affairs', CAB 129/21, C.P. (47) 259, 18 September 1947.

66 Memorandum by Burrows, 5 June 1948, FO 371/68559/E7376.

direct terms on 11 June 1948, the day the truce came into force:

> I venture to suggest … that the best line we could adopt would be to say that we are partners in adversity on this question. A Jewish State is no more in our interest than it is in the Arabs. We could point for evidence to the persistent hostility shown to us by the Zionists in recent years whether in Palestine or in the United States as well as to the fear which we share with the Arabs that a Jewish State may become a spearhead of Communism in the Middle East. But we could truthfully point out that neither we nor the Arabs, either in isolation or in co-operation, are able at the moment to stand up to the combined power of the United States and the USSR, nor is it in anyone's interest that the United Nations should founder on this rock. If the Arabs defy the United Nations they will be beaten. We should not be able to supply them or prevent others from supplying the Jews. The only possible course therefore seems to us that we should both bow to the inevitable and acquiesce in an arrangement which neither of us pretends to think just or in accordance with our long term interests. But there are times when the short term interest is of such overriding importance that the long term interest has to be sacrificed.[67]

In a London meeting with an Iraqi delegation at the end of January 1948, Bevin reprimanded his guests for failing to heed his advice. 'We would never have been faced with the partition plan if the Arabs had accepted his latest proposals at the London Conference in February, 1947', he complained.

67   From Cairo (B.M.E.O) to Foreign Office, 11 June 1948, telegram 20, FO 371/68650.

Yet 'he still thought that, if in the end partition proved a failure, they would have to go back to the "Bevin Plan"'.[68] As late as 19 April 1948, less than a month before the completion of the British withdrawal from Palestine, the Foreign Secretary found it difficult to accept in his heart of hearts the inevitability of partition. 'If the principle of a unitary Palestinian State was accepted, the Arab volunteers from outside Palestine would be withdrawn', he told US Ambassador Douglas. 'Unfortunately I could not put forward such a proposal as I should then be accused of going against the decision of partition approved by the General Assembly on the insistence of the US Government who had put great pressure to bear on the other members of the United Nations to accept such a solution'.[69]

These bitter words reflected Bevin's blind fury at President Truman's support for partition, which he viewed as betrayal of America's true interests for the sake of Jewish votes and money.[70] It never occurred to the presumptuous Foreign Secretary that Truman might have viewed American interests in different colours from himself, or for that matter from the oil companies and the bureaucrats of the State Department and the Pentagon; nor could he imagine, given his total lack of compassion for the tragedy of European Jewry, that the President might have been profoundly shocked by the Holocaust to the extent of seeing the point of the Jewish yearning for statehood in their ancestral homeland.

Bevin never overcame his obsession with the perceived Jewish sway over US policy ('the midsummer madness in New York', or 'the interest of New York in Jewish affairs', as he called it),[71] despite all evidence to the contrary provided by

---

68 The Iraqi delegation included Prime Minister Salih Jabir, Foreign Minister Fadil al-Majali and 'strongman' Nuri al-Said. H. Beeley, 'Discussion with the Iraqi Delegation on Palestine', 22 January 1948, FO 816/116.
69 Bevin to Lord Inverchapel, 19 April 1948, telegram 574, PREM, 8/859, II.
70 Bullock, *Ernest Bevin*, p. 175. Bullock takes for granted the validity of Bevin's blind fury against Truman.
71 'Record of Meeting with the U.S. Ambassador to Discuss the Palestine Situation', 25 May 1948, FO 800/487; 'Record of Conversation between the Secretary of State and Edgar Gallad Bey'.

the Washington Embassy, among other sources. On 28 November 1947, a day before the adoption of the UN Partition Resolution, the Washington Embassy reported the results of a Gallup Poll on Palestine revealing overwhelming support of 65 per cent for the partition of Palestine into two states and the immediate admission of 150,000 Jewish refugees into the country, as against a mere 10 per cent opposed to the idea.[72] Yet Bevin remained oblivious to such facts. In his view, the New York 'madness' involved the double-jeopardy of spoiling Anglo–American and Anglo–Arab relations at one and the same time. As a result he came to regard the Palestine conflict as very much a confrontation between an American–Zionist coalition and an Anglo–Arab one.[73] In his view, it was the Jewish refusal 'to admit that the Arabs were their equals'[74] that created the Palestine quagmire; and it was Truman's subservience to New York's Jewish voters that perpetuated the conflict. Had the Americans allowed Britain to have its way, the crisis would have long been resolved;[75] as things were, the Arabs had to be protected against an 'aggressive' and 'totalitarian' Jewish predator.[76]

'While there was some resentment in the Arab countries at the attitude adopted by the United Kingdom representative in the Security Council, the main bitterness was against the United States', Bevin reported to the Cabinet on 22 July 1948. 'The Governments of the Arab States seemed to recognize that we had acted in their best interests'.[77] This indeed they did, and nothing would seem to epitomize the British identification with the Arab cause better than the tenor of their contacts with the US administration. Take, for example, the

72   See FO 371/61891. See also Washington to Foreign Office, 22 May 1948, telegram 2451, FO 371/68649.
73   See, for example, Bevin to Inverchapel, 20 May 1948, telegram 5459, FO 371/68649.
74   Bevin to Inverchapel, 19 April 1948, telegram 574, PREM 8/859, II.
75   See, for example, 'Palestine – Strategic Appreciation', prepared by Bevin for Attlee, 24 May 1948, FO 371/68650.
76   See, for example, 'Conversation between the Secretary of State and the United States Ambassador', 29 April 1948, FO 800/487.
77   CAB 128/13, C.M. (48), 53rd Conclusions, 22 July 1948.

meeting between Bevin and Attlee with Ambassador Douglas on 28 April 1948. When the latter raised the question of the threatened invasion of Palestine by the Arab Legion, his interlocutors rallied to Abdullah's defence. 'What was Abdullah to do?', they asked, squarely laying the blame for the deterioration in the Palestine situation on Jewish 'aggression':

> First of all, he had never been admitted to the United Nations. His application had been vetoed by the Russians each time, and therefore how did the Charter of the United Nations apply to him? Secondly, were the Jews to be allowed to be aggressors on his co-religionists and fellow Arabs in the State of Palestine while he had to stand idly by doing nothing? ... What really was Abdullah to do?

Coming from the politicians who had acquiesced in Abdullah's invasion of Palestine and who were scheming to divide the Arab parts of Palestine between Transjordan and Egypt, and possibly other Arab States, this feigned interest in the fate of the Palestine Arabs sounds very hollow indeed. Yet Bevin and Attlee unabashedly sustained their duplicitous line of defence. 'It seemed to me that the United States policy was to allow no Arab country to help their fellow Arabs anywhere, but for the U.S. themselves to assist the Jews to crush the Arabs within Palestine and to allow the slaughter to go on, and then to ask the British Government to restrain Abdullah', claimed Bevin, totally ignoring the fact that the Jews had received no weapons from the United States due to the American arms embargo on the Middle East while the Arab armies, notably the Legion, were armed, trained and led by the British:

> Did this not seem a very illogical position? ... How was such a position to be met unless the U.S. put strong pressure on the Jews, who appeared to us to

be aggressive and arrogant, and disregard all the
appeals that had been made by the United Nations
... the number of Arabs who had infiltrated into
Palestine was not large and any acts they had
committed had been exaggerated. After all, Palestine
was an Arab country.

Attlee then took over from his Foreign Secretary. 'What was
aggression?' he asked. 'Was it aggression for Arabs to come
into Palestine from their own countries, and non-aggression
for Jews to come in by sea to the tune of thousands?' To the
Ambassador's claim that the Jews were coming in unarmed,
and were not fighting men, Attlee gave the 'winning argument'. 'That was just Hitler's method', he retorted. 'He put
people in as tourists, but they were soon armed once they got
in. The Jews would put them in as immigrants but they would
soon become soldiers, and it was known that they were
already being drilled and trained'.[78]

In his biography of Bevin, Bullock fends off contemporary
accusations of anti-Semitism levelled at the Foreign Secretary
on account of pieces of 'friendly advice' he gave the Jews such
as the suggestion that they should refrain from 'getting too
much to the head of the queue' in seeking a solution for the
remnants of European Jewry. He points out that this was a
phrase which Attlee had used two months earlier in a letter
to Truman and attributes Bevin's negative image to his
impetuosity: 'Bevin's personalization of British policy by
staking his own political future on its success, his egocentric
and emotional temperament, his disposition to fight when
faced with opposition and not to guard his tongue when
angered all combined to make him vulnerable to such charges
in a way that would not have been plausible if Attlee had been
the spokesman. He shared Bevin's views and the responsibility for British policy, but said little in public, did not become

78   'Record of Conversation which the Prime Minister and Secretary of State had with the
United States Ambassador on the 28th April 1948', FO 800/487.

emotionally involved, and so did not attract the lightning'.[79]

In mathematics two negatives can make a positive. But in human relations two wrongs do not make a right. That Attlee was as prejudiced as Bevin does not detract one iota from the Foreign Secretary's bigotry; the only difference between them is that Bevin 'did not guard his mouth when angered' while Attlee was careful not to give public airing to bigoted views such as the comparison of Holocaust survivors seeking refuge in their ancestral homeland to Nazi troops bent on the subjugation of an entire continent.

Nor did the Prime Minister and his Foreign Secretary hold the monopoly over bigotry. In a conversation at the War Office's Department of Military Intelligence on 30 January 1948, for example, Glubb Pasha made the preposterous suggestion that, if provoked into action, Jewish tactics 'would be on the Nazi lines – for one Jew killed, ten Arabs would be lined up and shot. Some even went further and said that whole villages, men, women, and children, should be wiped out and their lands ploughed up'.[80] And Sir John Troutbeck never shrank from the vilest of anti-Semitic diatribes. 'It is difficult to see that Zionist policy is anything else than unashamed aggression carried out by methods of deceit and brutality not unworthy of Hitler', he wrote on 18 May 1948.[81] In his perception Israel was a mirror image of Nazi Germany driven by an insatiable thirst for *Lebensraum*, and the Arab States a hapless Czechoslovakia.[82] Did it ever occur to him that just as Britain had surrendered Czechoslovakia to Nazi Germany a decade earlier, it was yet again supporting a concerted attempt to destroy a small State?

This perverted thinking was by no means Troutbeck's exclusive preserve but was widely shared by his colleagues in

---

79 Bullock, *Ernest Bevin*, pp. 181–2. For the strong response by the usually mildly-mannered Chaim Weizmann to Bevin's statement on the Jews as 'queue jumpers' see FO 371/51128.
80 'Transjordan – A Possible Forecast of Events in Palestine', 30 January 1948, FO 371/68369.
81 Troutbeck to Wright, 18 May 1948, FO 371/68386/E8738.
82 Troutbeck to Bevin, 2 June 1948, FO 371/68559/E7376; and on 24 January 1949, FO 371/75054/E3518; Troutbeck to Wright, 3 March 1949, FO 371/75064.

Whitehall. 'The analogy with Munich suggested in BMEO telegram should perhaps not be pressed too far', Burrows commented on one of Troutbeck's cables, 'but it is a timely reminder of the responsibilities which we have undertaken by using so much influence with the Arab States in favour of them accepting the ceasefire'.[83] And Sir Orme Sargent, the Permanent Under-Secretary at the Foreign Office, put the same analogy to Ambassador Douglas on 17 November 1947, during a discussion on the post-war settlement.[84]

The alarming thing is that all these people took their bigotry as the natural order of things. Had they been confronted with the accusation of anti-Semitism, they would have undoubtedly been genuinely astonished. In a conversation with Golda Meir (Meyerson), the British Chief Secretary in Palestine, Sir Henry Gurney, once remarked amiably: 'You know, Mrs. Meyerson, if Hitler persecuted Jews, there must be some reason for it'. He never understood why Meir was so incensed with his comment as to disconnect all contacts with him for some time. 'Why is Mrs. Meyerson so angry? I think highly of her', he queried a Jewish colleague of hers.[85]

BRITAIN AND THE JEWS: 'IT'S NOT PERSONAL –
IT'S STRICTLY BUSINESS'

In one respect Bullock is correct. Bigoted and virulently anti-Jewish as British decision-makers were, this did not form the cornerstone of their Palestine policy, something that Ben-Gurion recognized already at the height of the Yishuv's struggle for national liberation. 'Bevin is anti-semitic, the Foreign Office is a political opponent', he told a JAE meeting on 11 April 1948, to give one example; however, 'England has a policy to weaken us, to expose our weakness for [the

---

83 Memorandum by Burrows, 5 June 1948, FO 371/68559/E7376.
84 *Foreign Relations of the United States*, 1948, vol. 5, p. 1602.
85 Syrkin, *Golda Meir*, p. 153.

promotion of] a political goal. This is not only psychological anti-semitism ... political considerations determine [the adoption of] a human or inhuman attitude'.[86] 'Bevin and his colleagues had to see the Palestine problem in wider context than the Jews', Shlaim writes. 'They had to consider the need for peace in the Middle East, the need to keep an eye on Russia, the need to keep the friendship of the Arabs and not to alienate the Muslims in the British Empire'.[87] This patronizing claim puts the cart before the horse. The White Man's Burden may indeed be heavier than that of his subjects: for Britain, Palestine was yet another colonial trouble-spot that had to be evacuated, and not the most important of them all – India had that honour; for the Zionist movement, the fate of their only homeland was a matter of life and death. Yet the real point is not that Britain had to see the Palestine problem in a wider context than the Jews, but rather that it saw it in a different context. To put it more bluntly: in the order of things of the captains of British foreign policy, Jewish national aspirations counted for nothing, Arab sensitivities for everything.

There were many reasons for this outlook. No imperialist power enjoys being ejected from its colonies by a national liberation movement, and in the late 1940s it was the Zionists who were steadily pushing Britain out of Palestine through a combined political and armed struggle, thus leaving a lasting scar on Anglo–Israeli relations for many years to come. As the veteran British diplomat, Sir Anthony Parsons, candidly admitted: 'Many of us, including myself, who spent the last years of the British Mandate in Palestine will never recover fully from the shame and humiliation of the dismal retreat in the spring of 1948'.[88] This humiliation was compounded by the failure of British officialdom to grasp the phenomenon of

---

86   Meeting of the JAE, 11 April 1948, p. 8 (12549).
87   Shlaim, *Collusion*, p. 161.
88   Anthony Parsons, *From Cold War to Hot Peace: UN Interventions 1947–1994* (London: Michael Joseph, 1995), p. 3.

nationalism in general, and of Jewish nationalism (i.e., Zionism) in particular. Bullock attributes Bevin's inability to view the Jews as a people rather than as members of another religious group to the Foreign Secretary's Baptist upbringing and to his days as trade union organizer, during which he became familiar with Jewish special customs.[89] But this is only part of the explanation – the more important being Bevin's imperialist mindset. Like most of his fellow ministers and Whitehall bureaucrats, not to mention British colonial men on the spot, he could not grasp the yearning of peoples and communities for national liberation. For them, Third World nationalists were all thankless natives who failed to appreciate the 'civilizing message' articulated by the White Man.

'That's a fine tan you've got there, Colonel. Where did you get it?', Lord Inverchapel asked American Second World War veteran Mickey Marcus during a reception at the British Embassy on April 20, 1948, in which Marcus was made Honorary Commander of the British Empire. 'Travelling, sir', answered Marcus, who had just returned from Palestine where he had advised the Yishuv's military leadership on how to prepare for the imminent Arab invasion.

'Indeed. Any place I'd be interested in?'

Mickey smiled. 'I should think you'd be interested in practically every place. Isn't that what they say – the sun never sets on the British Empire?'

Inverchapel pursed his lips, then returned a smile. 'Not if we can help it, it doesn't.'[90]

In the case of Jewish nationalism, this slighted imperialist pride mingled with the virulent anti-Semitism within British officialdom as well as with the frustration of the colonial officials in Palestine over their inability to patronize the Jews in the way they patronized the Arabs (even the venomously anti-Zionist Troutbeck viewed the Arabs as 'silly, feckless

---

89   Bullock, *Ernest Bevin*, p. 167.
90   Berkman, *Cast a Giant Shadow*, p. 159.

people ... of medieval outlook' incapable of 'the same kind of loyalty to each other that one expects but does not always get from Europeans'),[91] in order to create a caricature image of the Jewish national movement. 'These officials aren't really anti-Semitic', wrote Richard Crossman on his meetings with British officials in Palestine during his tour of duty on the Anglo-American special commission of 1946, 'but they certainly are anti-Jewish and they are either pro-Arab or strictly impartial in detesting both sides ... Off the record, most of the officials here will tell you that the Jews are above themselves and want taking down a peg'.[92]

A note by the High Commissioner for Palestine, Sir Alan Cunningham, presented at a Cabinet meeting in January 1947, described Zionism as a movement where 'the forces of nationalism are accompanied by the psychology of the Jew, which it is important to recognise as something quite abnormal and unresponsive to rational treatment'.[93] On another occasion, having failed to induce Ben-Gurion to see things his way, the exasperated Cunningham wrote that the head of the Zionist movement 'remained Jewishly unconvinced'.[94]

Given this outlook of the top man on the spot, who was by no means on the most anti-Zionist extreme of British officialdom in Palestine, it is scarcely surprising that decision-makers in London had a totally distorted view of the Jewish national movement. 'The majority of Jews in Palestine have come from Germany, Russia, Poland, and Rumania and are more familiar with totalitarian than democratic regimes', warned a Chiefs-of-Staff memorandum of 26 February 1948;[95] and Bevin himself subscribed to an equally distorted view of

91 Troutbeck to Wright, 18 May 1948, 371/68386/E8738; Troutbeck to Bevin, 24 January 1949, FO 371/75054/E3518; Troutbeck to Wright, 3 March 1949, FO 371/75064.
92 Richard Crossman, *Palestine Mission: A Personal Record* (New York: Harper, 1947), p. 131.
93 'Palestine: Future Policy', Secret Memorandum by the Secretary of State for the Colonies, 16 January 1947, Annex I, CAB 129/16, C.P. (47) 31. See also Crossman, *Palestine Mission*, pp. 130–3.
94 Cunningham to Creech-Jones, 9 March 1948, telegram 583, Cunningham Papers, III/2.
95 'Memorandum by the Chiefs of Staff to the Minister of Defence', 26 February 1948, C.O.S. (48) 45 (0), FO 800/487.

the Jewish community in Palestine. In a conversation with US Ambassador Douglas on 29 April, he claimed that a totalitarian regime had been put in place in the Yishuv. 'Persecution of Christians Jews and others who offend against national discipline has shown a marked increase, and in some cases has reached medieval standards', he claimed. 'Detention and interrogation are common features of life in Yishuv today'.[96]

Another reason which made British officialdom hostile to Zionism was the belief, shared by the US foreign and defence establishments, that this movement was a 'communist stooge' and that, if established, a Jewish State would become a Soviet forward detachment in the Middle East. Even President Truman, who overruled the view of his bureaucrats to support the establishment of a Jewish State, and then to render it an immediate *de facto* recognition, was sufficiently alarmed by this misconception to dispatch a special envoy to the Israeli Prime Minister, David Ben-Gurion, to enquire whether Israel was going to become a 'red state'.[97] That such fears reflected gross ignorance of the essence of Zionism mattered little – it was translated into anti-Zionist and anti-Israeli policy, particularly on the part of Britain.

But above all, Britain's total disregard of Jewish concerns and interests was due to the simple fact that as occupiers of vast territories endowed with natural resources (first and foremost oil) and sitting astride strategic waterways (e.g., the Suez Canal), the Arabs had always been far more meaningful for British imperialist and post-imperialist interests than the Jews. To Bevin and his advisers, Jewish national aspirations were nothing but a nuisance which unnecessarily marred Britain's relations with its Arab clients and had therefore to be neutralized. As a memorandum written for Sir Alan Cunningham put it: 'Zionism has exhausted its usefulness to

---

96 Bevin to Inverchapel, 29 April 1948, telegram 633, 800/487.
97 Ben-Gurion, *Yoman Ha-milhama*, vol. III, pp. 846–7. The envoy, Samuel Klaus, reported back that all fears in this respect were groundless and that there was no 'immediate Soviet danger'.

Great Britain and has become more of a liability than an asset'.[98]

In a Strategic Appreciation for Attlee, Bevin wrote that

The Arabs are largely Muslims and that there is a closer affinity from a religious point of view between them than between almost any other peoples in the world. This religious or communal feeling extends from Morocco, Egypt and the Lebanon as far as Pakistan and Indonesia. I would add that the Christian Arabs feel as strongly as the Muslims on the Palestinian issue ... This cohesion might well at any moment cause the unification of the Muslim world. Muslims are fanatical people when roused ... It is true that they [i.e., the Arabs] blame the United Kingdom for the Balfour Declaration, and for introducing the Jews to Palestine at all. But they have developed a respect for our impartial attitude, especially since the question has been referred to the United Nations ...

Moreover, there are tremendous material resources, especially oil, involved. This may sound very mercenary, but our experience of Russia's pressure on Persia indicated a desire on her part to get into the Middle East and the Persian Gulf. If she could detach the Eastern world from the West she would gobble up Iraq and make Turkey a satellite, and oil, one of the great resources essential for the material and political recovery not only of Europe but of other parts of the world will be gone, and enormous power will be placed in the hands of Russia.

For these reasons, I am convinced that the future peace of the world depends to an enormous extent on a British and American understanding of the

98   'An Analysis of the Palestine Situation, April 1948'.

Middle East, India and Pakistan, Burma and South-East Asia. I regard the whole of this great area as one. We have therefore throughout urged the policy of not using force against Jew or Arab, but of promoting a settlement which we still believe can be done, if Jewish expansion is checked and if the Arabs can be made to feel that they will get justice and security.

The whole strategic position of the Western Powers is dependent on how and in what way we handle this Middle East situation.[99]

In this sweeping strategic vision, where world peace rested on the containment of 'Jewish expansion' and the satisfaction of Arab natural right for 'justice and security', Jewish national aspirations, let alone *their* right for 'justice and security', were totally ignored. 'No solution of the Palestine problem should be proposed which would alienate the Arab States', the Chiefs-of-Staff advised the Cabinet meeting of 11 July 1946, which approved a provisional autonomy plan for Palestine;[100] and seven months later the Chief of the Air Staff told the British Cabinet that if 'one of the two communities had to be antagonized, it was preferable, from the purely military angle, that a solution should be found which did not involve the continuing hostility of the Arabs; for in that event our difficulties would not be confined to Palestine but would extend throughout the whole of the Middle East'.[101]

One will be hard pressed to find the slightest consideration for Jewish wishes and concerns in the countless memoranda, briefs and working papers written by Bevin and his advisers during the seven critical months preceding the end of the British Mandate; nor did the Foreign Secretary, in his numerous

---

99 Bevin, 'Palestine – Strategic Appreciation'.
100 CAB 128/6, C.M. (46), 71st Conclusions, 22 July 1946.
101 CAB 128/11 C.M. (47), 6th Conclusions, Minute 3, 15 January 1947.

communications with his representatives in the Middle East and the United States, let alone in his Cabinet presentations, even hint that the Jews might have a point in their struggle for self-determination. Similarly the number of favourable references to the Jewish cause in Cabinet meetings can be easily counted on the fingers of one hand. In the Cabinet meeting of 5 February 1948, to mention one such rare occasion, it was argued (apparently by Colonial Secretary Arthur Creech-Jones who was among the least hostile ministers to the Jewish cause) that the British refusal to give the prospective Jewish State a free port as stipulated by the UN Partition Resolution 'seriously prejudiced the Jews by depriving them of freedom to import arms; and the suggestion was made that it was unfair to impose a rigid control over the importation of arms for use by the Jews in view of the ease with which the Palestinian Arabs could obtain arms from neighbouring countries. The general view of the Cabinet was, however, that no relaxation of control over the importation of arms would be justified'.[102]

The idea that 'world peace' could be achieved through some measure of collaboration with the Jews, rather than their containment, did not even cross the minds of most British policy-makers except the isolated few. At the Cabinet meeting of 17 January 1949, the Minister of Health, Aneurin Bevan, questioned the prudence of Britain's continued reliance on the 'unstable and reactionary Governments of the Arab States' in securing its strategic interests in the Middle East. By then Israel had turned the tables on its Arab enemies, and Bevan argued that this course of events confirmed his long-standing suspicion that the Government's political and military advisers had seriously overestimated the Arab strength, and that Britain 'should have done better to base our position in the Middle East on the friendship of the Jews, who, if we had pursued a different policy, would have been glad to give us

102 CAB 128/12, C.M. (48), 12th Conclusions, 5 February 1948.

all the facilities we needed to establish strong military bases in Palestine'.

This was the only instance during the two-year Palestine crisis in which a Cabinet member 'dared' raise the 'heretical idea' that the Jews not only had a point but had also some strategic value, and he came under an immediate assault by his colleagues. It was argued that British strategic interests could not have been secured by supporting the Jews against the Arabs; it was also doubted whether Israel would be a strong State or whether it would be especially friendly to Britain. Some ministers reiterated the worn adage that 'most of the Jewish population in Palestine came from Central or Eastern Europe', reflecting the ignorant misconception that they were either sworn communists, or totalitarians, or both; others warned that 'the activities of Jewish terrorists during the latter days of the British Mandate should not be forgotten', reflecting the injured pride of an imperialist power unable to come to terms with its humiliation by a national liberation movement; others still emphasized that the Commonwealth connection with the Muslim world made it imperative that Britain 'should support fair play for the Palestine Arabs, who had been in possession of Palestine for centuries'.[103]

Since it was this very Cabinet which four months earlier had approved Bernadotte's plan to deprive those Palestinians 'who had been in possession of Palestine for centuries' from their patrimony by annexing them to Transjordan,[104] a plan which had been etched on the UN Mediator by the Foreign Office in the first place, this feigned concern for 'fair play for the Palestine Arabs' smacks of utter hypocrisy and can scarcely be taken at face value. If anything it underscored the extent to which British foreign policy became enmeshed in the Arab cause; an intricate web where ulterior motives, self-righteousness and patronizing affinities were indistinguish-

103 CAB 128/15, C.M. (49), 3rd Conclusions, 17 January 1949.
104 CAB 128/13, C.M. (48), 61st Conclusions, 22 September 1948.

able. As Richard Crossman put it: 'Somehow we like the Arabs even though they fight us, and we dislike the Jews even if our interests run together'.[105] Furthermore a Chiefs-of-Staff memorandum warned against any moves that could alienate 'the Arabs to whom we shall be allied in sympathy arising out of economic and strategic interest'.[106] In this self-serving sympathy, there was – begrudgingly – room only for a minuscule Jewish State, occupying a fraction of the territory awarded by the UN Partition Resolution.

---

105 Crossman, *Palestine Mission*, p. 130.
106 'Palestine – Memorandum by the Chiefs of Staff to the Minister of Defence', 26 February 1948, FO 800/487.

Conclusions

> Bad history is written by the historian who has a
> passionate interest about what ought to have
> happened and chooses his materials and quotations
> by seeing only what he wants to see.
>
> ALBERT HOURANI

This book has conclusively demonstrated that the self-styled
'new historians' are neither new nor true historians but
partisans seeking to provide academic respectability to long-
standing misconceptions and prejudices relating to the
Arab–Israeli conflict. They are scarcely 'new' since most of
their 'factual discoveries' (and some of their interpretations)
are effectively nothing more than an attempt to reinvent the
wheel; and they are anything but historians because, taking
in vain the name of the archives, they violate all tenets of bona
fide research in their endeavour to rewrite Israeli history in
an image of their own devising.

Moreover, not only have the new historians failed to chart
new territory unknown to earlier generations of scholars, but
their foremost claim to 'newness', namely, access to 'hundreds
of thousands, perhaps millions, of state documents' declassified by the Israeli Government since the early 1980s[1] is
patently false. Rather, they have made but eclectic and
superficial use of this indispensable source-material. Thus, for
example, while portraying the Hagana and its successor – the

1 Morris, *1948 and After*, p. 7.

Israeli Defence Forces (or Zahal) – as the main culprits of the Palestinian exodus, Benny Morris's *Birth of the Palestinian Refugee Problem* fails to consult the archives of these two military organizations which truly do contain 'hundreds of thousands, perhaps millions' of relevant documents. Similarly, the discussion of the pan-Arab invasion of Israel in mid-May 1948 and the ensuing war operations in Avi Shlaim's *Collusion Across the Jordan* (Chapters 8–10) makes scarce use of Israeli archival source-material – and none whatsoever of the most pertinent archives of the Hagana and Zahal, relying instead on secondary published sources, a handful of interviews, and some British documents. Finally, Ilan Pappé's *The Making of the Arab–Israeli Conflict* is virtually a synthesis of published writings on the topic, making no original archival discoveries. In short, what the 'new historians' have been doing, to borrow E.H. Carr's words, is to 'write propaganda or historical fiction, and merely use facts of the past to embroider a kind of writing which has nothing to do with history'.[2]

Nor have members of this group lived up to their self-proclaimed status as paragons of virtue. Morris, for example, has tirelessly sung the praise of 'objective' history-writing: 'The historian of the Israeli–Arab conflict must endeavour to write on this conflict as if [he was writing on] the war between Carthage and Rome, or as if he had just arrived from Mars and were observing the situation without any connections and commitments.'[3]

If this is indeed the case then why does Morris twist and distort virtually every single document he brings to substantiate his (mis)claims that the 'transfer solution' was etched in Jewish thinking since the late 1930s, and that the Zionist and Israeli establishments have systematically falsified archival source material to conceal the Jewish State's (allegedly)

2   Carr, *What is History?*, p. 29.
3   Morris, 'Objective History'.

less-than-immaculate conception?[4] Surely a viable thesis can stand on its own legs without such textual acrobatics. After all, has not Morris himself defined the lesser historian as the one who 'discovers only part of the facts (ignores others or hides them)'?[5]

Equally misconceived is the conspiracy theory of an Anglo-Hashemite–Jewish 'collusion' to divide Palestine between Transjordan and the prospective Jewish State in flagrant violation of the UN Partition Resolution. Apart from being an old hat adorned with flashy 'revisionist' feathers, this theory is fundamentally flawed in several critical respects.

First, a careful examination of the two documents used by Shlaim to substantiate the Hashemite–Jewish aspect of the 'collusion' myth – Ezra Danin's and Eliyahu Sasson's accounts of the Meir–Abdullah conversation of 17 November 1947 in which the 'collusion' was allegedly clinched – proves beyond a shadow of a doubt that Meir was implacably opposed to any agreement that would violate the letter and spirit of the imminent UN Partition Resolution, and that in no way, shape or form did she give her consent to Transjordan's annexation of the Arab areas of Palestine. Rather she made it eminently clear that the *sole purpose* of the Transjordanian intervention in post-Mandatory Palestine was 'to maintain law and order until the UN could establish a government in that area', namely *a short-lived law-enforcement operation aimed at facilitating the establishment of a legitimate Palestinian government*.

Second, Meir's own verbal account of her conversation with Abdullah, which Shlaim, despite his unquestioned awareness of its existence, 'forgets' to note in his book, further underscores the fact that Mandatory Palestine *was not* divided on 17 November 1947.

Third, the belief that such critical decisions as the making of war and peace or the division of foreign lands can be made

4 See Afterword, below.
5 Morris, 'Objective History'.

in the course of a single conversation between state officials reflects a fundamental lack of understanding of the nature of foreign policy-making in general and of the Zionist decision-making process in particular. As Acting Head of the Jewish Agency's Political Department, Meir was in no position to commit her movement to a binding deal with King Abdullah, especially since the alleged deal would have run counter to the Jewish Agency's contemporary efforts to bring about a UN resolution on partition. All that she could do was to try to convince Abdullah not to oppose with force the impending UN Partition Resolution and to give him the gist of Zionist thinking: nothing more, nothing less.

Fourth, the Jewish Agency with which Abdullah alleged-ly struck the deal on the 'partition of Palestine' was totally unaware of the existence of any such deal for many months after its alleged conclusion: it never authorized Meir to 'divide Palestine' with the king, and it did not approve any such action *post factum*. Actually, Meir's conversation with Abdullah was never discussed by the Jewish Agency Executive, the effective 'government' of the Yishuv, and there is no trace of the alleged deal in either the Yishuv's military operations during the war imposed on it by the Palestinians, or its planning for the anticipated invasion of post-Mandatory Palestine by the Arab states in mid-May 1948. On the contrary, the Zionist leadership remained deeply suspicious of Abdullah's expansionist ambitions until the Arab invasion, in which he participated.

Fifth, the Jewish Agency's unquestioned preference of Abdullah over the Mufti did not *ipso facto* preclude the possibility of a Palestinian state that would not be headed by this arch-enemy of the Jewish national cause. On the contrary, as late as December 1948, more than a year after Palestine had been allegedly divided by Abdullah and Meir, prominent Israeli leaders, notably Prime Minister David Ben-Gurion and Foreign Minister Moshe Sharett, preferred an independent Palestinian state over the annexation of the Arab parts of

Mandatory Palestine to Transjordan. In Ben-Gurion's words: 'An Arab State in Western Palestine is less dangerous than a state that is tied to Transjordan, and tomorrow – probably to Iraq.'[6] And Sharett presented the idea in a far more elaborate form at a Cabinet meeting on 16 June 1948. 'At a certain stage we committed ourselves *vis-à-vis* the international community to a specific arrangement – that of the 29th of November', he told his fellow ministers, describing this arrangement as a 'package deal' comprising four integrated components:

> a) A Jewish State in a certain part of Palestine within specific borders; b) A separate Arab State, unattached to Transjordan, let alone Syria, but rather a separate Arab–Palestinian State in a specific territory of Palestine and within specific borders; c) An international Jerusalem having an efficient international regime based on certain elements, such as ensuring equality and free access to holy sites etc.; d) An economic alliance *unifying* these three elements – the Jewish State, the Arab State, and International Jerusalem – into a single economic entity, thus *preserving* the country's unity and the interrelationship between those parts. This is what we have agreed to.

'I assume, therefore, that it is our unanimous view that an Arab Palestine is here to stay', Sharett continued,

> If Arab Palestine goes to Abdullah, this means unification with Transjordan; and a possible linkage with Iraq. And if this Palestine is a separate state, standing on its own – it is a wholly different issue. In the former case [i.e., unification with Transjordan] – an economic alliance is impossible ... We undertook

6 Ben-Gurion, *Yoman Ha-milhama*, vol. III (18 December 1948), p. 885.

> to associate ourselves with a specific partner, and we
> are prepared to negotiate with it. But not with
> another partner.[7]

Sixth, Abdullah and the Zionist movement were talking at cross-purposes: the former viewed Palestine as an integral part of the vast kingdom he had been seeking to establish throughout his political career, and its Jewish community as an autonomous subject province within this kingdom; the latter was striving to establish its own independent state, free from foreign control and subjugation. These two positions were mutually exclusive, and in their two decades of intermittent contacts Abdullah and the Jewish Agency never even came close to transcending this divide.[8]

Seventh, contrary to the 'new historiographical' claim, Britain *did not know* of the alleged Hashemite–Zionist agreement to divide up Palestine between themselves, not least because, as shown above, this agreement did not exist; hence it could not, and never did, give such an agreement its blessing.

Eighth, as Ernest Bevin's reports on his secret meeting with Transjordan's Prime Minister Tawfiq Abul Huda unequivocally show, he never warned his interlocutor not to invade those parts of Palestine allotted by the UN to the Jews. Shlaim's desperate attempt to prove the existence of such a warning by superimposing the old and partisan account by the far from reliable Glubb Pasha on a newly released official document is not only methodologically flawed but also unbecoming of a 'new historian' who bases his claim to 'newness' on access to hitherto untapped documents.

Ninth, Bevin and his advisers could not care less whether or not Abdullah transgressed Jewish territory, provided this

7   Israel's State Archives, 'Protocol of the Provisional Government Meeting of 16 June 1948',
      pp. 12–13, 23–4 (emphasis in the original).
8   See Efraim Karsh, 'The Collusion That Never Was: King Abdullah, the Zionist
      Movement, and the Partition of Palestine', *Journal of Contemporary History*, 34, 4 (October
      1999), pp. 569–85.

did not implicate Britain in an embarrassing international situation. Indeed, shortly after the Bevin-Abul Huda meeting, Bernard Burrows, Head of the Eastern Department, wrote with Bevin's approval that 'it is tempting to think that Transjordan might *transgress the boundaries of the United Nations Jewish State* to the extent of establishing a corridor across the Southern Negeb [i.e., Negev] joining the existing Transjordan territory to the Mediterranean and Gaza ... [thereby] cutting the Jewish State, and therefore Communist influence, off from the Red Sea'.[9]

More importantly, on 7 May 1948 – a week before the Arab attack on Israel – Burrows suggested that the Foreign Office intimate to Abdullah that '*we could in practice presumably not object to Arab Legion occupation of the Nejeb* [Negev]'.[10]

Finally, Shlaim's depiction of Bevin as 'the guardian angel of the infant [Jewish] State' could not be further from the truth. Not only has he failed to produce one single document proving the slightest intention on the part of Bevin and his advisers to act in this vein, but the British archives burst at the seams with evidence that the Foreign Office, indeed most of the British Cabinet, viewed Jewish national aspirations as detrimental to British imperial interests, and the Zionist movement as the 'bad guys' that had to be restrained. Put in a nutshell:

- Bevin and his advisers would rather not have seen an independent Jewish State in part of Mandatory Palestine; hence their relentless opposition to the idea of partition.
- Having realized their inability to prevent partition, British officialdom wished to see a far smaller and weaker Jewish State than that envisaged by the UN Partition Resolution and did their utmost to bring about such an eventuality, despite their keen awareness that 'life for the Jews in such

9 Burrows' memorandum of 9 February 1948 (emphasis added).
10 Burrows, 'Palestine After May 14'.

a small State would sooner or later become intolerable and it could be eliminated altogether'.[11] More specifically, the Foreign Office spared no effort to induce the UN Mediator, Count Folke Bernadotte, to devise a solution that would cut Israel to approximately the same size as that envisaged by the 1937 Peel Partition Plan – less than half the size allotted to the Jewish State by the 1947 UN Partition Resolution. This included the surrender of the Negev to Transjordan and Egypt, with all its attendant detrimental consequences for Israel's strategic and economic interests; the prevention of a Jewish land corridor between the coastal plain and Jerusalem; the surrender of some territories in the eastern Galilee to Syria; and the creation of a substantial ex-territorial enclave in the Haifa harbour, Israel's main naval outlet, that would serve as a 'free port' for the use of the Arab and the Western countries under the control of the UN Port Commissioner.

- So keen were British policy-makers to cut Israel down to size that they sought to forestall a separate Israeli–Transjordanian peace agreement which did not include the detachment of the Negev from the Israeli state.

- The British scheme for 'Smaller Israel' did not envisage the mere diminution of Israeli territory but also the disruption of its natural population growth through severe restrictions on Jewish immigration to Israel.

- Britain's anxiety to prevent Israel from establishing its sovereignty over the entire territory awarded by the United Nations was manifested in the suggestion of a four-week truce, including an arms embargo on the belligerents. This was designed to help the Arab war effort, both by preventing Israel from obtaining arms and by 'saving the Arabs from themselves', namely preventing them from violating the truce at the twin risks of losing further territories to Israel, first and foremost the Negev,

11   Burrows, 'Conversation with Musa el-Alami'.

and of undermining Britain's efforts to cut the best deal on their behalf in the political and diplomatic arenas. Indeed, during the truce the Foreign Office volunteered free advice to the Arab states on how to exploit this respite for effecting the diminution of the Israeli state, including the need to strangulate the Israeli settlements in the Egyptian-occupied Negev.

• In short, it would be no exaggeration to say that throughout the Palestine crisis, from the surrender of the British Mandate to the UN in February 1947 to the end of the 1947–49 War, Bevin and his advisers, and by extension the British Cabinet, identified with the Arab cause to the extent of viewing its failure as their own. In the words of Sir John Troutbeck, Head of the British Middle East Office in Cairo: 'We are partners in adversity.'

This book has not sought 'to shore up the crumbling walls of the Old Historiography',[12] which is in the first place an artificial edifice constructed by the self-styled 'new historians' to serve their polemical purposes. Nor, *à la* Edward Said, has it intended to cast Arabs and Israelis in the roles of 'good guys' versus 'bad guys'. Rather, it has attempted to set the record straight and to make the case for fair play in the study of the Arab–Israeli conflict in general, and of Israeli history in particular.

It is obviously a necessary requirement of the historian's craft to take a hard-nosed look at the past and, without political intent, to debunk old myths. Yet coming from the 'new historians', this pretension sounds very hollow indeed for the simple reason that they have been substituting newly created myths for the realities which they have sought to debunk as 'myths'. Not only do the recently declassified documents in Israeli and Western archives fail to confirm the phoney picture of the origins of the Arab–Israeli conflict

---

12 Morris, 'A Second Look at the "Missed Peace"', p. 87.

painted by the 'new historians', but this group's wholesale resort to foul play by way of 'proving' their ill-conceived theories has effectively taken them from the realm of fact to that of fiction.

In response to Aharon Megged's criticism of the 'new historiographical' gospel Morris claimed that 'the State of Israel and its institutions are strong enough to withstand an objective and accurate description of the Zionist past'.[13] The State of Israel surely is. But are the 'new historians'?

13   Interview with Benny Morris, *Yediot Aharonot*, 16 December 1994.

Afterword[1]

It is lamentable enough that the 'new historians' should rewrite Israel's early history in the image of their own choosing. But the distortion that lies at the heart of the 'new historiography' goes much further than that. Having attributed false intentions, plans, and actions to the Zionist Movement and the State of Israel, the 'new historians' charge them with conspiring to conceal these non-existent misdeeds. 'In trying to produce or maintain an unblemished record, nations and political movements sometimes rewrite not only their history but also, it appears, the documents upon which that historiography must necessarily be based', argued Benny Morris in the *Journal of Palestine Studies*. 'The Zionist Movement and the State of Israel are no exceptions; indeed, they may be among the more accomplished practitioners of this strange craft.'[2]

This assertion is a red herring. Since archival source-material constitutes the Archimedean point of the historical investigation there is no conceivable way to prove its falsification, had this actually been the case. Indeed, contrary to his above claim, Morris does not attempt to prove any Zionist rewriting of 'documents upon which ... historiography must necessarily be based'; only to expose alleged divergences and contradictions between several archival

---

1 A shorter and somewhat different version of this chapter was published in the March 1999 edition of *Middle East Quarterly* as 'Benny Morris and the Reign of Error'. Permission for expanding this material and incorporating it into this book is gratefully acknowledged.
2 Benny Morris, 'Falsifying the Record: A Fresh Look at Zionist Documentation of 1948', *Journal of Palestine Studies*, XXIV, 3 (Spring 1995), p. 44.

documents and later published accounts making (partial) use of these sources – a far cry from his original charge.

MISREPRESENTATION

The first problem concerns a faulty account of the contents of documents. Morris tells of statements never made, decisions never taken, events that never happened. Consider, for example, the Israeli Cabinet meeting of 16 June 1948, about which Morris commits a double misrepresentation: he misattributes a decision to bar the return of the Palestinian refugees to this meeting; then he charges the Israeli establishment with concealing this non-existent decision!

On the first matter, Morris writes that

> The cabinet meeting of 16 June 1948 was one of the war's most important. It was at that session that, without a formal vote, agreement was reached among the thirteen ministers of Israel's 'Provisional Government' to bar a refugee return. The decision in effect sealed the fate of the 700,000 or so Palestinians who had become, or were to become, dispossessed exiles.[3]

Did it seal their fate? This Cabinet meeting took place one month after the war began, at the time of the conflict's first armistice, with fighting to be resumed within three weeks. Its protocol tells nothing of a decision 'to bar a refugee return'. In fact, it indicates there was no discussion of this issue, much less a decision. Only three participants (Foreign Minister Moshe Sharett, Prime Minister David Ben-Gurion, and Agriculture Minister Aharon Tzisling) referred to refugees at all, and they did so only in the context of a general survey of

3   Ibid., p. 56.

the situation. All three Cabinet members feared that so long as the war was not over, the return of refugees would tilt the scales in the Arabs' favour. However, while two Cabinet members (Sharett and Ben-Gurion) believed that the refugees should not return after the war, the third (Tzisling) emphatically argued that they should. Where is the consensus of the Cabinet alleged by Morris?[4]

On the second matter, Morris charges that later published accounts of this Cabinet meeting hide what happened at it. But any examination of the works in question, notably two of David Ben-Gurion's books,[5] shows not a shred of evidence to support this contention. Ben-Gurion's account of the meeting (as quoted by Morris) is a near-verbatim reiteration of the original minutes, espousing Ben-Gurion's view that the refugees should not be allowed back.

The following discussion demonstrates the intricate dynamics of distortion, whereby one misrepresentation inevitably leads to another. Having falsely claimed the existence of an Israeli Cabinet decision to bar a refugee return, Morris has no choice but to distort not only the documents related to this meeting but also those of a subsequent Israeli consultation, about the possibility of refugee return, so as to avoid exposure of his original (mis)claim.

This high-level consultation was held on 18 August 1948. Morris writes that the meeting, which included Ben-Gurion, his Arab affairs advisers, and his key ministers, was called 'to discuss the problem of the Arab refugees and ways to prevent their return'.[6] In fact, as the meeting's agenda[7] and Ben-Gurion's diary[8] make clear, it attempted to determine the

4 Israel State Archives, 'Partikol – Yeshivat Ha-memshala Ha-zmanit', 16 June 1948.
5 *Be-hilahem Israel* (Tel-Aviv: Hotsaat Mifleget Poalei Eretz Israel, 1951), pp. 130–31 and *Medinat Israel Ha-mehudeshet* (Tel-Aviv: Am Oved, 1969), pp. 163–8.
6 Morris, 'Falsifyingthe Record', p. 49.
7 Yaacov Shimoni, 'Beayot Gush Bet: Hahzarat Plitim O Ii Hahzaratam'. Recorded in 'Tamtsit Dvarim Be-yeshiva Be-misrad Rosh Ha-memshala al Beayot Ha-plitim Ha-arvim Ve-shuvam, 18 August 1948', Israel State Archives, FM 2444/19, p. 2. The other item on the agenda was the question of abandoned Arab property.
8 Diary of David Ben-Gurion, 18 August 1948, Ben-Gurion Archive, Sde Boker (hereafter BGA); David Ben-Gurion, *Yoman Ha-milhama*, vol. II, p. 652.

wholly different issue of 'whether or not to return Arabs'. The preliminary remarks of another participant, Director of the Jewish National Fund's (JNF) Land Development Division Yosef Weitz, confirm this point: 'We should not discuss the [abandoned] property here: there is a custodian attached to the treasury. Discussion of this matter will divert us from the main issue: to return [the refugees] or not to return?'[9] In the event, no collective recommendations were made on this issue, which was left for a government decision.[10] Morris withholds these facts from his readers.[11]

Rather than give the full title of the meeting's original minutes, as recorded by Yaacov Shimoni of the foreign office ('A Précis of a Meeting at the Prime Minister's Office on the Problems of the Arab Refugees and their Return'), Morris truncates it to merely 'A Précis',[12] thereby omitting any mention of a possible Palestinian return.

Morris also hides from his readers the widespread consensus among participants at this August 1948 meeting to allow Arabs who had fled to other parts of Israel from their places of residence to return to their original dwellings. In the words of Minister of Police and Minorities Bechor Shalom Shitrit: 'The Arabs of *Israel* who had left their places but remained inside – those should be returned.'[13] Under a section of the discussion titled 'The return of Arabs who had fled their places but remained inside Israel?' Sharett presented the idea in far more elaborate form:

> *These should be returned to their places*, with full owner-ship of their lands etc., and with full [citizenship] rights. We should not, as a matter of principle, discriminate against an Arab who had stayed inside [Israel] and thereby accepted its rule. He should

9   Shimoni, 'Tamtsit', p. 1.
10   Ibid., p. 4; BGA; Ben-Gurion, *Yoman Ha-milhama*, vol. II, p. 654.
11   Morris, 'Falsifying the Record', p. 49.
12   Ibid., p. 61, fn. 21.
13   Shimoni, 'Tamtsit', p. 2 (emphasis in the original).

enjoy full rights, including his property [rights] –
unless there are decisive emergency considerations,
security-wise. This should be the instruction to
governors, commanders, etc.[14]

To return to the Cabinet meeting of 16 June 1948, the original,
untruncated text of Foreign Minister Sharett's words as
recorded by Ben-Gurion reads:

Apart from the boundaries question, namely the
external perimeter of the state's territory, there is the
question of the future of the Arab community which
had existed in Israel's territory prior to the outbreak
of the present war: Do we imagine to ourselves [ha-
im anahnu metaarim le-atsmenu] a return to the
status quo ante, or do we accept the [present] situation
as a fait accompli and fight over it?[15]

Morris presents it this way:

'Can we imagine to ourselves a return to the status
quo ante?' the foreign minister asked rhetorically.
'They are not returning [or 'they will not return' –
'hem einam hozrim'], and that is our policy: they are
not returning.'[16]

Morris omits both the beginning of Sharett's presentation,
which places his words in context, and the second half of his
question (about accepting the situation or fighting it). These
changes permit him to turn a weighty issue for decision into
a rhetorical question. He further exacerbates the distortion by
mistranslating Sharett's genuine question, 'Do we imagine to
ourselves', as the rhetorical assertion 'Can we imagine to

14 Ibid., p. 3 (emphasis in the original).
15 Ben-Gurion, *Medinat Israel,* p. 164.
16 Morris, 'Falsifying the Record', p. 57.

ourselves'. Moreover, by linking Sharett's conclusion to his truncated question, he jumps over the lengthy consideration of the pros and cons of each option (three pages in the original protocol; nearly a page in Ben-Gurion's book).[17] Revealingly, in a Hebrew version of this same article, Morris did not misrepresent Sharett's words,[18] perhaps because Hebrew readers can check for themselves the veracity of his citation.

PARTIAL QUOTES

Through the omission of key passages, Morris repeatedly distorts many quotations. He makes a specialty of partial quotes from Ben-Gurion's books, in the process turning their original intention upside down. Morris claims that Ben-Gurion sought to hide his own views,[19] but this is also wrong.

Departed Palestinians

Consider, for example, the following partial quote, about the same meeting and from a book by Ben-Gurion, in which he discusses the departed Palestinians. The original text reads as follows:

> And we must prevent at all costs their return meanwhile [i.e., until the end of the war]. We, as well as world public opinion cannot ignore the horrible fact that 700,000 [Jewish] people are confronted here with 27 million [Arabs], one against forty. Humanity's conscience was not shocked when 27 million attacked

---

17 Ben-Gurion, *Medinat Israel*, pp. 164–5; 'Partikol – Yeshivat Ha-memshala Ha-zmanit', 16 June 1948, pp. 19–20.
18 Benny Morris, '"U-sfarim U-gvilim Be-zikna Regilim": Mabat Hadash al Mismachim Zioni'im Merkazi'im', *Alpayim*, 12 (1996), p. 98.
19 Morris, 'Falsifying the Record', pp. 50–51.

700,000 – after six million Jews had been slaughtered in Europe. It will not be just if they demand of us to allow back to Abu Kabir and Jaffa those who tried to destroy us.[20]

Morris provides only this truncated text:

And we must prevent at all costs their return meanwhile ... It will not be just if they demand of us to allow back to Abu Kabir and Jaffa those who tried to destroy us.[21]

The innocent-looking ellipsis hides an insightful glimpse into Ben-Gurion's mindset, namely, his perception of the 1948 War as a concerted attempt by the Arab world to destroy the Yishuv (the Jewish community in Mandatory Palestine) shortly after the Holocaust. This was a central component in the Prime Minister's thinking, one that Morris and the 'new historians' must deny in their attempt to misrepresent the 1948 War as a confrontation between a Jewish Goliath and an Arab David. And again, by omitting a key passage, Morris misleads his readers into thinking that this paragraph in Ben-Gurion's book differs from the original meeting protocol; in fact, it is a near-verbatim rendition of it, and not the 'falsification' that Morris claims to find.

Jaffa

Here is the complete text of a paragraph from a book Ben-Gurion published in 1951:

Jaffa will become a Jewish city. War is war; it is not us who wanted war. Tel-Aviv did not wage war on Jaffa,

---

20 Ben-Gurion, *Be-hilahem Israel*, p. 131. See also 'Partikol – Yeshivat Ha-memshala Ha-zmanit', 16 June 1948, p. 36.
21 Morris, 'Falsifying the Record', p. 57.

Jaffa waged war on Tel-Aviv. And this should not happen again. We will not be 'foolish hasidim'. Bringing back the Arabs to Jaffa is not just but rather is foolish. Those who had gone to war against us – let them carry the responsibility after having lost.[22]

As quoted by Morris, this paragraph reads:

Jaffa will become a Jewish city ... Bringing back the Arabs to Jaffa is not just but rather is foolish. Those who had gone to war against us – let them carry the responsibility after having lost.[23]

By dropping the middle part of this passage, Morris withholds from his readers Ben-Gurion's elaborate reasoning for barring an Arab return to Jaffa. He also hides the striking similarity between this later rendition and the original protocol – which would refute his charge that Israelis falsify the historical record.

In another passage, Morris writes:

Interestingly, in *Medinat Yisrael* Ben-Gurion did not republish his statement that 'Jaffa will become a Jewish city'. Perhaps he felt in 1969 that Israel – or the world – had become somewhat more sensitive than it had been in 1952 to anything smacking of racism.[24]

Leaving aside the curious expectation that two books on different subjects should precisely replicate each other, a glance at Ben-Gurion's account of the Cabinet meeting reveals that 'Jaffa will become a Jewish city' meant that through the vicissitudes of the war, Jaffa would become part of the Jewish State rather than of an Arab State, as envisaged by the UN

22   Ben-Gurion, *Be-hilahem Israel*, pp. 130–31.
23   Morris, 'Falsifying the Record', p. 57.
24   Ibid.

Partition Resolution. Morris omits Sharett's words at the same meeting that explain this:

> As regards Jaffa, a very serious question arises yet again: can we agree, after the experience we had just gone through, to the restoration of the status quo ante: that Jaffa will return to be an Arab city, at a time when the risk is so great? Even then, when we agreed to the exclusion of Jaffa from the territory of the [Israeli] state, many [people] questioned [our decision]; but there was the assumption that just as they held [Jewish] Jerusalem [hostage], we held Jaffa. But now we realize what a fifth column it was! And having removed this troublesome spot, returning Jaffa to foreign sovereignty, which is likely to be [our] enemy for many years to come – is a very grave question.[25]

Arab rights

Ben-Gurion had the following to say about Arab rights, according to the original protocol of a meeting:

> We must start working in Jaffa. Jaffa must employ Arab workers. And there is a question of their wages. I believe that they should receive the same wage as a Jewish worker. An Arab has also the right to be elected president of the state, should he be elected by all. If in America a Jew or a black cannot become president of the state – I do not believe in the quality of its civil rights. Indeed, despite the democracy there, I know that there are plots that are not sold to Jews, and the law tolerates this; and a person can sell his plot to a dealer on condition that it not be bought

25 'Partikol – Yeshivat Ha-memshala Ha-zmanit', 16 June 1948, pp. 15–16.

by a Jew … Should we have such a regime – then we
would have missed the purpose of the Jewish State.
And I would add that we would have denied the
most precious thing in Jewish tradition. But war is
war. We did not start the war. They made the war.
Jaffa waged war on us, Haifa waged war on us, Bet
She'an waged war on us. And I do not want them
again to make war. That would be not just but foolish.
This would be a 'foolish hasid'. Do we have to bring
back the enemy, so that he again fights us in Bet
She'an? No! You made war [and] you lost.[26]

His published account of his words read:

Jaffa must employ Arab workers. And there is a
question of their wages. I believe that they should
receive the same wage as a Jewish worker. An Arab
has also the right to be elected president of the state,
should he be elected. If in America a Jew or a black
cannot become president of the state – I do not believe in the quality of its civil rights. But war is war.[27]

But then here is Morris reporting on Ben-Gurion's views:

He favoured giving work to the Arabs who had
remained in Jaffa (about 3,000 of the original 70,000):
'I believe that they should receive the same wage as
a Jewish worker. An Arab has the right also to be
elected president of the state … But war is war.'[28]

Why Morris omitted key passages from his article is easy to
guess, for it was precisely Ben-Gurion's relentless commitment to democracy and his perception of Israel's Arabs as full

26 Ibid., pp. 34–5.
27 Ben-Gurion, *Medinat Israel*, p. 167.
28 Morris, 'Falsifying the Record', p. 57.

and equal members of the Jewish State (i.e., Israel as a genuine 'state of all its citizens') that Morris and his fellow 'new historians' have so vehemently denied. Moreover, the original protocol offers a more elaborate exposition of Ben-Gurion's democratic values than the shorter account he chose to bring in his book. Where, then, is Ben-Gurion's attempt at a cover-up?

WITHHOLDING VITAL EVIDENCE

The Yishuv's war strategy

Morris repeatedly omits key words or even sentences from his quotations, thus distorting their meaning; or he places the quotes out of context; or he portrays them in false light. At times he even omits entire passages, then has the nerve to castigate the speaker or writer for the absence of these very passages!

Take Ben-Gurion's discussions with his advisers on 1–2 January 1948, to determine the strategy of the Yishuv against Palestinian attempts to subvert violently the UN Partition Resolution of November 1947. Morris compares the 13-page description of these deliberations in Ben-Gurion's diary with the 81-page stenographic typescript of the proceedings and finds a 'few but telling' differences.[29] Leaving aside the fact that it is technically impossible for a 13-page diary entry fully to replicate an 81-page stenographic typescript, Morris neglects to inform his readers of much key information.

The first of these differences concerns a statement by Gad Machnes, one of Ben-Gurion's advisers on Arab affairs. Morris writes that

> [Gad] Machnes kicked off the discussion by stating:
> '... The Arabs were not ready when they began the

29 Morris, 'Falsifying the Record', p. 51.

disturbances. Moreover, most of the Arab public did not want them.' Ben-Gurion, in his diary, rendered this passage thus: 'The Arabs were not ready' – completely omitting Machnes's opinion that 'most' of the Arabs did not want the disturbances.[30]

Morris does not mention that Ben-Gurion's diary entry is replete with references to the Arab masses' lack of interest in war. Quoting Eliyahu Sasson, Director of the Arab Section of the Jewish Agency's Political Department, Ben-Gurion wrote: 'It is true that the wider Arab public was not swayed by the disturbances; the villager, the merchant, the worker, and the citrus-grower did not want [war] and do not want [it] now. But the Mufti wanted – and succeeded in implicating the country.' Shortly afterwards Ben-Gurion recorded a similar comment by yet another Arab specialist, Ezra Danin: 'He [Danin] disputes Sasson's opinion that the Mufti achieved more than he had hoped. To the contrary, he expected the Arabs to follow him more than it actually happened.' And yet another comment in the same vein, this time by Joshua [Josh] Palmon: 'Are there or are there not disturbances? In the vicinity of Beit-Govrin, in the south up to Yazur there are no disturbances. Most of the Arabs want peace.'[31]

Indeed, Ben-Gurion repeatedly tells of his conviction that the Palestinian masses did not want war but had it imposed on them by an intransigent leadership. He reiterated this theme both in his private meetings with Sir Alan Cunningham, the British High Commissioner in Palestine,[32] and in public. On 25 November 1947, for example, he stated that 'it should

---

30   Ibid.
31   BGA, 1 January 1948; Ben-Gurion, *Yoman Ha-milhama*, vol. I, pp. 99, 100, 101, 102.
32   Thus, for example, in his meeting with Cunningham on 2 October 1947, Ben-Gurion argued that 'he himself felt that the mass of the people in Palestine wished peace'. Eleven days later he told Cunningham that 'there were a large section of Arabs who were against the Mufti and wished to co-operate'. On 6 January 1948, four days after the meeting cited by Morris, Ben-Gurion claimed that 'the felaheen did not want trouble and the Jews were not going to provoke them'. Cunningham Papers, St Antony's College, Oxford, V/1.

be borne in mind that the masses of the Arab people – forcibly silenced and deprived of political expression – are not keen to rush to battle'.[33]

Second, Morris writes that 'Machnes went on to enjoin the Hagana to retaliate against Arab provocations "with strength and brutality", even hitting women and children.'[34] Morris withholds from his readers, however, that 'strength and brutality' refers here not to indiscriminate attacks against Palestinian society as a whole, but as a means of last resort and to pinpoint retaliation against specific and well-identified perpetrators of armed attacks on Jews. Here is the full citation of Machnes's words from the meeting's original protocol:

> I think that today there is no question whether or not to respond. But for the response to be effective, it must come in the right time and the right place and take the form of a strong punishment. Blowing up a house is not enough. Blowing up a house of innocent people is certainly not enough! The response must be strong and harsh because it must create the [right] impression, must punish [the perpetrators of violence] and must serve as a warning. If our responses are not impressive – they will create the opposite impression. These matters necessitate the utmost precision – in terms of time, place, and whom and what to hit ... If we operate against, say, a specific family in a known place, a known village [i.e., identified perpetrators of violence], then there should be no mercy! But only a direct blow and no touching of innocent people! We have already reached a position that necessitates a strong response. Today one should not even avoid hitting women and children. For otherwise, the response cannot be effective.[35]

33   Ben-Gurion, *Ba-ma'araha*, p. 254.
34   Morris, 'Falsifying the Record', p. 51.
35   'Partikol Meha-yeshiva Be-inyanei Shem', 1–2 January 1948, Ha-kibbutz Ha-meuhad Archive, Ramat-Efal, Israel, Galili Section, Box 45, File 1–4, pp. 3–4.

Whereas Machnes recommended a highly discriminate response, to the totally indiscriminate Arab attacks on the Yishuv, Morris misquotes him as suggesting precisely the opposite.

Third, Morris misrepresents Yigal Allon, commander of the Palmach, as advocating political assassinations: '... Eliminating a few personalities at the right time – is very important.'[36] The actual text reads as follows:

> In conclusion, I would like to say that we cannot shift
> to a pattern of personal terrorism. But the elimination
> of a few individuals at the right time is a very
> important thing.[37]

By removing Allon's first sentence Morris turned his position upside down. Allon rejected political assassination as a *modus operandi*, as opposed to the targeting of specific individuals who had a direct bearing on the prosecution of the war.

Finally, Morris withholds Ben-Gurion's summation of the same discussion:

- To hit attackers, be they a family, a village, or a neighbourhood;
- Not to touch under any circumstances any peaceful Arab;
- To operate in close co-operation with the SHAI [the Hagana's intelligence service) and the [Jewish Agency's] Arab Section.[38]

Ben-Gurion underscored the vital importance of avoiding innocent casualties and spelled out some means to this end, notably improved intelligence co-ordination. This by no means self-evident strategy in a war for survival against an enemy which made not the slightest distinction between

36 Morris, 'Falsifying the Record', pp. 51–2.
37 'Partikol Meha-yeshiva Be-inyanei Shem', p. 46.
38 Ibid., p. 36.

belligerents and non-belligerents was not purely based on moral considerations, but also on the above assessment by Ben-Gurion and his Arab advisers that most Palestinians wanted peace but were being drawn into war by the militant Hajj Amin al-Husseini; hence a strong but accurate response could deter wider violence while stopping short of alienating Palestinian society, whereas indiscriminate retaliation would have the opposite effect. Indeed, the recommendations presented to the same forum the next day by a special committee, appointed at the end of the 1 January meeting, made a conscious effort to specify the means of avoiding indiscriminate retaliation. Thus, for example, it was suggested that retaliation against 'holy places, hospitals, schools, and similar objects' be withheld, even in the event of Arab attacks on such Jewish targets. In the words of Danin, who sat on this committee: 'The spirit of these things was that it is possible that in many instances we will not respond. We do not have an accounting system of "debit" and "credit".'[39]

Palestinian flight

In his endeavour to 'prove' a Zionist design to disinherit the Palestinians from their land, Morris extensively misrepresents the diaries of Yosef Weitz, a secondary Zionist figure whom Morris inflates into a straw man of gigantic proportions. Here is how Morris reports Weitz's alleged role in the Arab departure from the town of Bet She'an:

> On 4 May, he complained to the local Jewish leaders that 'the valley was still seething with enemies ... I said – the eviction [of the Arabs] from the valley is the order of the day.'[40]

Weitz's diary as found in the archive has much more to tell about the same episode:

39 Ibid., 'Second Meeting, 2.1.1948', pp. 51–2, 54.
40 Morris, 'Falsifying the Record', p. 47.

A delegation from the Jezreel Valley and Bet She'an informs that the Arab Legion entered the [Arab] town of Bet She'an; ordered the women and children to leave the town and barricaded itself inside it. The question arose: should we attack the town or lay siege to it? This issue was discussed yesterday at the regional headquarters. An attack necessitates far larger forces than those available at the area, while the siege might take a long time and might trigger an invasion of foreign forces from Transjordan and an increase of the [Arab] Legion's forces [in the area]. No decision was reached. The local committee [of Jewish settlements] supports an attack, and came to ask me to influence the commanders here. I complained that this valley was still seething with enemies. And I am afraid that we are on the verge of defeat, because the British army, which had suddenly returned to the country, intends forcefully to impose 'peace' on both parties and will prevent us from undertaking vigorous actions at a time when we have the upper hand. 'The Bet She'an Valley is the gate to our state in the Galilee, and nobody should stand on its threshold to disturb us', – I said – 'the evacuation of the valley [pinuyo shel ha-emek] is the order of the day.'[41]

Note that Morris mistranslates 'evacuation' of the valley as 'eviction [of the Arabs]', though Weitz clearly refers to the valley, not the Arabs. Even if Weitz implies their eviction, Morris undoubtedly has taken liberties with the translation. Also, by quoting a tiny fraction of this lengthy paragraph out of its real context, Morris withholds from his readers Weitz's thinking about the strategic importance of the Bet She'an Valley for Israel's security and his recurrent fears of Jewish

41   Yosef Weitz Diary, 4 May 1948, Central Zionist Archives, A246/13, pp. 2,373–4.

defeat (a far cry from the militant mood misattributed to him by Morris).

Above all, Morris hides revealing information about the departure of Palestinians as a result of Arab pressure – a central bone of contention in the historiography of the 1948 War. He repeats this distortion in both the English and Hebrew versions of his book on the birth of the Palestinian refugee problem, where he mentions the Arab Legion's entry into Bet-She'an, but not its ordering the women and children out of the town.[42]

Needless to say, this is not the only time that Morris withholds such information regarding the Palestinian exodus. On 28 March 1948, for example, Weitz recorded in his published diary:

> Haifa – R. Baum told me that the inhabitants of Qumia, about three hundred people, left the village yesterday having asked the [British] authorities to vacate them. They were in a difficult economic position and the [Arab] gangs had struck fear into them. The people cried on Baum's shoulders about the difficulty of leaving their place.[43]

Morris ignores this entry altogether.

MAKING FALSE ASSERTIONS

Unconcerned with the necessities of scholarly rigour, at times Morris does not even take the trouble to provide evidence for his charge of Zionist wrongdoing. He expects his readers to take on trust his assertions that fundamental contradictions exist between published accounts and the underlying documents. In fact, these contradictions do not exist.

For example, Morris charges Ben-Gurion with omitting

---

42 Morris, *The Birth*, p. 106; idem, *Leidata*, p. 148.
43 Yosef Weitz, *Yomani Ve-igrotai La-banim* (Tel-Aviv: Masada, 1965), vol. III, p. 257.

passages from the protocol of the (above-noted) consultation on 18 August 1948:

> Both Shitrit and Weitz spoke of the need to buy land. As Shitrit put it: 'There are many Arabs who wish to leave – they must be found and bought out.'

Morris goes on to recount what other participants said and then returns to these two:

> Ben-Gurion's three-and-a-half page diary description of that meeting completely omits mention of Weitz's proposals to destroy the villages and prevent Arab harvesting. It also fails to mention Weitz's and Shitrit's proposal to encourage Arab emigration through offers to purchase land.[44]

But did Ben-Gurion's diary actually not mention these proposals? Here is the original text:

> *Shitrit*: Many Arabs do not want to return to the country and we must immediately buy their land.
>
> *Weitz*: As for the cultivation of the land: if we do not wish the Arabs to return, and we require only food – then we should cultivate only the land necessary for growing food – 100,000 dunams of the best land, and from the rest – lease and buy as much as possible … one has to prepare plans for settling the Arabs in the neighbouring states.[45]

In fact, Ben-Gurion scrupulously recorded the meeting in his diary.

Similarly, Morris charges Yosef Weitz with another distortion:

44   Morris, 'Falsifying the Record', p. 49.
45   BGA; Ben-Gurion, *Yoman Ha-milhama*, vol. II, pp. 653–4.

On 12 January 1948, six weeks into the war, Weitz travelled to Yoqne'am, an agricultural settlement southeast of Haifa, where he discussed with Yehuda Burstein, the local Hagana intelligence officer, 'the question of the eviction of [Arab] tenant-farmers from Yoqne'am and [neighbouring] Daliyat [al-Ruha] with the methods now acceptable. The matter has been left in the hands of the defense people [the Hagana] and during the afternoon I spoke with the [Hagana] deputy district commander.' This whole passage was omitted from the published diary.[46]

Was it? Let us look at the published diary:

Haifa, 11.1: I discussed with the Haifa people [i.e., officials] the question of the [Arab] tenant-farmers in Yoqne'am and Daliya. Is it not the time now to get rid of them? Why should we continue to keep these thorns among us, at a time when they pose a threat to us? Our people weigh and reflect [on the matter].[47]

Equally false is Morris's claim that Weitz omitted from the published diary his advocacy that Bedouin tenant-farmers from the Ghawarna clan be vacated from Jewish land in the Haifa bay. As Morris puts it:

A member of [kibbutz] Kfar Masaryk came to see Weitz in Tel Aviv and complained, 'astonished', that these bedouin had not yet been evicted. Weitz promptly wrote a letter 'to the [Hagana] commander there and to [Mordechai] Shachevitz [Weitz's land-purchasing agent in the area] to move

---

46 Morris, 'Falsifying the Record', pp. 46–7.
47 Weitz, *Yomani*, vol. III, p. 223. Though dated 11 January 1948, rather than 12 January, as in the original diary, there is no doubt that this is the meeting referred to by Morris, not least since Weitz held his meetings in Haifa (and not in Yoqne'am as Morris states). See, Yosef Weitz Diary, 12 January 1948, A246/12, p. 2290.

quickly in this matter.' A week later, Shachevitz informed Weitz that 'most of the bedouins in the [Haifa] bay [area] had gone, [but] some fifteen–twenty men had stayed behind to guard [the clan's property]. I demanded that they also be evicted and that the fields be plowed over so that no trace of them remains.' Again, no trace of any of this is to be found in Weitz's published diary entries.[48]

Really? A look at Weitz's published account reveals the following:

> Haifa, 27.3 – Today we discussed the Ghawarna Bedouins in our bay, who must be sent away from there so as to prevent them from joining our enemies ...
>
> Haifa, 26.4 – ... In the bay [area] I saw the lands cleared of the Ghawarna, most of whom had left. In the northern part [of the bay] the shacks had been destroyed and the land was being plowed over. In the southern part, the operation had yet to be completed. In war – as in war.[49]

It gets worse. Morris misrepresents the latter entry from Weitz's diary. He holds that Weitz 'recorded that the northern part of the Zevulun Valley was completely clear of bedouin'.[50] Not so: as we have just seen, Weitz's published account specifically refers to the departure of the Ghawarna Bedouins, rather than of Bedouins as a whole, and from the Haifa Bay, rather than the Zevulun Valley – precisely as it appears in the original diary.[51] Had Morris quoted the diary correctly, he would have negated his false claim that no trace of this

48   Morris, 'Falsifying the Record', p. 47.
49   Weitz, *Yomani*, vol. III, pp. 257, 273.
50   Morris, 'Falsifying the Record', p. 47.
51   Yosef Weitz Diary, 26 April 1948, A246/13, p. 2367.

episode is to be found in the published diary entries, since he had himself acknowledged that 'Weitz included this passage in his published entry for 26 April'.[52]

Morris then accuses Weitz of wholesale falsification of the personal diaries of Yosef Nahmani, longtime director of the JNF Office in the eastern Galilee, which Weitz edited after Nahmani's death. Morris writes:

> On 30 December 1947, a squad of IZL [Irgun Zvai Leumi] terrorists threw a bomb at a bus stop outside the oil refinery complex just north of Haifa, killing about half a dozen Arabs, some of them workers at the plant, and wounding others. Within hours, in a spontaneous act of vengeance, Arab workers at the plant turned on their Jewish colleagues with knives and sticks, slaughtering thirty-nine of them. Nahmani jotted down in his diary (on 30 December):
>
> > ... [I] was told about the bomb that Jews threw into a crowd of Arab workers from the refinery and there are dead. The Arabs [then] attacked the Jewish clerks ... and killed some of them ... This incident depressed me greatly. After all, the Arabs [in Haifa] had declared a truce and why cause the death of innocent people and again ignite the Arabs ...

Morris quotes more of Nahmani, musing on the significance of this event, then adds his own comment:

> Weitz, in *Nahmani*, completely omitted this passage (though he did include a brief excerpt from Nahmani's entry for 30 December – dealing with other matters altogether). However, he published part of Nahmani's entry for 31 December, reading:

52   Morris, 'Falsifying the Record', p. 47.

'The disaster that struck the workers at the Haifa oil refinery depressed me greatly.' For Israeli readers in 1969, this passage, in the way it appears, could only be taken to refer to the massacre of the Jewish refinery workers and not to the killing of the Arab workers at the bus stop that preceded it.[53]

But did Weitz really seek to shield his fellow Israelis from the less savoury aspects of their past by expunging all traces of Jewish-initiated violence? Hardly. The page in Nahmani's published diary that Morris quotes contains no fewer than two other entries specifically dedicated to this issue:

> Tiberias, 19.12 – this morning we learnt from the Galileans who came to Tiberias about the bombing of houses in Kasas [in retaliation for a mob attack on a Jewish guard] and there are fatalities: ten dead Arabs, including five children. This is appalling. Indiscriminate acts of retaliation hitting innocent people will mobilize all of the Arabs against us and help the extremists who will immerse the country in a whirlpool of bloodletting. The Kasas incident greatly depressed me.

> Tiberias, 21.12 – I participated in a meeting of representatives of those Galilee settlements which maintain contacts with Arabs and propagate the preservation of relations with them [i.e., the Arabs]. I raised the Kasas incident and said that this act indicated that the generation at the helm had no moral inhibitions against bloodshed.[54]

Further showing the complete inaccuracy of Morris's claim that Weitz hid the less savoury episodes, Weitz's own

---

53   Ibid., pp. 53–4. The Irgun Zvai Leumi was also known as the National Military Organization.
54   *Yosef Nahmani – Ish Ha-Galil* (Ramat-Gan: Masada, 1969), p. 246.

published diary offered a candid description of the refinery
episode four years before Nahmani's was published:

> What happened this week at the Haifa refinery
> shocked all of us, on both accounts: the bomb throw-
> ing into a crowd of Arab workers was a crime on the
> part of our 'secessionists' [i.e., the Irgun Zvai Leumi].
> For while we favour 'a retaliatory action', we are
> totally opposed to a provocative attack. I do not find
> any supportive circumstances, not even one in a
> thousand, to justify this act by the secessionists,
> which caused to a certain extent the Arab riots in the
> refinery and the massacre of forty Jews. I said to a
> certain extent, because it is argued that incitement
> for an attack of the Jewish workers has been sensed
> for quite some time and that the attack would
> probably have occurred in any event. However, it is
> clear today that this provocative act caused the
> spilling of our precious blood.[55]

Thus did Weitz make not the slightest attempt to cover up the
IZL's responsibility for what he called a 'crime' in the refinery.
His omission of the above entry in Nahmani's diary obviously
had nothing to do with the 'political and propagandistic
intent' Morris attributes to him.[56] On the contrary, as activists
in the Labour movement, Weitz and Nahmani had no
compunction about publicly disowning the activities of the
smaller underground groups, the IZL and Lohamei Herut
Israel (LEHI, Fighters for Israel's Freedom), which they
deemed as morally reprehensible and politically detrimental.
Hence the striking similarity in Weitz's and Nahmani's
responses to the IZL attack at the refinery; hence the negative
references to IZL terrorist acts recurring in their published

---

55   Weitz, *Yomani*, vol. III, p. 218 (entry for 3 January 1948).
56   Morris, 'Falsifying the Record', p. 53.

diaries. Indeed, on 30 December 1947, the same day as the refinery attack, Weitz recorded in his diary a similar bomb attack on Arab civilians, this time in Jerusalem: 'The hour is 12.30. Ten minutes later a strong explosion reverberates throughout the city. Unidentified people have thrown a bomb into an Arab crowd at the Shechem [Nablus] Gate, and there is anticipation in the city for whatever will be forthcoming, though not in anxiety.'[57] This entry also appears in his published diary.

Where is the cover up?

REWRITING ORIGINAL DOCUMENTS

Falsification means the reader is presented with allegedly direct quotations from original documents that are in fact rewritten texts containing at best altered words or sentences, and at worst sentences invented by Morris and then misrepresented by him as authentic.

Take Morris's citation of Prime Minister Ben-Gurion's words at the Israeli Cabinet meeting of 16 June 1948:

> But war is war. We did not start the war. They made the war, Jaffa went to war against us. So did Haifa. And I do not want those who fled to return. I do not want them again to make war.[58]

The key sentence here ('I do not want those who fled to return') is simply not found in the text of the meeting protocol. It is entirely of Morris's own making. The actual text reads as follows:

> But war is war. We did not start the war. They made the war. Jaffa waged war on us, Haifa waged war on us, Bet She'an waged war on us. And I do not want

57   Weitz, *Yomani*, vol. III, p. 214.
58   Morris, 'Falsifying the Record', p. 58.

them again to make war. That would be not just but foolish. This would be a 'foolish hasid'. Do we have to bring back the enemy, so that he again fights us in Bet-She'an? No! You made war [and] you lost.[59]

It bears noting that in the Hebrew version of his article, Morris did not put words into Ben-Gurion's mouth.[60] Is it because Hebrew readers could check for themselves the veracity of his citation?

On another occasion, Morris rewrites words or sentences in primary documents to misrepresent their meaning. He quotes the 12 January 1948 entry in Yosef Weitz's diary and has Weitz discussing the eviction of Arab tenant-farmers from 'Daliyat',[61] which he identifies as 'Daliyat al-Ruha', an Arab locality. Weitz's diary in fact refers to Dalia, a Hebrew kibbutz – a neighbouring and wholly different place from 'Daliyat'. By Arabizing the name of a Hebrew settlement Morris creates the absolutely false impression that the tenant-farmers were to be evicted from Arab, rather than from Jewish land.

On other occasions, Morris rewrites entries in the Weitz and Ben-Gurion diaries to implicate the Prime Minister in Weitz's (alleged) activities. Writes Morris:

> According to the original Weitz diary entry for 5 June, Weitz had informed Ben-Gurion that the committee had already begun 'here and there destroying villages'. In the published diary, Weitz had amended this to 'here and there "improving" villages' (the [double] quotes presumably designed to signal his more perceptive readers what was actually meant). In both versions, Weitz wrote that Ben-Gurion 'gave his approval' to this work.[62]

59 'Partikol – Yeshivat Ha-memshala Ha-zmanit', 16 June 1948, pp. 35–6.
60 Morris, '"U-sfarim U-gvilim Be-zikna Regilim"', p. 99.
61 Morris, 'Falsifying the Record', pp. 46–7.
62 Ibid., p. 48.

Morris goes on to characterize these as 'the Transfer Committee's proposals', and to indicate that Ben-Gurion approved of them.[63] But did Weitz really tell Ben-Gurion that the 'committee had already begun' destroying villages? Did Ben-Gurion authorize 'the Transfer Committee's proposals'? Not at all, as Weitz himself explains:

> I said that I [and not the 'Transfer Committee' as misquoted by Morris] had already given instructions to start here and there 'improving' villages – and he approved it. I contented myself with this.[64]

Weitz's resort to the first person is important: as director of the Jewish National Fund's Land Development Division he was directly involved in the question of abandoned Palestinian villages; as representative of a non-existent committee he had no relevance whatsoever to this issue. For the 'Transfer Committee' Morris writes of never came into being. During this same meeting, Ben-Gurion specifically told Weitz that he rejected outright the very existence of such a committee. As Weitz put it: 'He would like to convene a narrow meeting and to appoint a committee to handle the issue. He does not agree to the [existence] of our temporary committee.'[65]

Having withheld these critical facts, Morris then has the nerve to charge Ben-Gurion with taking great care 'to avoid leaving footprints of his own involvement'[66] in the activities of the non-existent Transfer Committee. To substantiate this false claim, Morris rewrites the entry in Ben-Gurion's diary pertaining to the meeting. The actual text reads as follows:

---

63   Ibid.
64   Weitz, *Yomani*, vol. III, p. 298 (diary entry for 5 June 1948). See also Yosef Weitz Diary, 5 June 1948, A246/13, p. 2411.
65   Weitz, *Yomani*, vol. III, p. 298 (diary entry for 5 June 1948). See also Yosef Weitz Diary, 5 June 1948, A246/13, p. 2411.
66   Morris, 'Falsifying the Record', p. 49.

> He [i.e., Weitz] proposes to discuss with the Arab
> Governments help in settling these Arabs in the Arab
> states. This is [far too] premature and untimely.[67]

Morris turns this into:

> But how did Ben-Gurion record the self-same meet-
> ing? 'It is too early and untimely ... to discuss with
> the Arab Governments help in resettling these Arabs
> in the Arab states ...'[68]

Morris restructures Ben-Gurion's diary entry to remove the
fact that Weitz proposed resettling refugees in the Arab states
and Ben-Gurion rejected the idea. This permits Morris to
conceal Ben-Gurion's rejection of a pivotal component of
Weitz's thinking and to paint a false picture of a complete
meeting of minds, if not a straightforward collusion. As Morris
puts it:

> Indeed, according to Weitz, Ben-Gurion had not only
> approved the 'whole policy', but had thought that
> the proposed actions in Israel (destruction of villages,
> prevention of harvesting, settlement of Jews in aban-
> doned sites) should take precedence over efforts to
> resettle refugees elsewhere (meaning negotiating
> with Arab countries about resettlement, assessing
> compensation and so forth).[69]

The reality was quite different. Ben-Gurion did not accept
Weitz's suggestions about settling the Arabs abroad. Rather,
Ben-Gurion deemed the latter issue irrelevant and unwar-
ranted because the war was far from over and he had not yet
made up his mind about the solution to the refugee problem.
But then, why be bothered about the facts?

67 BGA, entry for 5 June 1948; Ben-Gurion, *Yoman Ha-milhama*, vol. II, p. 487.
68 Morris, 'Falsifying the Record', p. 49.
69 Ibid., p. 48.

Index